Palgrave Explorations in Workplace Stigma

Series Editor
Julie Gedro, Empire State College, Rochester, NY, USA

This series is a call to action for organizations to not only recognize but include, support, and value employees of all walks of life, regardless of the social stigmas that might create material, affective, or psychological divisions between them and their ostensibly "normal" counterparts. It fills the gap in scholarship surrounding the difficult issues employees or job seekers might face based on their demographics, life events, or other factors. The series explores issues such as mental illness and wellness; and alcohol and drug addiction and recovery. It explores the complex and often times nuanced issues that face sexual minorities, or those who are formerly incarcerated, or military veterans in the context of employment or career decision making.

Through rigorous research and contributions from the foremost scholars in human resources, books in the series will provide an in-depth exploration of each population and challenge HR scholars and practitioners to effectively consider and embrace these explorations and consider expanding their own awareness. The series speaks on behalf of anyone who has ever been affected–directly or indirectly–by discrimination or exclusion in the context of work, and promotes a positive, productive, and purposeful working environment for employees at all levels.

Jacqueline H. Stephenson · Natalie Persadie

Disability in the Workplace

A Caribbean Perspective

palgrave
macmillan

Jacqueline H. Stephenson
University of the West Indies
St. Augustine, Trinidad and Tobago

Natalie Persadie
University of Trinidad and Tobago
Point Lisas, Trinidad and Tobago

ISSN 2662-3625 ISSN 2662-3633 (electronic)
Palgrave Explorations in Workplace Stigma
ISBN 978-3-031-19339-2 ISBN 978-3-031-19340-8 (eBook)
https://doi.org/10.1007/978-3-031-19340-8

This Palgrave Macmillan imprint is published by the registered company Springer Nature Switzerland AG
The registered company address is: Gewerbestrasse 11, 6330 Cham, Switzerland

Contents

List of Figures

List of Tables

CHAPTER 1

Introduction—Disability and Discrimination

Introduction

In this book, we explore the workplace experiences, opportunities and challenges as it relates to the heterogeneity of persons with disabilities. In this chapter, we outline the scope of the text and importantly, the interrelated nature of diversity, discrimination, inclusion and equality in the English-speaking Caribbean, specifically in relation to persons with disabilities, within the context of employment. Many of the islands of the Commonwealth Caribbean have signalled their commitment to inclusivity, diversity and the reduction of disparate treatment for persons with disabilities, by becoming signatories to the United Nations (UN) Convention on the Rights of Persons with Disabilities (CRPD), which entered into force in 2008 and aims to "*promote, protect and ensure the human rights, dignity and fundamental freedoms of all persons with disabilities*". To date, the following Anglophone Caribbean islands are signatories to and have ratified this UN Convention—Antigua *and* Barbuda, the Bahamas, Trinidad *and* Tobago, Barbados, St. Vincent *and* the Grenadines, Dominica, Grenada, Guyana, Jamaica and consequently, they are legally bound by the directives outlined therein.

Moreover, some Anglo-Caribbean islands have enacted legislation that (congruent with the directives of the CRPD) prohibit discrimination on the basis of disabilities, within the context of education, employment

J. H. Stephenson and N. Persadie, *Disability in the Workplace*, Palgrave Explorations in Workplace Stigma,
https://doi.org/10.1007/978-3-031-19340-8_1

and the provision of goods and services. These islands include—Antigua and Barbuda, Jamaica, and the Bahamas, where legislation has been enacted solely to prohibit discrimination on the basis of disabilities *and* Trinidad and Tobago, St. Lucia, and Guyana, where broad-based anti-discrimination legislation has been enacted, with disabilities representing only a single element of the multiple grounds of discrimination outlawed therein. Notwithstanding this, less than 50% of the islands of the Commonwealth Caribbean have to date, actively taken steps to comply with the obligations of the CRPD, i.e. to adopt legislative measures to prohibit discriminatory, disparate and unequal treatment for persons with disabilities. Indeed, initial efforts by the aforementioned islands to establish such legislation, represent a positive migration towards the establishment and implementation of equitable policies and practices in relation to persons with disabilities and may act as a catalyst towards facilitating greater inclusion and acceptance of PWD in the Anglophone Caribbean (Karpur et al., 2014).

Disability and Discrimination

"*Nothing about us, without us*" is the motto globally associated with persons with disabilities and used by them, their advocates and allies, to convey the desire of persons with disabilities (PWD), to actively participate in the development and implementation of any policies and plans designed to help them. However, every day, the rights and autonomy of persons with disabilities are routinely ignored, for example when individuals push an individual's wheelchair out of their way (instead of politely engaging the wheelchair user); yelling at a person with hearing impairment or getting frustrated that they are unable to read lips (instead of perhaps learning sign language ourselves); grabbing a person with a sight impairment *to help them*, without asking if they need or want your assistance or support; telling a person with a mental illness like clinical depression that *they simply need to get over it* (mental illnesses are just as legitimate as physical illnesses and one cannot simply get over a diabetes diagnosis, without the requisite medical treatment). These actions occur every day, and far from being perceived as helpful by PWD, they are viewed as disrespectful and dismissive and may be interpreted by PWD as attempts to marginalise and infantilise them, by imposing the will of others on them, based on an erroneous assumption that they are incapable of making autonomous decisions. In reality, these acts convey stigma and pity rather than allowing PWD the dignity and autonomy of making their own decisions (Andrews et al., 2021; Thomas, 2022). In addition, researchers (Andrews et al., 2021) have advocated for "*disability humility*" which suggests that deference to PWD as "authority and experts about their own lives".

Persons with disabilities are discriminated against when they are treated less favorably than others on the basis of their disability (i.e. real or perceived). Within the context of PWD, ableism describes the discrimination of PWD in favour of persons without known disabilities, which may be explicit or implicit acceptance of preconceived notions or implicit biases (Andrews et al., 2021; Gayle-Geddes, 2016; Morris, 2018). With respect to persons with disabilities, advocacy is typically associated with equality of treatment, equality of opportunity and equality of outcome. The evolution of the concept of equality to the prevailing notion of diversity suggests with respect to equality of treatment that it is essential to treat each person with disabilities, as an individual with unique concerns. Otherwise stated, PWD are heterogenous hence even if two employees have been diagnosed with the same disabling condition, it cannot be assumed that they would benefit from the same access provisions. Hence it is incumbent on every employer to inquire as to whether accommodations are needed and investigate the associated costs rather than to assume in the absence of supporting evidence whether accommodations would be required, and the type and nature of said accommodations.

Equality, Diversity and Inclusion

Equality, diversity and inclusion (EDI) are recognised as concepts that are interrelated and evolving (Garg & Sangwan, 2021; Kirton, 2020; Köllen et al., 2018; Nair & Vohra, 2015; O'Donovan, 2018; Özbilgin, 2009; Tomlinson & Schwabenland, 2010), this has been extended to include access when discussing PWD, hence equality, diversity, inclusion and access (EDIA). Access has special relevance to persons with disabilities and may be interpreted variously, *to wit* access to employment, opportunities, education, the provision of goods and services and appropriate accommodations (Konur, 2002; Vanderheiden, 1998; Vornholt, et al., 2018). In short, the EDI discourse has evolved from "*equality (*everyone is treated equally*), equity (*individual needs are met*), and justice (*the removal of systemic embedded barriers*)*" (Andrews et al., 2021: 452; Tomlinson & Schwabenland, 2010).

Turning to *equality*, simply asserting that everyone is treated the same does not mean that the outcomes are the same nor does it mean that everyone can access the same opportunities. As an example, if during an organisation wide (*in person*) staff meeting, information is verbally shared by the Human Resource Manager, indicating that the organisation has updated its performance measures, an employee with a hearing impairment may be disadvantaged, if accommodations are not made to ensure that this employee is also able to access this information (*for example* failure to provide a sign language interpreter, or failure to provide the employee the updated procedures in an alternative format, i.e. via a printed document), then by a preponderance of the evidence, the affected employee has not been afforded equality of treatment, opportunity or outcome. Three primary categories of equality are: equality of outcome, treatment and opportunity (Jewson & Mason, 1986; Laci et al., 2017; Peragine & Biagi, 2019). It has been suggested that addressing inequality within the workplace, with the stated intention to treat everyone the same could be ineffective and result in the failure of some equality initiatives (Coleman et al., 2013; Liff & Wajcman, 1996). Moreover, there is an absence of irrefutable evidence to support any assertion that equal treatment approaches have resulted only in benefits in relation to equality in part because prevailing prejudicial stereotypes appear to create some difficulty for workplace managers to conceptualise job requirements in neutral terms (Collinson et al., 1990; Curran, 1988; Köllen et al., 2018; Roemer, 2002; Schaar, 2017).

In their 1996 article, Liff and Wajcman (1996) discussed equal opportunities from the perspective of sameness or equality as well as the viewpoint of differences or managing diversity. Accordingly, equality based on sameness is deemed to occur where one person is treated the same as another who may differ in some way (the differences may be based on immutable characteristics). However, one of the challenges with such an approach is that those persons who are different from the dominant group invariably minimise their differences in order to be treated in the same manner as the dominant group. Where equality based on sameness is concerned, such an approach to equality would be difficult to attain where minority groups are represented in the workplace, as this may require consideration of differences in experiences, skills and abilities. The alternative to such an equality approach would be managing diversity which requires acknowledging differences in the workplace. This approach in contrast to the equality model suggests that employees may not wish to be treated equally but may value different treatment or working arrangements, based on their needs.

Inclusion as a concept is associated with the following attributes: feeling valued, involved and engaged at work, feeling accepted as your authentic self, high-quality dyadic relationships with organisational members including managerial staff and executives (Bernstein & Bilimoria, 2013; Köllen et al., 2018; Miminoshvili & Černe, 2021; Ng & Sears, 2020; Sabharwal, 2014; Shore et al., 2011). This is similar to the sense of belonging or acceptance desired by employees to ensure that they remain motivated at work (see theories of motivation theories: Maslow's hierarchy of needs and Alderfer's ERG theory) and feel a sense of fitting in and a part of the in-group as predicted by social identity theory (Mor Barak, 2015; Mor-Barak & Cherin, 1998; Sabharwal, 2014), rather than isolation and marginalisation because of their differences as suggested by the similarity attraction paradigm (Colella & Stone, 2005). This would require the promotion of organisational citizenship behaviours (Benuyenah, 2021; Bergeron, 2007; Bizri, 2018) and organisational inclusive behaviours (Gasorek, 2000; Mor-Barak & Cherin, 1998; Sabharwal, 2014) patterned after the actions of the organisation and its leaders (Özbilgin, 2009).

One of the challenges with group-related theories as it relates to persons with disabilities is an assumption that all members of a group are homogeneous, which is a fallacy. Persons with disabilities are a heterogeneous group and, as such, any assumptions about this group based on generalisations and the erroneous application of stigmas and stereotypes to all PWD, will invariably result in ineffective organisational decision-making, and employees with disabilities who are left feeling isolated, abandoned, derided, ineffective, devalued, physically and emotionally unwell (Leach et al., 2010; Miminoshvili & Černe, 2021; Shore et al., 2011). The extent to which PWD are excluded, as where for example, they are not offered the same opportunities for training, development and promotion, as a result of their organisational contributions not being recognised and valued, may cause them to experience a "sticky floor" effect. This effect refers to a phenomenon where employees with disabilities (EWD) are concentrated at lower positions in the organisational hierarchy, where they are overqualified and this could be a catalyst for them to leave the organisation, to seek opportunities elsewhere, where their skills and valued, utilised and rewarded (Shore et al., 2011; Yap & Konrad, 2009).

An alternative approach to equality of treatment is to find a way to value and utilise differences between employees. By managing diversity, organisations are encouraged to strengthen the workforce and the competitive advantage by employing different people from those already in the workforce [status quo] (Hossain et al., 2020; Köllen et al., 2018; Larkey, 1996; Robertson, 2004; Tomlinson & Schwabenland, 2010). This approach challenges the equality framework, suggesting that people do not necessarily wish to be treated the same in every aspect of their working life but by offering different working arrangements or benefits, employers facilitating the diversity approach may realise greater benefits within their workplaces relative to those pursuing an equality approach (Liff & Wajcman, 1996). Diversity policies and practices within organisations, encourage inclusivity and the multiple skills and talents of all different types of employees (Bernstein & Bilimoria, 2013; Shore et al., 2011; Soni, 2000; Thomas, 1990), which may involve changing workplace policies and practices such that there are no exclusions (intentional or unintentional) according to an employee's immutable characteristics. Rather, the goal of organisational diversity initiatives is to foster cohesion with a collective organisational focus on achieving the goal of the organisation (Soni, 2000). Diversity has been broadly categorised as surface level and deep level diversity, the former refers to obvious differences for example race, age, etc., while the latter refers to differences in attitudes, opinions, information, values, etc. (Bell et al., 2018; Nkomo et al., 2019; Phillips & Loyd, 2006; Phillips et al., 2006).

An alternative approach to equality of treatment is to find a way to value and utilise the differences between people (employees). This approach is the managing diversity approach where businesses are encouraged to strengthen the workforce and the competitive advantage by employing different people from those already in the workforce. This approach challenges the equal treatment model suggesting that people do not necessarily wish to be treated the same in every aspect of their working life but by offering different working arrangements or benefits, employers facilitating the diversity approach may realise greater returns within their workplaces relative to those pursuing an equality approach (Liff & Wajcman, 1996).

According to Dover et al. (2020), the adoption of diversity initiatives within contemporary organisations may send fairness (which groups of employees are treated fairly/unfairly), inclusion (which groups of employees are included/excluded) and competency signals (which groups of employees are competent/incompetent) to organisational stakeholders including PWD. Diversity initiatives are not only espoused by the organisation but must also be actively enacted in order to be effective in the achievement of their goals (Ng & Sears, 2020). In assessing the efficacy of diversity initiatives, Leslie (2019) categorised diversity practices as ***non-discrimination practices*** (merit-based decision-making; providing diversity training); ***resource practices*** (preferential treatment for marginalised groups, targeted recruitment, issuing diversity statements, targeted training for marginalised groups, diversity networking groups to improve access and support, diversity mentoring programmes to assist marginalised employees), **and *accountability practices*** (diversity plans, diversity performance evaluations, diversity managers and/or departments, grievance systems) (see also, Kalev et al., 2006; Richard et al., 2013).

Consistent across these diversity/equality-related paradigms are elements that must be present within the organisation in order for these workplace initiatives to succeed, namely commitment from the organisation's leaders who foster an inclusive fair diverse culture, diversity and inclusion policies that are actively implemented and enforced, challenge ableist norms, engage in an ongoing destigmatisation process (Köllen et al., 2018; Kreiner et al., 2022; LeBlanc-Omstead & Kinsella, 2019; Özbilgin, 2009; Sabharwal, 2014; Tomlinson & Schwabenland, 2010).

Diversity Motives

Research (Ely & Thomas, 2001) has proposed three perspectives of diversity, namely (i) *discrimination and fairness*; (ii) *access and legitimacy* and (iii) *integration and learning*. The former is associated with the ***moral arguments*** for pursuing diversity which are centred around ensuring "justice and fair treatment" the second is based on embracing diversity such that the composition of an organisation staff complement is reflective of the societies they serve and the final perspective, is related to ***business case*** arguments, since organisations are expected to engage in cost–benefit analysis of the use of their resources (Tomlinson & Schwabenland, 2010), where the outcome of such an analysis suggests that adopting diversity policies would result in net organisational benefits such as better decision-making, increased innovation, complex problem solving, increased cost-effectiveness, reduction of inefficiencies (Bernstein & Bilimoria, 2013; Dover et al., 2020; Ely & Thomas, 2001; Hossain et al., 2020; Ozeren, 2014; Seierstad, 2016; Tomlinson & Schwabenland, 2010; Van Dijk et al., 2012). Similarly, Dover et al. (2020) suggest that organisations may adopt diversity policies and practices to create fairer workplaces (***justice*** *rationale*), create more efficient and effective workplaces (***instrumental*** *rationale*) and to communicate non-discriminatory and diversity values to stakeholders (***signalling*** *rationale*).

The realisation by organisations of the benefits of the business imperative is not without controversy, indeed it has been argued that some organisational factors may moderate whether and the extent to which the business benefits are accrued, i.e. its efficacy is context contingent (Barmes & Ashtiany, 2003; Robinson & DeChant, 1997; Tomlinson & Schwabenland, 2010). This includes whether these diversity policies are actively implemented; whether there is management support for diversity initiatives, etc. Further, it has been argued that business motives are more likely to be cited by private sector organsations in support of diversity initiatives, whereas public sector organisations are more likely to identify a combination of business case reasons and moral arguments in support of the pursuit of diversity (Jansen et al., 2021; Tomlinson & Schwabenland, 2010). Notwithstanding this, there is no policy panacea that may be applied resulting in success for all organisations, thus organisations would be well advised to select the most appropriate ones from the available options (Tomlinson & Schwabenland, 2010).

Social justice arguments for diversity are related to fairness, equity and moral legitimacy within organisations (Hill et al., 2018; Noon, 2007). Thus, when considering a PWD for an employment vacancy, the candidates background, qualifications and aptitude should be evaluated as far as they are required by all applicants in order to be considered for placement (Johns et al., 2012; Johnson & Miller, 2002; Tomlinson & Schwabenland, 2010). Hence, if a data entry clerk post is vacant and an applicant has mobility limitations, this should not preclude that candidate from consideration because it is unlikely that mobility is directly related to the daily duties of a data entry clerk.

Turning now to legislative arguments, as previously indicated, the legislative response in the Anglophone Caribbean has been somewhat varied, such that whereas the islands of the Bahamas, Antigua and Barbuda, Jamaica and Guyana have enacted laws specifically outlawing discrimination against PWD, Trinidad and Tobago, St. Lucia and Guyana, have enacted more broad-based laws to prohibit discrimination on a wide variety of grounds, including but not limited to disabilities. The salient question in relation to these laws is whether and the extent to which they are efficacious and for those islands where legislation either does not exist or is still in the developmental stage, how are they ensuring that they are fulfilling their obligation as a signatory to the CRPD. A quick and dirty approach to determine this could be to compare the number of PWD employed prior and subsequent to the enactment of relevant legislation and/or adoption of the CRPD (via policy changes) to determine whether the number has increased. However, such an approach lacks rigour and fails to take into account the complexity of the environment in which organisations function. This approach as such is replete with pitfalls as changes to employment levels which are observed after such a comparison may or may not be attributable to legislative changes but to other environmental factors (Bennington & Wein, 2000; Hornstein et al., 2001; Loretto & White, 2006; Smedley & Whitten, 2006).

Discrimination cases are typically civil law cases that are filed in a court of law or employment tribunal, where the standard of proof is a preponderance of the evidence, here the aggrieved party (or victim of discrimination) shoulders responsibility for proving their claims. This refers to a balance of probabilities, where the charging party must show that the alleged acts and/or omissions are more likely to have occurred in the manner alleged than not. There are also civil matters where the burden of proof requires the charging party to provide "clear and convincing evidence" to support the act/omission being alleged in the legal filing(s). Civil matters such as discrimination claims do not rise to the level of the provision of proof "beyond a reasonable doubt", as is required for a successful conviction in criminal cases. In practice, the burden of proof in cases of discrimination is first on the aggrieved party, who must not only assert that discriminatory action has been perpetuated against them but must also offer evidence in support of their assertions. Where this is done the burden of proof may then be passed on to the workplace or responding party to the action, whose responsibility it then becomes to show that their behaviour was not unlawful.

The primary exception associated with anti-discrimination legislation is the genuine and determining occupational requirement (GDOR), which mandates that the absence of specific disabilities is required for a specific job and within the organisation, it is appropriate to apply this requirement. This suggests that where either the employee or applicant fails to meet this requirement, or the employer is not satisfied that it is met, discrimination is permissible, and any legal remedy sought is unlikely to succeed. Finally, the punitive remedies available to the claimant must be severe enough to deter organisations from engaging in discriminatory behaviour and to dissuade other organisations from engaging in reprehensible discriminatory practices.

Even with these change agents, changing institutionalised systemic behaviour socially and specifically within the organisational context is not without challenge. There are many change models after which societal and organisational changes may be patterned, including but not limited to Lewin's change model (Hussain et al., 2018), Kotter's change model (Kritsonis, 2005). In advocating for the initiation and pursuit of a change agenda across the Caribbean region to ensure the eventual achievement of the United Nation's strategic goals and the objectives of the CRPD to which the islands are signatories, a change model proposed by Prochaska and DiClemente (1983) may be instrumental. The model's proposed stages of change consist of the following four (4) steps: ***Pre-contemplation*** (targets of change maintain the status quo); ***Contemplation*** (targets of change develop an intention to change); ***Preparation*** (targets of change develop a plan to change); ***Action*** (targets of change start and continue to make changes in the immediate term; and ***Maintenance*** (targets of change resist reverting to old patterns of thinking and modes of behaviour and continue with the changed behaviour) (Lecube et al., 2019; Manaf, 2019; Prochaska & DiClemente, 1983).

Comprehensive changes in discriminatory behaviour are unlikely to occur in isolation. With phenomenon such as discrimination and disparate treatment, cognitive, emotional and behavioural changes are required, however, where prejudicial attitudes are embedded culturally, the emergence of change will inevitably be slow and methodical, and its realisation would likely be hastened by repeated island-wide re-education and sensitisation campaigns across the region; incentives offered to organisations to increase the number of employees with disabilities (e.g. offering government subsidies for any required accommodations), comprehensive enactment of anti-discrimination laws (in relation to disabilities) which are enforced, with punitive consequences for any and all breaches (by organisations and individuals), *inter alia*.

Current Disability Challenges

According to the World Bank's World Health Report on Disability, at the time of writing there are over 1 billion persons with disabilities globally which accounts for 15% of the world's population. This number continues to grow globally due to poor environmental conditions, inability to access adequate health care, unsafe working conditions and increase in chronic untreated health conditions. The number of PWD is not equally distributed globally and in fact, 80% of PWD live in developing countries and women disproportionately report higher incidents of disability than men. According to the International Labour Organisation (ILO), approximately 386 million persons of working age are PWD, with employers typically assuming that they are unable or unwilling to work. Such assumptions, based on preconceived notions rather than proven reality exacerbates the challenges of unemployment and underemployment faced by this marginalised group and as a result, PWD who are adversely affected are forced to rely on the state for access to social services and welfare payments.

Consequently, the benefits associated with work are not realised, not only the monetary payments and economic benefits but the abilities to use one's knowledge, skills and abilities in a productive way, but there is a resulting deterioration of their mental wellness, social inclusion, self-esteem and self-worth. In promoting access to employment for PWD, the ILO has proposed a useful three-pronged framework, which proposes (i) *inclusive employment*, (ii) *enabling environments* and (iii) *increasing employability* as areas of concentration for governments, employers and trade unions (and other workers organisations), with a view of promoting inclusion of PWD in the labour market.

As it relates to *inclusive employment*, the ILO echoes some of the previously supported research findings namely a business case for diversity, disability sensitisation via knowledge sharing. Turning to the promotion of *enabling environments*, the ILO supports the enactment of anti-discrimination legislation, social protection schemes and employment placement services for PWD. The final prong of the ILO framework is the focus on *increasing employability* of PWD by promoting inclusive skills development and entrepreneurship, and in so doing PWD are not dependent on employers for offers of gainful employment but create opportunities for themselves by scanning the marketplace and identifying areas of service or product deficiencies. According to independent reports by the United Nations Educational, Scientific and Cultural Organisation (UNESCO) and the Economic Commission for Latin America and the Caribbean (ECLAC), at the time of writing there are approximately 1.3 million persons in the Caribbean with disabilities facing discrimination, exclusion and systematic barriers which curtail their ability to actively participate in social, economic and political life.

Models of Disability

The above-referenced ILO framework points to an understanding of disabilities and PWD from the perspective of the impact of the environmental conditions on PWD, rather than the physical or mental challenges faced by the individual being considered. Within extant literature there are several models of disabilities which are considered. Perhaps the model which is most ubiquitous (in the Caribbean) is the ***medical*** model, where PWD are assessed based on their physical and/or psychological medical diagnoses. However, in addition to this, the social model of disability regards disability as a socially constructed problem, such that it is not the medical condition of the individual but rather the extent to which the social environment in which the individual resides (and is employed) is able and willing to make environmental modifications to ensure that all persons may actively take part and be integrated. The ***human rights model*** of disability recognises disability as a part of human diversity and as such PWD should be included and not excluded from the rights and freedoms afforded to any other. There is also the International Classification of Functioning, Disability and Health (**ICF**) model of disability which asserts that a person's level of functioning is determined by environmental factors, personal factors and the state of their health (or health conditions). In the Caribbean when referencing PWD, the medical model is the most commonly used approach, this results in employers' inability to see the role of the social/environmental structures, limiting the engagement of PWD in accessing and retaining gainful employment.

The medical model of disability focuses on the physical and/or mental impairment with which an individual has been diagnosed. It defines disability as "the attribute(s) of a person who is functionally and biologically limited" (Jongbloed, 2003), these may be categorised as physical, visual, auditory, psychosocial, and intellectual. This perspective of disability aligns disabilities with individuals and as a result, the individual is seen as defective, dependent and stigmatised (Foster & Scott, 2015; Sullivan & Artiles, 2011).

The accommodations which may be required for this heterogenous group, are regarded as potentially imposing a burden on organisations, such that its profitability and sustainability are adversely affected. This is typically in the absence of supporting evidence. In fact, this prevailing wisdom has not found support in empirical research, in fact, it has been argued that many of the accommodations required are minimal in costs (Bonacio, 2020) and due to the heterogeneity in nature and scope of disabilities, all possible accommodations will not be the same for all members of this marginalised group (Schartz et al., 2006; Solovieva & Walls, 2013). Where discrimination has been institutionalised in a society or an organisation, prejudicial patterns of employment practice may be followed without question, as a result of norms and expectations within the workplace (Renskin, 2000). Indeed, the embeddedness of discrimination within societies (Banaji, 1999) may make it more challenging for movement towards inclusion to occur.

Theoretically, there exist many models through which we can enrich our understanding of persons with disabilities and employment (Coker, 1995). Though the acceptance of stereotypes may be an efficient shortcut to aid our understanding of persons whom we regard as "other" (i.e. those persons who do not fit within the preconceived parameters of a typical stereotyped employee), it must be emphasised that heterogeneity exists within all groups and by extension within all marginalised groups. For the avoidance of doubt, it would be erroneous to assert that all persons with disabilities are the same and have the same needs, the same accommodation requirements, the same levels of productivity, and the same limitations as it would be to assert that all humans are the same.

The disability employment model developed by Bonaccio et al. (2020) highlights some concerns that employers may have in relation to the employment of persons with disabilities. Specifically, regarding recruitment and selection employers are concerned with (*i*) the qualifications of applicants with disabilities; (*ii*) the number of qualified people with disabilities; (*iii*) the attractiveness of vacancies to people with disabilities; (*iv*) the selection process for applicants with disabilities; (*v*) the cost of potential accommodations. Employers also have concerns about the social organisational integration of employees with disabilities and the potential impact of workers with disabilities on colleagues. Finally, as it relates to performance concerns, employers may be concerned with the job performance of PWD, the occupational health and safety behaviours of workers with disabilities, occupational health and safety behaviour and disciplinary action and termination of workers with disabilities.

It is common for published annual reports to include a statement of inclusivity but while it will typically explicitly include race, age, gender, ethnicity, *inter alia*, disabilities are frequently omitted. In the Caribbean, there exist five (5) dominant conglomerates, namely Ansa McAl Ltd., Barbados Shipping and Trading Ltd., Grace Kennedy and Company and Neal and Massy Holdings Ltd. Of these in their published annual reports over the period 2015–2020, each conglomerate included statements indicating their commitment to inclusion, equality and diversity and in so doing positioned their companies as tolerant of persons with disabilities and companies who would be willing to engage current or potential members of staff /stakeholder group members with disabilities. These statements have not yet been tested in the Caribbean but where companies based in other jurisdictions have made similar statements, empirical research has found that espoused policies are incongruent with enacted practice (Cooke & Saini, 2010; Gilbert & Ivancevich, 2000; Ng & Sears, 2012; Nyambegera, 2002; Prasad & Mills, 1997).

Concluding Comments

This book is important at this time, because there is a paucity of literature on issues of discrimination and diversity in the English-speaking Caribbean region specifically, on the grounds of disabilities and, where such publications exist, they fail to provide a comprehensive analysis of the issues relating to employment of this marginalised group. This point of departure of this text is that it covers persons with disabilities in the Caribbean by reason of its comprehensive and exclusive evaluative analysis of employment in relation to persons with disabilities, simultaneously examining socio-economic and legal factors. These issues will be examined from the perspective of Stone and Colella's (1996) seminal model, which "provides a framework for understanding and studying the way persons with disabilities are perceived and treated at work", and via the framework of the theory of social categorisation, where individuals categorise others into groups with the objective of identifying those who are similar to and/or different from themselves (Wenzel, 2004) and hence those with whom they anticipate successful work and other relationships (Kurzban et al., 2001). There are three (3) primary models of disability, namely the medical, social and human rights models. Within the island states of the Caribbean, the medical model of disability is relied on and as such, physical or mental impairments are perceived to differentiate persons with disabilities from persons with no known disabilities. This is reflected in the legislation (in the Anglophone Caribbean) enacted to prohibit discrimination on the basis of disabilities, and as such is influential in the way in which disabilities are perceived by societal members and stakeholders.

Legislators and policymakers may wish to consider the analysis of this text in making legislative amendments or enacting new laws, with a view to broadening the range of persons protected as it relates particularly to disabilities. Moreover, organisational practitioners may find these discussions useful, where current policies/practices are shown to be unlikely to further their organisation's objective vis-à-vis productivity and sustainability. Moreover, academics may also find this text useful in facilitating the delivery of contemporary data, literature and analysis as it relates to the current challenges faced by persons with disabilities in the region, how they are perceived within Caribbean society and community stakeholders and whether and the extent to which this has evolved over time. Students seeking to understand the challenges faced by persons with disabilities as a marginalised group in contemporary Caribbean society may also find the analysis in this text enlightening. Academics and students from outside the Caribbean region may find this text useful in conducting comparative analyses of what obtains in this region as compared to what obtains in theirs, in terms of both the content of the law and policy as well as their real-life application. This book also establishes a benchmark for future researchers, from within the region as well as outside, who may explore further the issues of discrimination in relation to persons with disabilities and the extent to which sustained employment of this group is affected. In the Caribbean region, specifically, as it relates to persons with disabilities and much of what is accepted as representative of reality is based on anecdotal evidence and historical assumptions about this marginalised group.

In the succeeding chapters, the authors examine from the perspective of the Anglophone Caribbean: the nature of disabilities; education and persons with disabilities; disabilities, information technology, assistive devices, and employment; mental health disabilities and work; neurodiversity and employment; disability, employment and law; prohibiting discrimination against persons with disabilities—lessons from other jurisdictions and the experiences of disabled persons in employment.

References

Andrews, E. E., Ayers, K. B., Brown, K. S., Dunn, D. S., & Pilarski, C. R. (2021). No body is expendable: Medical rationing and disability justice during the COVID-19 pandemic. *American Psychologist, 76*, 451–461.

Banaji, M. R. (1999). *The roots of prejudice*. Kendon Smith Lectures, University of North Carolina, Greensboro. NC.

Barmes, L., & Ashtiany, W. S. (2003). The diversity approach to achieving equality: Potential and pitfalls. *Industrial Law Journal, 32*(4), 274–296.

Bell, S. T., Brown, S. G., Colaneri, A., & Outland, N. (2018). Team composition and the ABCs of teamwork. *American Psychologist, 73*(4), 349.

Bennington, L., & Wein, R. (2000). Anti-discrimination legislation in Australia: Fair, effective, efficient or irrelevant? *International Journal of Manpower, 21*(1), 21–33.

Benuyenah, V. (2021). Theorising an organisational citizenship behaviour model for managerial decision-making: From history to contemporary application. *Management Research Review, 44*(8), 1182–1198.

Bergeron, D. M. (2007). The potential paradox of organizational citizenship behavior: Good citizens at what cost? *Academy of Management Review, 32*(4), 1078–1095.

Bernstein, R. S., & Bilimoria, D. (2013). Diversity perspectives and minority nonprofit board member inclusion. *Equality, Diversity and Inclusion: An International Journal, 32*(7), 636–653.

Bizri, R. (2018). Diversity management and OCB: The connection evidence from the Lebanese banking sector. *Equality, Diversity and Inclusion: An International Journal, 37*(3), 233–253.

Bonaccio, S., Connelly, C. E., Gellatly, I. R., Jetha, A., & Ginis, K. A. M. (2020). The participation of people with disabilities in the workplace across the employment cycle: Employer concerns and research evidence. *Journal of Business and Psychology, 35*(2), 135–158.

Coker, C. C. (1995). *A comparison of job satisfaction and economic benefits of four different employment models for persons with disabilities*. University of Wisconsin-Stout, Rehabilitation Research and Training Center on Improving Community Based Rehabilitation Programmes. Menomonie, Wisconsin, USA.

Collinson, D. L., Knights, D., & Collinson, M. (1990). *Managing to discriminate*. Routledge.

Coleman, N., Sykes, W., & Groom, C. (2013). *Barriers to employment and unfair treatment at work*. Equality and Huma Rights Commission.

Cooke, F. L., & Saini, D. S. (2010). Diversity management in India: A study of organizations in different ownership forms and industrial sectors. *Human Resource Management: Published in Cooperation with the School of Business Administration, the University of Michigan and in Alliance with the Society of Human Resources Management, 49*(3), 477–500.

Curran, M. (1988). Gender and recruitment: People and places in the labour market. *Work, Employment and Society, 2*(3), 335–351.

Dover, T. L., Kaiser, C. R., & Major, B. (2020). Mixed signals: The unintended effects of diversity initiatives. *Social Issues and Policy Review, 14*(1), 152–181.

Ely, R. J., & Thomas, D. A. (2001). Cultural diversity at work: The effects of diversity perspectives on work group processes and outcomes. *Administrative Science Quarterly, 46*(2), 229–273.

Foster, D., & Scott, P. (2015). Nobody's responsibility: the precarious position of disabled employees in the UK workplace. *Industrial Relations Journal, 46*(4), 328–343.

Garg, S., & Sangwan, S. (2021). Literature review on diversity and inclusion at workplace, 2010–2017. *Vision, 25*(1), 12–22.

Gasorek, D. (2000). Inclusion at Dun & Bradstreet: Building a high-performance company. *Diversity Factor, 8*, 25–29.

Gayle-Geddes, A. (2016). A situational analysis of persons with disabilities in Jamaica and Trinidad and Tobago: Education and employment policy imperatives. *Occupying disability: Critical approaches to community, justice, and decolonizing disability* (pp. 127–141). Springer, Dordrecht.

Gilbert, J. A., & Ivancevich, J. M. (2000). Valuing diversity: A tale of two organizations. *Academy of Management Perspectives, 14*(1), 93–105.

Hill, J., Philpot, R., Walton-Fisette, J. L., Sutherland, S., Flemons, M., Ovens, A., Phillips, S., & Flory, S. B. (2018). Conceptualising social justice and sociocultural issues within physical education teacher education: International perspectives. *Physical Education and Sport Pedagogy, 23*(5), 469–483.

Hornstein, Z. (2001). Age discrimination legislation: Choices for the UK, joseph rowntree foundation findings. http://www.jrf.org.uk/Knowledge/findings/socialpolicy/pdf/spr711/pdf.

Hossain, M., Atif, M., Ahmed, A., & Mia, L. (2020). Do LGBT workplace diversity policies create value for firms? *Journal of Business Ethics, 167*(4), 775–791.

Hussain, S. T., Lei, S., Akram, T., Haider, M. J., Hussain, S. H., & Ali, M. (2018). Kurt Lewin's change model: A critical review of the role of leadership and employee involvement in organizational change. *Journal of Innovation & Knowledge, 3*(3), 123–127.

Jansen, W. S., Kröger, C., Van der Toorn, J., & Ellemers, N. (2021). The right thing to do or the smart thing to do? How communicating moral or business motives for diversity affects the employment image of Dutch public and private sector organizations. *Journal of Applied Social Psychology, 51*(7), 746–759.

Jewson, N., & Mason, D. (1986). The theory and practice of equal opportunities policies: liberal and radical approaches. *The Sociological Review, 34*(2), 307–334.

Johns, N., Green, A., & Powell, M. (2012). Diversity in the British NHS: The business versus the'moral'case. *Equality, Diversity and Inclusion: An International Journal, 31*(8), 768–783.

Johnson, D. G., & Miller, K. W. (2002). Is diversity in computing a moral matter? *ACM SIGCSE Bulletin, 34*(2), 9–10.

Jongbloed, L. (2003). Disability policy in Canada: An overview. *Journal of Disability Policy Studies, 13*(4), 203–209.

Kalev, A., Dobbin, F., & Kelly, E. (2006). Best practices or best guesses? Assessing the efficacy of corporate affirmative action and diversity policies. *American Sociological Review, 71*, 589–617.

Karpur, A., VanLooy, S. A., & Bruyère, S. M. (2014). Employer practices for employment of people with disabilities: A literature scoping review. *Rehabilitation Research, Policy, and Education, 28*(4), 225–241.

Kirton, G. (2020). Diversity and inclusion in a changing world of work. In A. Wilkinson, & M. Barry (Eds.), *The future of work and employment* (pp. 49–64) Edward Elgar Publishing.

Köllen, T., Kakkuri-Knuuttila, M. L., & Bendl, R. (2018). An indisputable "holy trinity"? On the moral value of equality, diversity, and inclusion. *Equality, Diversity and Inclusion, 37*(5), 438–449.

Konur, O. (2002). Access to employment by disabled people in the UK: Is the Disability Discrimination Act working? *International Journal of Discrimination and the Law, 5*(4), 247–279.

Kreiner, G., Mihelcic, C. A., & Mikolon, S. (2022). Stigmatized work and stigmatized workers. *Annual Review of Organizational Psychology and Organizational Behavior, 9*(1), 95–120.

Kritsonis, A. (2005). Comparison of change theories. *International Journal of Scholarly Academic Intellectual Diversity, 8*(1), 1–7.

Kurzban, R., Tooby, J., & Cosmides, L. (2001). Can race be erased? Coalitional computation and social categorization. *Proceedings of the National Academy of Sciences, 98*(26), 15387–15392.

Laci, A., Maxhelaku, A., & Rusi, I. (2017). Equality at work and discrimination in employment and occupation. *Journal of Educational and Social Research, 7*(2), 67–67.

Larkey, L. K. (1996). Toward a theory of communicative interactions in culturally diverse workgroups. *Academy of Management Review, 21*(2), 463–491.

Leach, L. S., Butterworth, P., Strazdins, L., Rodgers, B., Broom, D. H., & Olesen, S. C. (2010). The limitations of employment as a tool for social inclusion. *BMC Public Health, 10*(1), 1–13.

LeBlanc-Omstead, S., & Kinsella, A. E. (2019). Shedding light on a 'hidden prejudice': Considering sanism in occupational therapy. *Occupational Therapy Now, 21*(2), 15–16.

Lecube, A., Sánchez, E., Andrés, A., Saldaña, C., Morales, M. J., Calañas, A., ... Vilarrasa, N. (2019). Assessing motivational stages and processes of change for weight management around bariatric surgery: A multicenter study. *Obesity Surgery, 29*(10), 3348–3356.

Leslie, L. M. (2019). Diversity initiative effectiveness: A typological theory of unintended consequences. *Academy of Management Review, 44*(3), 538–563.

Liff, S., & Wajcman, J. (1996). Sameness and difference revisited: Which way forward for equal opportunity initiatives. *Journal of Management Studies, 33*(1), 79–94.

Loretto, W., & White, P. (2006). Employers' attitudes, practices and policies towards older workers. *Human Resource Management Journal, 16*(3), 313–330.

Manaf, R. A. (2019). A cluster randomised controlled trial on effectiveness of carbon monoxide measurement feedback among college smoker: A study protocol. *Medical Journal Malaysia, 74*(1), 62.

Miminoshvili, M., & Černe, M. (2021). Workplace inclusion–exclusion and knowledge-hiding behaviour of minority members. *Knowledge Management Research & Practice, 20*(3), 422–435.

Mor Barak, M. E. (2015). Inclusion is the key to diversity management, but what is inclusion? *Human Service Organizations: Management, Leadership & Governance, 39*(2), 83–88.

Mor-Barak, M. E., & Cherin, D. (1998). A tool to expand organizational understanding of workforce diversity. *Administration in Social Work, 22*, 47–64.

Morris, F. (2018). An inclusive, equitable and prosperous Caribbean: The case of persons with disabilities. *Social and Economic Studies, 67*(4), 95–119.

Nair, N., & Vohra, N. (2015). Diversity and inclusion at the workplace: A review of research and perspectives. *IIMA Working Papers* (WP2015-03-34).

Ng, E. S., & Sears, G. J. (2012). CEO leadership styles and the implementation of organizational diversity practices: Moderating effects of social values and age. *Journal of Business Ethics, 105*(1), 41–52.

Ng, E. S., & Sears, G. J. (2020). Walking the talk on diversity: CEO beliefs, moral values, and the implementation of workplace diversity practices. *Journal of Business Ethics, 164*(3), 437–450.

Nkomo, S. M., Bell, M. P., Roberts, L. M., Joshi, A., & Thatcher, S. M. (2019). Diversity at a critical juncture: New theories for a complex phenomenon. *Academy of Management Review, 44*(3), 498–517.

Noon, M. (2007). The fatal flaws of diversity and the business case for ethnic minorities. *Work, Employment and Society, 21*(4), 773–784.

Nyambegera, S. M. (2002). Ethnicity and human resource management practice in sub-Saharan Africa: The relevance of the managing diversity discourse. *International Journal of Human Resource Management, 13*(7), 1077–1090.

O'Donovan, D. (2018). Diversity and inclusion in the workplace. In *Organizational behaviour and human resource management* (pp. 73–108). Springer.

Özbilgin, M. (2009). Equality, diversity and inclusion at work: A research companion. In M. F. Ozbilgin (Ed.), *Equality, diversity and inclusion at work: Yesterday, today and tomorrow* (p. 1–16). Edward Elgar.

Ozeren, E. (2014). Sexual orientation discrimination in the workplace: A systematic review of literature. *Procedia-Social and Behavioral Sciences, 109*, 1203–1215.

Peragine, V., & Biagi, F. (2019). *Equality of opportunity: Theory, measurement and policy implications*. Publications Office of the European Union.

Phillips, K. W., & Loyd, D. L. (2006). When surface and deep-level diversity collide: The effects on dissenting group members. *Organizational Behavior and Human Decision Processes, 99*(2), 143–160.

Phillips, K. W., Northcraft, G. B., & Neale, M. A. (2006). Surface-level diversity and decision-making in groups: When does deep-level similarity help? *Group Processes & Intergroup Relations, 9*(4), 467–482.

Prasad, P., & Mills, A. J. (1997). From showcase to shadow: Understanding the dilemmas of managing workplace diversity. In *Managing the organizational melting pot: Dilemmas of workplace diversity* (pp. 3–27), Sage Publications.

Prochaska, J. O., & DiClemente, C. C. (1983). Stages and processes of self-change of smoking: Toward an integrative model of change. *Journal of Consulting and Clinical Psychology, 51*(3), 390.

Renskin, B. F. (2000). The proximate causes of employment discrimination. *Contemporary Sociology, 29*, 319–328.

Richard, O. C., Roh, H., & Pieper, J. R. (2013). The link between diversity and equality management practice bundles and racial diversity in the managerial ranks: Does firm size matter? *Human Resource Management, 52*, 215–242.

Robertson, Q. M. (2004). *Disentangling the meanings of diversity and inclusion*. CAHRS, Cornell University.

Robinson, G., & Dechant, K. (1997). Building a business case for diversity. *Academy of Management Perspectives, 11*(3), 21–31.

Roemer, J. E. (2002). Equality of opportunity: A progress report. *Social Choice and Welfare, 19*(2), 455–471.

Sabharwal, M. (2014). Is diversity management sufficient? Organizational inclusion to further performance. *Public Personnel Management, 43*(2), 197–217.

Schaar, J. H. (2017). Equality of opportunity, and beyond. In *Equality* (pp. 228–249). Routledge.

Schartz, H. A., Hendricks, D. J., & Blanck, P. (2006). Workplace accommodations: Evidence based outcomes. *Work, 27*(4), 345–354.

Seierstad, C. (2016). Beyond the business case: The need for both utility and justice rationales for increasing the share of women on boards. *Corporate Governance: An International Review, 24*(4), 390–405.

Shore, L. M., Randel, A. E., Chung, B. G., Dean, M. A., Holcombe Ehrhart, K., & Singh, G. (2011). Inclusion and diversity in work groups: A review and model for future research. *Journal of Management, 37*(4), 1262–1289.

Smedley, K., & Whitten, H. (2006). *Age matters—employing, motivating and managing older employees*. Gower Publishing, Hampshire.

Solovieva, T. I., & Walls, R. T. (2013). Implications of workplace accommodations for persons with disabilities. *Journal of Workplace Behavioral Health, 28*(3), 192–211.

Soni, V. (2000). A twenty-first-century reception for diversity in the public sector: A case study. *Public Administration Review, 60*(5), 395–408.

Stone, D. L., & Colella, A. (1996). A model of factors affecting the treatment of disabled individuals in organizations. *Academy of Management Review, 21*(2), 352–401.

Sullivan, A. L., & Artiles, A. J. (2011). Theorizing racial inequity in special education: Applying structural inequity theory to disproportionality. *Urban Education, 46*(6), 1526–1552.

Thomas, G. M. (2022). A legacy of silence: The intersections of medical sociology and disability studies. *Medical Humanities, 48*(1), 123–132.

Thomas, R. R. (1990, March–April). From affirmative action to affirming diversity. *Harvard Business Review*, 107–117.

Tomlinson, F., & Schwabenland, C. (2010). Reconciling competing discourses of diversity? The UK non-profit sector between social justice and the business case. *Organization, 17*(1), 101–121.

Van Dijk, H., van Engen, M., & Paauwe, J. (2012). Reframing the business case for diversity: A values and virtues perspective. *Journal of Business Ethics, 111*(1), 73–84.

Vanderheiden, G. C. (1998). Universal design and assistive technology in communication and information technologies: Alternatives or complements? *Assistive Technology, 10*(1), 29–36.

Vornholt, K., Villotti, P., Muschalla, B., Bauer, J., Colella, A., Zijlstra, F., Van Ruitenbeek, G., Uitdewilligen, S., & Corbière, M. (2018). Disability and employment–overview and highlights. *European Journal of Work and Organizational Psychology, 27*(1), 40–55.

Wenzel, M. (2004). An analysis of norm processes in tax compliance. *Journal of Economic Psychology, 25*(2), 213–228.

Yap, M., & Konrad, A. M. (2009). Gender and racial differentials in promotions: Is there a sticky floor, a mid-level bottleneck, or a glass ceiling? *Industrial Relations, 64*, 593–619.

CHAPTER 2

The Nature of Disabilities in the Caribbean

Introduction

This chapter will examine the causes of disabilities in the English-speaking Caribbean region and the extent of their impact on the life of the affected person(s), specifically as it relates to employment. Generally, the causes of disabilities include birth defects, congenital conditions, accidents, chronic illnesses, gun and physical violence, gender-based violence and other health conditions (Autor, 2011; Barnes, 2014; Büttner & Hasselhorn, 2011; de Lucas & Navarro, 2020; Grünke & Cavendish, 2016; Pinilla-Roncancio & Gallardo, 2022). In the Caribbean region, the frequently reported causes of disabilities include accidents (work related and vehicular), chronic illnesses (e.g. diabetes) and other health conditions, gun violence and gender-based violence (ECLAC, 2019; Gayle & Palmer, 2005; World Bank, 2019). Within the context of employment, it has been argued that knowledge of the nature and origin of an individual's disability, may influence whether and the extent to which a person with disabilities is engaged by an organisation and treated fairly. Stone and Colella's (1996) seminal model has identified these as influential intervening factors in the way that persons with disabilities are perceived at work. They argue that the value of members of this group is assessed through various characteristics including but not limited to their aesthetic qualities, the origin of their disability, the extent to which their disability

J. H. Stephenson and N. Persadie, *Disability in the Workplace*, Palgrave Explorations in Workplace Stigma,
https://doi.org/10.1007/978-3-031-19340-8_2

can be concealed and whether or not making accommodations for PWD is likely to be disruptive and the potential danger which persons with disabilities are either known to or, believed to pose (Stone & Colella, 1996). It must be noted that there is no legal requirement for persons with disabilities to declare their disability to their employer in the Caribbean, and as such, where persons with disabilities believe (given the prevailing organisational and/or societal culture) that they may be demeaned, ridiculed, bullied or otherwise unfairly treated as a result of their disability, they are unlikely to declare their disability to their employer, thus avoiding disparate treatment.

Categorising Disabilities

Let us start by understanding the term persons with disabilities (PWD) within the employment context, these are "*individuals whose prospects of securing, returning to, retaining and advancing in suitable employment are substantially reduced as a result of a recognized physical, sensory, intellectual or mental impairment*" (Suresh & Dyaram, 2020: 1560). This is consistent with the definition used within the Convention on the Rights of Persons with Disabilities (CRPD) which defined PWD as those "who have long-term physical, mental, intellectual or sensory impairments which, in interaction with various barriers, may hinder their full and effective participation in society on an equal basis with others". Relatedly, Article 2 of the CRPD defines discrimination as "*any distinction, exclusion or restriction on the basis of disability which has the purpose or effect of impairing or nullifying the recognition, enjoyment or exercise, on an equal basis with others, of all human rights and fundamental freedoms in the political, economic, social, cultural, civil or any other field*", and reasonable accommodation as "*necessary and appropriate modification and adjustments not imposing a disproportionate or undue burden, where needed in a particular case, to ensure to persons with disabilities the enjoyment or exercise on an equal basis with others of all human rights and fundamental freedoms*". This is echoed by extant Caribbean anti-discrimination legislation, for example, Trinidad and Tobago's Equal Opportunities Act, 2000 has defined discrimination as where one individual is treated less favourably than another, on the basis of immutable characteristics.[1]

[1] In the case of Trinidad and Tobago's Equal Opportunity Act (2000), the protected grounds are disability, sex, race, ethnicity, origin, religion and marital status.

It is imperative to recognise PWD as a highly heterogeneous group, with impairments that vary with respect to their nature and severity. To this end, the Pan American Health Organisation (PAHO), reported the top 20 causes of disability (Table 2.1), in the Anglophone Caribbean, which may be broadly categorised as follows: ***Noncommunicable diseases*** (diabetes, depressive disorders, back and neck pain, anxiety disorders, gynecological diseases, oral conditions, migraine, uncorrected refractive errors, skin and subcutaneous diseases, osteoarthritis, bipolar disorder, asthma, kidney diseases, schizophrenia, alcohol use disorders, epilepsy); ***Communicable, maternal, perinatal and nutritional conditions*** (neonatal conditions, iron deficiency anaemia, diarrheal diseases); and ***Injuries*** (exposure to mechanical forces).

In the Anglophone Caribbean, the top seven (7) causes of disabilities in 2019 were ***noncommunicable diseases*** (diabetes, depressive disorders, back/neck pain, anxiety disorders, gynaecological diseases, oral conditions), followed by ***communicable conditions*** (neonatal conditions and iron deficiency anaemia). The 10th to 18th causes of disabilities are ***noncommunicable diseases*** (refractive errors, skin diseases, osteoarthritis, bipolar disorder, asthma, kidney diseases, schizophrenia, alcohol disorders and epilepsy. Finally, the 19th cause is diarrheal (***communicable, maternal perinatal and nutritional conditions***), and the 20th cause is exposure to mechanical forces (***injuries***). Over the period from 2000 to 2019, these causes of disability have not varied significantly, though the order of importance has fluctuated over time. Figure 2.1 and Table 2.2 record these causes for Antigua & Barbuda, the Bahamas, Barbados, Grenada, Guyana, Jamaica, St. Lucia, St. Vincent and the Grenadines and Trinidad and Tobago, with the corresponding proportion of each disability in 2000, identified for each island.

Below (see Fig. 2.2 and Table 2.3) the same data is presented for the above-mentioned islands, 19 years hence, i.e. in 2019. A comparison of the graphs for 2000 and 2019, reveals a significant difference in the appearance of the graphs, indicating that over the 19-year period, the incidence of all of the identified causes of disability increased across the English-speaking Caribbean (see Fig. 2.2 and Table 2.3). Notably, the primary cause of disabilities across the region was diabetes mellitus, which is attributed to lifestyle choices, primarily the content of our diet and the low incidence of exercise (Hennis et al., 2002), while the incidence of injuries (which affect physical mobility) are relatively low and are typically associated with road traffic accidents or work-related incidents (e.g. in

Table 2.1 Causes of disabilities in the Anglophone Caribbean (2000 vs 2019)

No.	2000		2019	
	Causes (2000)	Proportion of all causes (%)	Causes (2019)	Proportion of all causes (%)
1.	Diabetes mellitus (excluding CKD due to Diabetes)	6.5	Diabetes mellitus (excluding CKD due to Diabetes)	9.6
2.	Depressive disorders	6.4	Depressive disorders	6.3
3.	Back and neck pain	4.7	Back and neck pain	4.8
4.	Iron-deficiency anaemia	4.2	Anxiety disorders	3.8
5.	Anxiety disorders	4.1	Gynecological diseases	3.5
6.	Gynecological diseases	3.8	Oral conditions	3.2
7.	Migraine	3.5	Migraine	3.2
8.	Oral conditions	3.1	Neonatal conditions	3.1
9.	Neonatal conditions	2.9	Iron-deficiency anaemia	3.1
10.	Skin and subcutaneous diseases	2.6	Uncorrected refractive errors	2.4
11.	Asthma	2.6	Skin and subcutaneous diseases	2.2
12.	Uncorrected refractive errors	2.6	Osteoarthritis	2.1
13.	Bipolar disorder	2.1	Bipolar disorder	2.0
14.	Alcohol use disorders	1.8	Asthma	1.9
15.	Schizophrenia	1.8	Kidney diseases	1.9
16.	Epilepsy	1.6	Schizophrenia	1.8
17.	Osteoarthritis	1.6	Alcohol use disorders	1.7
18.	Kidney diseases	1.5	Epilepsy	1.4
19.	Exposure to mechanical forces	1.4	Diarrhoeal diseases	1.4
20.	Diarrhoeal diseases	1.3	Exposure to mechanical forces	1.3

Broad cause groups:

GREEN: Communicable, maternal, perinatal and nutritional conditions

BLUE: Noncommunicable diseases

PINK: Injuries

Source Global Health Estimates (2019). World Health Organisation (2020). https://www.paho.org/en/enlace/leading-causes-death-and-disability; Leading causes of mortality and health loss at regional, subregional, and country levels in the Region of the Americas, 2000–2019. ENLACE data portal. Pan American Health Organization (2021)

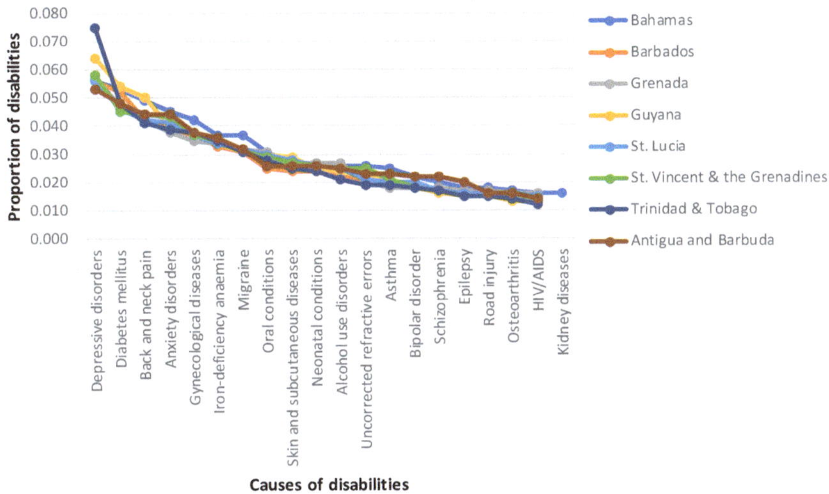

Fig. 2.1 Top 20 causes of disability in the Anglophone Caribbean (2000)

manufacturing, construction, etc.). WHO (2011) notes that *"disability disproportionately affects vulnerable populations. Lower income countries have a higher prevalence of disability barriers in accessing services, (health, education, employment, transport as well as information), including inadequate policies and standards, negative attitudes, lack of service provision, inadequate funding, lack of accessibility, inadequate information and communication and lack of participation in decisions that directly affect their lives"*.

Factors Influencing Employment of Persons with Disabilities

It has been established that work is important to daily life, including the ability to socially engage with others, to service one's financial obligations and to use one's skills and expertise in an efficient manner (Berrigan et al., 2020; Hendricks, 2010; Krzeminskà et al., 2019; Purc-Stephenson et al., 2017; Scott et al., 2017; Solomon, 2020). To this end, PWD want to work and may be prevented from doing so due to: ***(a) work environment challenges*** related to finding and retaining gainful employment—*(i)* limited job opportunities, *(ii)* willingness to

Table 2.2 Top causes of disability—Islands of the Anglophone Caribbean (2000)

		Proportion of disabilities (2019)								
No	*Causes of disability, 2000 (Listed in alphabetical order)*	*Antigua and Barbuda (%)*	*Bahamas (%)*	*Barbados (%)*	*Grenada (%)*	*Guyana (%)*	*Jamaica (%)*	*St. Lucia (%)*	*St. Vincent and the Grenadines (%)*	*Trinidad and Tobago (%)*
1.	Alcohol use disorders	2.6	2.60	1.80	1.80	2.10	1.50	2.10	2.50	1.80
2.	Alzheimer disease	0.0	0.00	1.60	0.00	0.00	0.00	0.00	0.00	0.00
3.	Anxiety disorders	4.4	4.50	4.20	4.20	3.90	4.10	4.20	4.30	3.90
4.	Asthma	2.2	2.50	2.50	3.10	2.90	3.00	3.20	2.50	1.50
5.	Back and neck pain	4.8	4.90	5.20	4.70	3.80	4.90	4.60	4.50	4.80
6.	Bipolar disorder	2.3	2.20	2.10	2.00	1.80	2.20	2.00	2.10	2.10
7.	Childhood behavioural disorders	0.00	0.00	0.00	0.00	0.00	1.30	0.00	0.00	0.00
8.	Depressive disorders	5.3	5.60	5.60	5.70	8.20	5.30	5.60	5.80	7.50
9.	Diabetes	5.8	5.30	7.20	6.50	5.40	6.00	8.00	6.90	8.60
10.	Diarrhoeal diseases	1.4	0.00	1.50	1.70	1.50	0.00	1.60	1.50	0.00
11.	Epilepsy	2.3	1.80	1.60	1.60	1.60	1.40	2.00	1.80	1.90
12.	Exposure to mechanical forces	2.5	0.00	0.00	1.60	0.00	1.90	0.00	1.30	0.00
13.	Falls	0.0	0.00	0.00	0.00	1.30	0.00	0.00	0.00	0.00

		Proportion of disabilities (2019)								
No	*Causes of disability, 2000 (Listed in alphabetical order)*	*Antigua and Barbuda (%)*	*Bahamas (%)*	*Barbados (%)*	*Grenada (%)*	*Guyana (%)*	*Jamaica (%)*	*St. Lucia (%)*	*St. Vincent and the Grenadines (%)*	*Trinidad and Tobago (%)*
14.	Gynecological diseases	4.4	4.20	3.90	3.50	3.40	3.90	3.70	3.70	3.80
15.	HIV/AIDS	0.0	1.60	0.00	0.00	0.00	0.00	0.00	0.00	0.00
16.	Iron-deficiency anaemia	3.8	3.70	2.20	3.80	6.40	3.70	4.10	4.40	4.10
17.	Kidney diseases	1.6	1.60	1.70	1.80	1.30	1.60	1.60	1.50	1.40
18.	Lymphatic filariasis	0.0	0.00	0.00	0.00	5.00	0.00	0.00	0.00	0.00
19.	Migraine	3.6	3.70	3.30	3.40	3.10	3.60	3.40	3.50	3.50
20.	Neonatal conditions	2.2	2.70	3.10	2.70	3.00	3.10	2.80	2.90	2.50
21.	Oral conditions	3.2	3.10	3.70	3.20	2.50	3.30	3.00	3.10	3.10
22.	Osteoarthritis	1.6	1.70	2.40	1.80	0.00	1.70	1.60	1.50	1.70
23.	Refractive errors	2.6	2.60	0.00	0.00	0.00	2.70	2.50	2.60	2.80
24.	Road injury	0.0	1.80	1.40	0.00	0.00	0.00	1.50	0.00	1.50
25.	Schizophrenia	2.0	2.00	2.00	1.70	1.50	1.80	1.70	1.70	1.90
26.	Skin diseases	2.6	2.70	2.40	2.70	2.40	2.70	2.60	2.70	2.40
27.	Stroke	0.0	0.00	0.00	0.00	0.00	0.00	0.00	0.00	1.20
28.	Uncorrected refractive errors	0.0	0.00	0.00	2.70	2.20	0.00	0.00	0.00	0.00

Source Global Health Estimates (2019). World Health Organisation (2020). https://www.paho.org/en/enlace/leading-causes-death-and-disability; Leading causes of mortality and health loss at regional, subregional, and country levels in the Region of the Americas, 2000–2019. ENLACE data portal. Pan American Health Organization (2021)

Abbreviated causes: **Diabetes**—Diabetes mellitus (excluding CKD due to Diabetes); **Skin diseases**—Skin and subcutaneous diseases

Pulmonary diseas—Chronic obstructive pulmonary disease; **Refractive errors**—Uncorrected refractive errors; **Alzheimer disease**—Alzheimer disease and other dementias

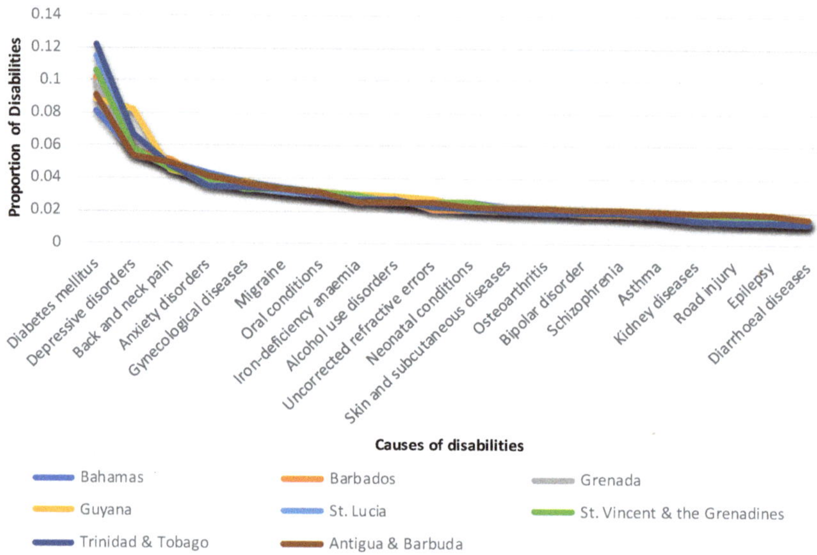

Fig. 2.2 Top 20 causes of disability in the Anglophone Caribbean (2019)

adapt to the workplace—e.g. architectural modifications, special equipment, organisational policy barriers limiting what they would be allowed to participate in—based on institutionalised discrimination or accepted stereotypes); ***(b) self-perceptions and symptom management*** *(iii)* ability to cope with symptoms at work, *(iv)* resisting the label of being considered a PWD, *(v)* defining the personal meaning of work) and ***(c) social climate*** issues *(vi)* gaining peer support, confronting social reactions to disability, *(vii)* managing whether to disclose the nature of the disability, *(viii)* the extent to which the organisational culture is disability-friendly) (Purc-Stephenson et al., 2017).

While all of these challenges are important to employees with disabilities, the decision as to whether or not to disclose their impairment to their employer, is a fundamental decision with which PWD must contend, particularly where the impairment is not clearly observable. It is acknowledged that disabilities may be categorised into *visible* and *invisible* disabilities; physical and mental disabilities or a combination thereof (Martz, 2003; Norstedt, 2019; Prince, 2017; Santuzzi et al., 2014; Ysasi et al., 2018). With visible disabilities (for example mobility challenges),

Table 2.3 Top causes of disability—Islands of the Anglophone Caribbean (2019)

		Proportion of Disabilities (2019)								
No	*Causes of disability, 2019 (Listed in alphabetical order)*	*Antigua and Barbuda (%)*	*Bahamas (%)*	*Barbados (%)*	*Grenada (%)*	*Guyana (%)*	*Jamaica (%)*	*St. Lucia (%)*	*St. Vincent and the Grenadines (%)*	*Trinidad and Tobago (%)*
1.	Alcohol use disorders	2.50	2.50	1.50	1.80	2.10	1.40	2.10	2.50	1.70
2.	Alzheimer disease	0.00	4.30	2.00	0.00	0.00	0.00	0.00	0.00	0.00
3.	Anxiety disorders	4.10	2.00	3.80	3.90	3.70	3.90	3.90	3.90	3.50
4.	Asthma	1.90	4.90	2.00	2.40	2.20	2.00	2.10	1.90	1.40
5.	Back and neck pain	4.90	2.10	5.10	4.70	4.00	4.90	4.80	4.60	4.80
6.	Bipolar disorder	2.10	5.60	1.80	1.90	1.70	2.10	2.00	1.90	1.90
7.	Depressive disorders	5.40	8.10	5.60	5.60	8.20	5.50	5.70	5.80	6.70
8.	Diabetes	9.10	1.40	10.20	9.80	8.80	8.90	11.50	10.60	12.20
9.	Diarrhoeal diseases	1.60	1.50	1.70	1.80	0.00	1.30	1.70	1.50	0.00
10.	Epilepsy	1.80	0.00	0.00	0.00	1.50	1.30	1.50	1.50	1.50
11.	Exposure to mechanical forces	2.30	0.00	0.00	1.70	0.00	1.60	0.00	0.00	0.00
12.	Falls	0.00	0.00	1.40	1.50	1.60	0.00	0.00	1.50	0.00
13.	Gynecological diseases	3.70	3.80	3.20	3.40	3.10	3.70	3.50	3.30	3.40
14.	Iron-deficiency anaemia	2.50	2.90	1.50	2.70	4.50	2.90	2.70	3.20	2.70

(continued)

Table 2.3 (continued)

		Proportion of Disabilities (2019)								
No	*Causes of disability, 2019 (Listed in alphabetical order)*	*Antigua and Barbuda (%)*	*Bahamas (%)*	*Barbados (%)*	*Grenada (%)*	*Guyana (%)*	*Jamaica (%)*	*St. Lucia (%)*	*St. Vincent and the Grenadines (%)*	*Trinidad and Tobago (%)*
15.	Kidney diseases	2.10	1.90	2.10	2.30	1.90	1.90	2.00	2.00	1.90
16.	Lymphatic filariasis	0.00	0.00	0.00	0.00	3.30	0.00	0.00	0.00	0.00
17.	Migraine	3.20	3.40	2.90	3.00	2.90	3.30	3.00	3.00	3.00
18.	Neonatal conditions	1.90	2.50	3.10	2.80	3.00	3.80	2.60	2.50	2.20
19.	Oral conditions	3.30	3.20	3.80	3.20	2.70	3.30	3.20	3.30	3.30
20.	Osteoarthritis	2.20	2.20	2.90	2.10	1.60	2.10	2.10	2.10	2.30
21.	Refractive errors	2.50	2.50	0.00	2.50	2.20	2.50	2.40	2.50	2.70
22.	Road injury	0.00	1.50	0.00	0.00	0.00	0.00	1.40	0.00	1.40
23.	Schizophrenia	2.00	2.00	1.80	1.80	1.50	1.80	1.80	1.70	1.90
24.	Skin diseases	2.20	2.30	2.10	2.20	2.20	2.30	2.00	2.10	2.00
25.	Stroke	0.00	0.00	1.40	0.00	0.00	0.00	0.00	0.00	1.30

Source Global Health Estimates (2019). World Health Organisation (2020). https://www.paho.org/en/enlace/leading-causes-death-and-disability; Leading causes of mortality and health loss at regional, subregional, and country levels in the Region of the Americas, 2000–2019. ENLACE data portal. Pan American Health Organization (2021)

Abbreviated causes: **Diabetes**—Diabetes mellitus (excluding CKD due to Diabetes); **Skin diseases**—Skin and subcutaneous diseases

Pulmonary disease—Chronic obstructive pulmonary disease; **Refractive errors**—Uncorrected refractive errors; **Alzheimer disease**—Alzheimer disease and other dementias

disclosure may not be necessary as the disabilities are observable (Purc-Stephenson et al., 2017). On the other hand, invisible disabilities are those that can be easily concealed, and where PWD decide not to disclose the nature and severity of their disability, it can remain unknown to organisational members for the duration of the employee's tenure with the organisation. In current anti-discrimination Caribbean legislation, there is no explicit mandate requiring self-disclosure, unlike that which is obtains in developed nations like the United Kingdom (*within the parameters of the U.K.'s Equality Act, 2010*). This means that if employees choose to disclose their diagnosis at a later time, during their employment tenure, the organisation has neither recourse nor can they refuse to provide any accommodations later sought. Some employees may make the decision to withhold reporting disabilities if they are invisible, preferring to try to navigate the organisation independently using their accessible resources, because of the prevailing stigma and discrimination perpetuating the organisation's policies and practices.

Disclosure

In the absence of legislative protections, employees with disabilities (EWD) must consider the net benefits of disclosing to their employer and/or colleagues. It is important to note that as it relates to recruitment and selection, organisations interested in hiring the best talent, should develop policies and engage in policies that are meritorious, with a view to hiring the most efficient and effective employees. As such, to the extent that an individual's conditions are unlikely to have an adverse impact on their ability to perform their assigned duties, they should neither be precluded from consideration for the vacancy, nor from accessing promotional and developmental opportunities. Thus, Purc-Stephenson et al. (2017, *see also* MacDonald-Wilson et al., 2011) found that PWD primarily disclosed because of evident physical symptoms or atypical behaviour which resulted from their diagnosed condition, for example, frequent fatigue, frequent use of the bathroom, unexplained tics (characteristic of Tourette's syndrome), however, it was noted that such employees would delay disclosure until they were able to prove themselves as committed, engaged, effective, dependable and indispensable to the organisation (Charmaz, 2010; Santuzzi et al., 2014; Von Schrader et al., 2014; Wilton, 2006).

As it relates to the existence of a disability-friendly culture, prior to applying to an organisation, applicants will typically engage in personal reconnaissance by reviewing the organisation's website, browsing and reading annual reports and other published reports, speaking to current and/or former employees, scouring the internet (specifically social media) for any scurrilous or commendable stories/reports involving the organisation.

Today's contemporary organisations acknowledge the import of diversity and as such, diversity/inclusion statements are often included in the company's website and/or published annual reports. For example, IBM's website states as follows: *"IBM is committed to creating a diverse environment and is proud to be an equal opportunity employer. All qualified applicants will receive consideration for employment without regard to race, color, religion, gender, gender identity or expression, sexual orientation, national origin, genetics, disability, age, or veteran status. IBM is also committed to compliance with all fair employment practices regarding citizenship and immigration status"*.[2] Similarly, Apple's website includes the following "*Different together. At Apple, we're not all the same. And that's our greatest strength. We draw on the differences in who we are, what we've experienced, and how we think. Because to create products that serve everyone, we believe in everyone*".[3]

Unwillingness to disclose one's disability status may also be attributed to Purc-Stephenson et al. and's (2017: 57) ***glass box model of disability***, which identifies the barriers for PWD in the workplace, resulting in employees with disabilities *"feeling "stuck" in generally lower-level positions with little job opportunity to advance or to move laterally within or between organizations regardless of qualifications"*. This is consistent with the existing concepts of the ***glass ceiling*** (Booth, 2006; Booth et al., 2003)—discrimination within the workplace based on gender and race bias, results in sluggish or an absence of promotions to senior/executive levels within organisations for these marginalised groups; the ***lavender ceiling*** (Landau, 1993; Ozturk & Tatli, 2018)—used by the LGBTQ+ community, refers to barriers within the workplace as a result of discrimination in relation to this group which prevents them from developing and

[2] IBM website for diversity—https://www.ibm.com/impact/be-equal/.

[3] Apple website for diversity—https://www.apple.com/diversity/#:~:text=We're%20continuing%20to%20build,workforce%20and%20a%20better%20world.&text=74%25Increase%20in%20the%20number,URCs)2%20in%20the%20U.S./.

being promoted to the executive positions in the organisations; and the ***sticky floor hypothesis*** (Booth et al., 2003; Yap & Konrad, 2009)—argues that for the same job and the same pay scale, women are appointed at the bottom of the scale and men are appointed at higher wages on the scale, thus the floor is said to be ***sticky*** for women as they seem to remain there for some time due to organisational policies and practices which are discriminatory.

Where an organisation is known to have institutionalised discriminatory policies, employees with disabilities (EWD) are unlikely to disclose for fear that they will face disparate treatment on the basis of their disability. It has been argued that persons with visible disabilities "*have their skills and training negated or disregarded due to the employer's misperception of their capabilities*" this results in a decreased likelihood of success in a job search and a greater likelihood of underemployment (Newton et al., 2021; Purc-Stephenson et al., 2017). Arguments in favour of disclosure include the perception of the employer as receptive to such discussions where the vacancy to be filled required significant communication and customer engagement (Lyons et al., 2018), further, it has been asserted that in doing so, the applicant allays some of the fears and hesitation of the employer regarding the probable limitations of the candidate with disabilities and boosts the candidates' perceived interpersonal attributes (Lipow, 2015), greater access to training and developmental opportunities (Martinez-Marrero, 2007; Purc-Stephenson et al., 2017), an organisation-wide re-education and inclusion drive in which the accepted stereotypes associated with PWD are challenged and the myths and assumptions about this marginalised group are addressed and debunked, and the benefits which are likely to be derived from PWD are emphasised. For persons with invisible disabilities, there seems to be a continuous implication that the PWD's claims of disabilities are not credible because the symptoms are not evident. This results in PWD and EWD always feeling the need to constantly prove that they do in fact, face challenges related to the particular medical health concerns (Dibben et al., 2002; Hernandez et al., 2000; Jasper & Waldhart, 2013; Purc-Stephenson et al., 2017).

Employment Outcomes

Work is important to maintain well-being and to practice and improve one's skills and expertise *inter alia* (Svinndal et al., 2020). Depending on its severity, employees with hearing impairments may require accommodations, to ensure that they have access to the same information and resources, as all other employees in a safe and reliable and timely manner. This may include assistance in communicating with others, to protect against information loss and to promote cordial and collegial relationships within the organisation (Pollard & Block, 2017; Svinndal et al., 2020). Further employment barriers for PWD include ignorance of how to effectively and successfully manage EWD and perceived potential legal exposure in the event that lack of familiarity with the relevant laws results in disparate treatment of PWD; perceived costs of accommodation, which organisations appear to anticipate, will be onerous, without either engaging in a comprehensive investigation or consultation with the EWD to determine what accommodations will be required (Kaye et al., 2011). While stereotypes and prevailing notions of the characteristics of PWD and EWD are heuristics and therefore offer a shortcut to decision-making, these may be ineffective in advancing the achievement of the organisation's strategic objectives. By accepting these stereotypical views as normative, organisations treat PWD as a homogeneous group, ignoring the diversity among the members of this marginalised group and depriving them of the opportunity of engaging in productive work (World Bank, 2011). Such an approach may not be limited to PWD but where this is institutionalised human resource policy and practice, an organisational throughline could result in employees, (with attributes or immutable characteristics that are not congruous with that of the status quo) who are "*othered*" in the organisation and experience less favourable treatment when compared to employees with whom managers, supervisors and colleagues are able to identify and with whom they share similar recognisable traits, attributes and characteristics.

Consistent with the strategies to improve employment opportunities suggested by Kaye et al. (2011),—*see* Table 2.4—are the recommendations advanced in the 2011 World Report on Disability, which include:- *(i)* enabling access to mainstream programmes and services to PWD (including but not limited to education, training, health, social services *inter alia*); *(ii)* investing in programmes and services for PWD (e.g. rehabilitation and support services) which improve their independence;

(iii) adopting a national disability strategy and implementation plan (to improve the well-being of PWD); *(iv)* when making policy and implementation decisions, consult with and include PWD in the decision process; *(v)* increasing awareness and understanding about disabilities (this may be achieved through funding of relevant disability research projects/grants which will provide reliable, verifiable data on which evidence-based decisions may be made regarding this group).

Assessing Diversity

The Disability Equality Index (DEI) developed in collaboration with the American Association of People with Disabilities (AAPD), is an organisational benchmarking measure that assesses whether and the extent to which organisations have established and implemented effective, disability-inclusive policies and practices. The core values of the DEI are: ***Inclusivity*** (celebrating differences), ***Integrity*** (transparency, quality and accountability), ***Impact & Quality*** (catalyst for businesses globally to take positive action that expands disability inclusion and equity) (AAPD, 2021). Each assessed company receives a score from 0 to 100, companies earning 80 and over are recognised as the "*best places to work for disability inclusion*" in the United States and these outstanding companies are published in an annual DEI Report. Each organisation is assessed using the following weighted categories: *(i)* culture and leadership (commitment to disability inclusion and visible leadership in this regard); *(ii)* enterprise-wide access (commitment to workplace accessibility); Employment Practices; *(iii)* employment practices (commitment to human resource practices which incorporate PWD); *(iv)* community engagement practices (practices which support PWD); and *(v)* supplier diversity (demonstrating supplier diversity such that businesses owned by PWD are included on the supplier lists). In 2021, a total of 319[4] companies were assessed via the DEI Report exercise (the highest number of participating companies since its inauguration). 272 of these companies scored 80% or more and were listed as the best companies to work for in relation to disability diversity. The list of companies that scored **100%**, includes (*but is not limited to*) 3M, Deloitte, Johnson and Johnson, Walgreens and Walmart; the list of companies that scored **90%** includes

[4] DEI website: https://disabilityin.org/what-we-do/disability-equality-index/.

Table 2.4 Hiring and retaining persons with disabilities (PWD)

	Reasons employers do not hire PWD	*Reasons employers do not retain EWD*	*Strategies for improving the number of PWD hired and retained by employers*
1.	Concerned with the cost of providing reasonable accommodations so that workers with disabilities can do their jobs	Don't know how to handle the needs of a worker with a disability on the job	More or better training on disability issues for supervisors and managers
2.	Ignorant as to how to handle the needs of a worker with a disability	Fear that workers who develop disabilities will become a liability to them	A central organization-wide source for expertise on accommodation issues
3.	Fear they won't be able to discipline or fire a worker with a disability for poor performance, because of potential discrimination lawsuits	Worried about the cost of providing reasonable accommodations so that workers with disabilities can do their jobs	Written guidelines for dealing with disability issues, including accommodation requests
4.	Precluded from asking about a job applicant's disability, making it hard to assess whether the person can do the job	Believe that workers who are poor performers only get worse once they acquire a disability	An organization-wide system for handling requests for reasonable accommodations
5.	Concerned with the extra time that supervisors or co-workers will need to spend to assist workers with disabilities	Worried about associated costs, such as increased health insurance premiums for PWD	External resources to get guidance on disability and accommodation issues
6.	Worried about other costs, such as increased health insurance or worker's compensation premiums	Can't ask about a worker's disability, making it hard to assess whether the person can still do the job	A diversity specialist who deals with disability issues
7.	Afraid the workers with disabilities won't work up to the same standards as other employees	Believe that workers who develop disabilities can no longer do the basic functions of their jobs	A centralized fund within the organization to pay for job accommodations
8.	Rarely see people with disabilities applying for jobs	Believe that workers who develop disabilities become less dependable	A written company policy of non-discrimination that includes disability

(continued)

Table 2.4 (continued)

	Reasons employers do not hire PWD	*Reasons employers do not retain EWD*	*Strategies for improving the number of PWD hired and retained by employers*
9.	Don't believe that people with disabilities can complete the basic functions of the jobs they apply for	Concerned about attitudes of co-workers toward the worker with a disability	
10.	Discriminatory attitudes towards PWD	Think of workers who develop disabilities as "problem employees"	
11.	Concerned with attitudes of co-workers toward the person with a disability	Believe that workers who develop disabilities become less dedicated to their jobs	
12.	Think of workers with disabilities as "problem employees"	Believe that workers who develop disabilities prefer not to return to work	
13.	Believe that job applicants with disabilities don't present themselves well in interviews		

Source Kaye, H. S., Jans, L. H., & Jones, E. C. (2011). Why don't employers hire and retain workers with disabilities? *Journal of Occupational Rehabilitation*, *21*(4), 526–536

(*but is not limited to*) Airbus, Amazon, Nike and Reed Smith. Finally, the list of companies that scored **80%** includes (but is not limited to) Lululemon, Pillsbury, Ralph Lauren and United States Steel (AAPD, 2021). Organisations that score 100% on the DEI have not achieved perfection in relation to disability diversity, but this high score denotes that these companies "*adhere to many of the numerous leading disability inclusion practices*" against which the companies are assessed in the DEI.

Although a global diversity index has also been published (by the AAPD, Forbes (USA) and Oxford (UK), the Caribbean is not represented. Indeed, from a review of the websites and published reports by some of the largest companies in the Caribbean, the inclusion of diversity/equality statements is limited, both in scope (typically very nebulous) and in the negligible number of companies that have created them. Further, the espoused company values and enacted values are sometimes fundamentally contradictory and a cursory review of the staff across the region, reflects typically homogeneous staff. Further, the filing of anti-discrimination cases in the Caribbean regions where discrimination on the basis of disabilities is prohibited continues, suggesting that discrimination has not yet been effectively addressed. This is not an atypical outcome, as models of change (Kotter, 2012; Laughlin, 1991; Lewin, 1947) suggest that a path to change is likely to be filled with obstacles, which must be overcome before the change goal is accomplished. Further, during the journey to change, the concerns of multiple stakeholders will need to be addressed, requiring a multifaceted approach. Consequently, there will be a variation in the resulting change, to wit, there may not be any change at all, as organisational members maintain the status quo; change may be the minimal required adjustments to policy and practice; changes which result may be to selected policies and practices; and finally, there may be comprehensive and proactive changes made within the workplace (Goss & Adam-Smith, 2001; Kirton & Greene, 2006; Laughlin, 1991). For employees with disabilities, desired changes will include accommodations via assistive technology, job sharing, flexible schedules, telecommuting and redesigned workstations *inter alia* (Kaye et al., 2011; Purc-Stephenson et al., 2017; Schartz et al., 2006; Solovieva et al., 2011).

Interestingly, an acronym designed to assist in understanding one's role and obligations as it relates to PWD, may also be applied in the organisational context and as such may be instructive to managers, employees and other organisational stakeholders (Berghs et al., 2016). The acronym is IDEAS and this represents Inclusion (**I**); Dignity (**D**); Equity (**E**); Accessibility (**A**) and Intersectionality (**S**). Barclay and Markel (2007) refer to an employee's assumed social identity, individual's imputed character, and an attribute that is discrediting, as stigma, which they suggest may be immediately evident or discovered over time. Similarly, Thornicroft et al. (2008) argue that stigma is associated with social exclusion and suggest that stigma is a function of lack of knowledge, prejudicial attitudes and discriminatory behaviour which targets a specific marginalised social group. PWD can experience discrimination at any stage of the employment process. To wit, discrimination at the stage of recruitment and selection, which is referred to as ***access discrimination*** and discrimination throughout one's tenure with the organisation, known as ***treatment discrimination*** (Perry et al., 2000). Examples of access discrimination include lower compensation package offered, lower-level jobs are more readily offered than managerial or executive positions (recall glass box of discrimination theory by Purc-Stephenson et al., 2017). Researchers (Perry et al., 2000) found that PWD reported more access discrimination relative to treatment discrimination, and the severity and type of disability was also found to be a factor in the type of discrimination experienced by PWD (Fuqua et al., 1984; Stone & Colella, 1996; Tringo, 1970), such that persons with visual impairments and those that are intellectual challenged, PWD who are visually impaired and those who use wheelchairs, frequently report access discrimination (Fichten & Amsel, 1986; Fuqua et al., 1984; Johnson & Baldwin, 1993; Perry et al., 2000).

Discriminatory attitudes may arise due to the acceptance of stereotypes, assumptions about the productivity of EWD relative to employees with no known disabilities and possible exploitation by employers (Mizunoya & Mitra, 2013). With the onset of the global pandemic in 2020, there was an increase in the number of persons turning to the gig economy,[5] as governments across the globe mandated the close of organisations and restricted the movements of all employees who were not involved in the provision of essential services (Dokko et al., 2015; Ekberg et al., 2016; Feingold, 2017). The gig economy also created opportunities for PWD to provide services and create products for end users by using their skills and talents, without being limited by the employment policies of organisations

[5] **What is the gig economy?** (Woodcock & Graham, 2019: 9–10)—The term "gig economy" refers to labour markets that are characterized by independent contracting that happens via *and* on digital platforms. The kind of work that is offered is contingent: casual and non-permanent work. It may have variable hours and little job security, involve payment on a piece-work basis. This relationship is sometimes termed "independent contracting", "freelancing" or "temporary work" ('temp' for short). The term has also been used to refer to a broader range of activities that happen in both digitally mediated, via *platforms such as Amazon Mechanical Turk (MTurk), Fiverr, Freelancer.com and Upwork*, and non-mediated ways (such as bike messengers and cab drivers). *Source* Woodcock, J., & Graham, M. (2019). The gig economy. *A Critical Introduction. Cambridge: Polity.*

What are gig workers? (Vallas & Schor, 2020: 275)—Gig workers are those whose services are engaged via platforms and generally performed offline, as in ride-hail, food delivery, home repair and care work. There is a robust market of this type for business, which includes delivery, day-labour, and odd-job tasks. This arrangement affords the provider with flexibility in terms of work schedules and autonomy; however, gig workers must not only assume responsibility for operating costs and risks and forego protections enjoyed by employees but also conform to the temporal rhythms of customer demand, which can reduce their autonomy substantially. *Source* Vallas, S., & Schor, J. B. (2020). What do platforms do? Understanding the gig economy. *Annual Review of Sociology*, *46*(1), 273–294.

or the limitations placed on them by others as a result of their perceived of their disabilities (Ekberg et al., 2016; Harpur & Blanck, 2020; Schur et al., 2020; Schroeder et al., 2021).

Visible and Invisible Disabilities

Visible disabilities refer to readily observable impairments, there are also disabilities which may be occasionally visible, and these are referred to as episodic disabilities (e.g. epilepsy, schizophrenia) (Lingsom, 2008; Norstedt, 2019; Tompa et al., 2015). Invisible or hidden disabilities are impairments which are not immediately obvious to onlookers (e.g. dyscalculia). Due to the nature of these broad groups of impairments, the way in which persons so diagnosed are perceived by managers, colleagues and other organisational members, varies. Hence for persons with visible disabilities, disclosure is not required as the impairment is apparent, and a paternalistic approach of being helpful to this group is often engaged, which though well intended, may be perceived by PWD as condescending and infantalising (Sabat et al., 2014). On the other hand, persons with invisible disabilities, within the organisational context, may be perceived as "lazy and unmotivated", and this is particularly so, where employees decide not to disclose to their organisation and colleagues, the nature and severity of their invisible impairment, for fear of being discriminated against or being denied opportunities for training and development at the organisation (Black, 2004; Tompa et al., 2015). In fact, research has found that persons with visible disabilities are 16 times less likely to be gainfully employed when compared to persons with invisible disabilities, even where such persons have the requisite knowledge, skills and abilities to efficiently performed their duties (Martz, 2003; Tompa et al., 2015).

PWD, particularly those with visible disabilities may engage in claiming or downplaying strategies in an effort to acknowledge their disabilities within the organisational context. These approaches reflect deliberate attempts by PWD to influence the narrative in the organisation about them as well as to affect the perceptions of organisational members variously, in relation to the EWD'S competence and warmth, instead of assuming upon meeting the PWD to know their capabilities and ability to fit within the organisation's social fabric. To this end, it has been found that some PWD believe that by either claiming or downplaying their visible disabilities allows them to control the narrative that is woven about them from the stage of recruitment and selection and throughout their tenure with the organisation. *Claiming* refers to emphasising positive aspects of the stigmatised identities of PWD and reframing associated stereotypical beliefs, while *downplaying* refers to minimising the negative aspects of the multifaceted stigmatised identity of PWD, promoting their competence and de-emphasising the presence of a disability (Jans et al., 2012; Lyons et al., 2018; Shih et al., 2013; Taub et al., 1999). These approaches are akin to impression and identity management as PWD are constructing a narrative and a lens through which they would prefer their organisation to view them and their potential contribution, competence and character. EWD may avoid disclosure as this could result in increased attention to the differences between EWD and other employees in the organisation (Svinndal et al., 2020).

Anti-discrimination legislation prohibits organisations from inquiring about the nature of an employee's disabilities. However, employers may inquire as to what accommodations if any would be necessary for the EWD to be able to do their job. For PWD then, acknowledging and disclosing their disabilities may be a strategic approach to gain acceptance as a transparent individual and to preempt any concerns about their attributes and to debunk any prevailing stereotypes about persons who share a similar impairment (Lyons et al., 2018). In fact, research has found that EWD have received more positive performance evaluations when they acknowledge their disabilities (Goodman, 2008; Hebl & Kleck, 2002; Hebl & Skorinko, 2005).

When there is a perceived poor fit with the nature and severity of a disability and the attributes believed to be required in order for the job to be carried out efficiently by the post holder, organisations may be more influenced by prevailing disability stereotypes. This is regrettable as PWD are not homogeneous and it would be more prudent to consider each applicant as an individual with unique talents and abilities. To obviate any potential inclination of hiring managers to simply accept prevailing stereotypes, PWD should be proactive and engage in either *claiming* or *downplaying* early in the recruitment and selection stage, with a view of drawing managers attention to the positive characteristics, attributes, skills and unique abilities which the applicant will bring to the organisation thus making the individual a suitable candidate for consideration and appointment. It must be cautioned here that deliberate attempts to emphasise a candidate's positive attributes and minimise any perceived deleterious effects the applicant's impairment might have on the organisation, could be viewed by the organisation as deceptive attempts to misguide, or mislead (Kaye et al., 2011; Roberts, 2005; Schur et al., 2005; Shier et al., 2009; Stone & Colella, 1996). Where the limitations of the impairment do not affect the candidate's ability to do the job, then the disability is not relevant and it should not be a determining factor in determining the candidate to be appointed in the post (for example a receptionist who is a wheelchair user, as a result of a diagnosed impairments should not be precluded from consideration because the job does not require the employee to be mobile in order to undertake the associated job tasks.

Passing

The concept of passing is typically associated with race, but within the context of invisible disabilities, an individual may desire to pass as a person with no known disabilities at work, which refers to "concealment and/or silencing" surrounding any impairments or disorders with which an individual has been diagnosed (Lingsom, 2008: 7). Typically, a PWD desires to pass in order to maintain bodily autonomy; to circumvent the stigma and discrimination associated with varying disabilities, insecurity and fear of the employer's possible response to disclosure and in relation to employment, successful passing may be regarded as essential in order to obtain and retain gainful employment, being offered opportunities for promotion and development at work (Brune et al., 2012; McDonald et al., 2007; Norstedt, 2019, Samuels, 2003). Further, where the organisation's employment policies and practices are actually inclusive, there is organisational wide commitment to diversity, all organisational members proactively provide support to EWD and where one's impairment results in a reduction of work ability such that accommodations need to be provided by the employer, even if passing could be successfully achieved, it might not be necessary (Jans et al., 2012; Samuels, 2017; Tregaskis, 2000).

Passing also requires continuous self-monitoring to ensure that no indication of impairment is ever revealed intentionally or unintentionally and may result in increased anxiety within the passing employee. In a practical sense, one of the primary challenges associated with passing, is that if work colleagues are unaware of the existence of a medical impairment (because of successful masking), should a medical emergency arise and an invisible disability becomes visible (e.g. an epileptic seizure, diabetes event), colleagues may not be prepared to immediately render assistance (Erevelles, 2014; Lingsom, 2008; Norstedt, 2019). In the aftermath of such an occurrence, organisational members may also view the "passer" as untrustworthy and lacking in integrity for failing to disclose (Durlak, 2017; Lingsom, 2008; Siebers, 2019). Employees who could benefit from accommodations, further disadvantage themselves when they fail to disclose, especially where their productivity levels are below par and they are regarded as inefficient or worse, incompetent (Emens, 2008; Hartnett et al., 2011; Stone, 2005), as they are unlikely to be offered support, if it is perceived that they are incompetent or have no work ethic. Where PWD disclose an invisible impairment, organisational members may not readily accept that the employee has been diagnosed with the stated condition, if the employee does not physically appear to have the outwardly presenting signs expected by societal convention (Cureton, 2018; Kulkarni, 2022; Stone, 2005). As a consequence, such reports may not be accepted as legitimate claims. Notwithstanding this, it has been noted that passing is an "attempt to achieve normality, but it also creates the risk of reinforcing ableist norms which suggest that persons with no known disabilities are the only suitable job candidates" (Norstedt, 2019: 20; *see also* Gjertsen et al., 2021).

Seminal Model on the Treatment of Persons with Disabilities

Stone and Colella (1996) proposed a model of factors affecting the treatment of PWD (see Fig. 2.3), in which they identified the nature of an employee's impairment to be an important consideration. Specifically, the model suggests that organisations consider the origin, severity, concealability, aesthetic qualities, associated danger and potential disruption of an impairment as important attributes of PWD, in relation to their potential employment outcomes. It is important to note that in addition to the impairment-related characteristics, other attributes are regarded as determining factors, these are performance level, gender, interpersonal style, race and status/social power. Interestingly, collectively, these attributes are immutable (in the main) and race, gender and class are recognised bases of disparate treatment. Therefore, where the PWD is also a member of a marginalised, race, gender or class, they may be subjected to discrimination on multiple grounds. Where this occurs, their likelihood of success may be quite low with their current or potential employer.

The antecedents of legislation and organisational characteristics will influence the way in which PWD are perceived and where anti-discrimination is effective, disparate treatment on these (or related) grounds may be deterred.

Stone and Colella's (1996) model is comprehensive in regarding the input and attributes of other organisation members, and the nature of the job performed by the PWD. Collectively, the interaction of these factors will have an impact on whether and the extent to which PWD are successful in being hired and where hired, the factors will impact their organisational success (i.e. promotions, access to training and developmental opportunities, pay increases, access to organisational citizenship behavioural support, *inter alia*). This model suggests that persons with no known disabilities or where disabilities are invisible and not disclosed are less likely to face disparate treatment on the basis of their impairment, though as mentioned other intersectional factors (where present),

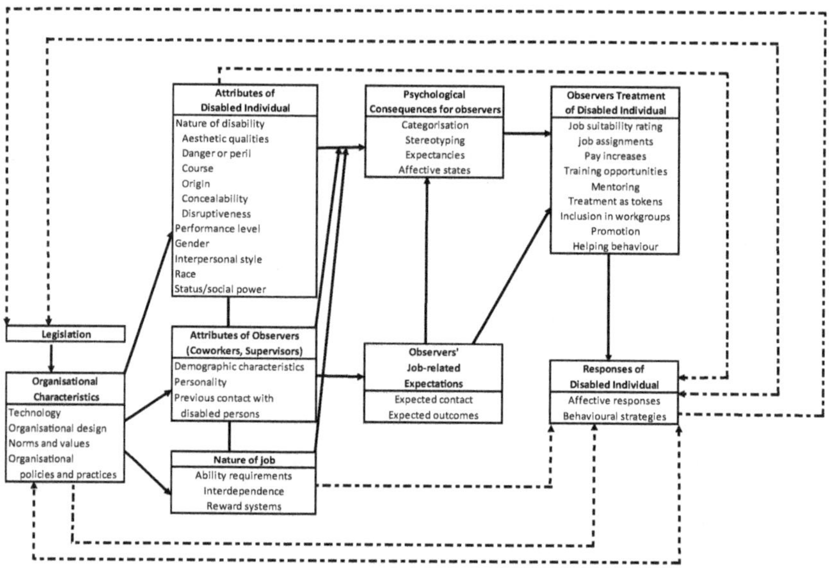

Fig. 2.3 Model of factors affecting the treatment of disabled individuals in organisations (*Source* Stone, D. L., & Colella, A. [1996]. A model of factors affecting the treatment of disabled individuals in organizations. *Academy of Management Review*, *21*(2), 352–401)

may create an organisational environment that is not inclusive, preferring employees who fit within the status quo. Mik-Meyer (2016) found that within organisations, employees refer to their colleagues with visible disabilities as *different*, which is in effect, a proxy for exclusion of members of this different group of employees, facilitates an organisational environment in which the disparate treatment of employees with known disabilities, is regarded as acceptable. "*Othering*"[6] of individuals because of their immutable differences, is neither useful in the organisational context nor in wider society, and it is, in fact, a reflection of fear which is projected onto someone else (Montrey et al., 2018; Norstedt, 2019), instead of engaging, without malice, in evidence-based decision-making. Ultimately, "*while disability correlates with disadvantage, not all people with disabilities are equally disadvantaged, People with more severe impairments often experience greater disadvantage*" (WHO, 2011).

Concluding Comments

The desire to work is one held by most. The reasons are wide and varied and may include a need to meet one's financial obligations, social interaction or simply to use one's skills, knowledge and attributes in a productive manner. In the Caribbean, our continued reliance on the medical model as the only lens through which we understand impairments creates disadvantages for PWD and EWD. As with all other societal groups, persons with disabilities are heterogeneous, and any effort by organisations to treat them as a homogeneous group, discredits their talent, experience and potential contribution. This could force PWD to no longer seek gainful employment or, where possible conceal any trace of impairment to give themselves the best probability of success. Just hearing the words, "I

[6] **What is othering?** (Mik-Meyer, 2016: 1343)—The othering process refers to the way in which co-workers talk about the impairments of their colleague in an implicit manner by referring to other "different" people. The *othering* or stereotyping of employees who "differ" from the norm may be done through co-workers' associations with other people who are (also) constructed as "different". Able-bodied norms, or "ableism" (Campbell, 2009), inform how co-workers think about a colleague with impairments. Therefore, when co-workers spontaneously associate with people whom they (also) construct as "different", when answering questions about their particular colleague with impairments (most likely in attempts to avoid reinforcing their colleague's status as 'other'), this may be viewed as an *othering process*. *Source* Mik-Meyer, N. (2016). Othering, ableism and disability: A discursive analysis of co-workers' construction of colleagues with visible impairments. *Human Relations*, *69*(6), 1341–1363.

have an impairment", appears to be enough to deter organisations from hiring a potential candidate, as after hearing these 4 words, organisations appear to believe that such a revelation is akin to "an inability to be productive". It is imperative that organisations go the extra mile and conduct some independent research, with a view to determining whether the declared disability is likely to have any impact on the employee's performance at work. If there is a vacancy for a tree surgeon, required to climb multiple trees a day, mobility challenges may present an obstacle, but if the available vacancy is sedentary (for example an Accountant), then efficient cognitive processing abilities should be the foremost consideration. The primary consideration for employers to consider must be whether, and the extent to which job applicants or employees possess the skills, education, abilities and competencies outlined in the job description, instead of the impairment. Ableism and its attempts to homogenise workforces, must be eliminated, in favour of the active pursuit of diversity and inclusion by organisations.

References

American Association of People with Disabilities (AAPD). 2021. Disability Equality Index. American Association of People with Disabilities and Disability:IN™ Initiative. https://disabilityin.org/what-we-do/disability-equality-index/

Autor, D. H. (2011). The unsustainable rise of the disability rolls in the United States: Causes, consequences, and policy options. *NBER Working Paper Series-National Bureau of Economic Research*, (17697).

Barclay, L. A., & Markel, K. S. (2007). Discrimination and stigmatization in work organizations: A multiple level framework for research on genetic testing. *Human Relations, 60*(6), 953–980.

Barnes, E. (2014). Valuing disability, causing disability. *Ethics, 125*(1), 88–113.

Berghs, M., Atkin, K., Graham, H., Hatton, C., & Thomas, C. (2016). Implications for public health research of models and theories of disability: A scoping study and evidence synthesis. *Public Health Research, 4*(8), 1–166.

Berrigan, P., Scott, C. W., & Zwicker, J. D. (2020). Employment, education, and income for Canadians with developmental disability: Analysis from the 2017 Canadian survey on disability. *Journal of Autism and Developmental Disorders*, 1–13.

Black, N. E. (2004). Blessing or curse? Distance delivery to students with invisible disabilities. *Journal of Library Administration, 41*(1–2), 47–64.

Booth, A. L. (2006). *The glass ceiling in Europe: Why are women doing badly in the labour market?* Centre for Economic Policy Research (CEPR), Research School of Social Sciences, The Australian National University.

Booth, A. L., Francesconi, M., & Frank, J. (2003). A sticky floors model of promotion, pay, and gender. *European Economic Review, 47*(2), 295–322.

Brune, J. A. (2012). The multiple layers of disability passing in life, literature, and public discourse. *Disability and Passing: Blurring the Lines of Identity, ed. Jeffrey A. Brune and Daniel J. Wilson (Philadelphia: Temple University Press, 2013), 36*, 33–57.

Büttner, G., & Hasselhorn, M. (2011). Learning disabilities: Debates on definitions, causes, subtypes, and responses. *International Journal of Disability, Development and Education, 58*(1), 75–87.

Campbell, F. A. K. (2009). Having a career in disability studies without even becoming disabled! The strains of the disabled teaching body. *International Journal of Inclusive Education, 13*(7), 713–725.

Charmaz, K. (2010). Disclosing illness and disability in the workplace. *Journal of International Education in Business, 3*(1/2), 6.

Cureton, A. (2018). Hiding a disability and passing. *Disability in Practice: Attitudes, Policies, and Relationships, 15*.

de Lucas, J. M., & Navarro, A. C. (2020). Permanent visual work disabilities: 321 cases review. *Archivos De La Sociedad Española De Oftalmología (English Edition), 95*(3), 130–137.

Dibben, P., James, P., Cunningham, I., & Smythe, D. (2002). Employers and employees with disabilities in the UK: An economically beneficial relationship? *International Journal of Social Economics*.

Dokko, J., Mumford, M., & Schanzenbach, D. W. (2015). Workers and the online gig economy. *The Hamilton Project*, 1–8.

Durlak, P. R. (2017). Disability at work: Understanding the impact of the ADA on the workplace. *Sociology Compass, 11*(5), e12475.

ECLAC (Economic Commission for Latin America and the Caribbean). (2019). *Social Panorama of Latin America, 2019* (LC/PUB.2019/22-P/Rev.1), Santiago.

Ekberg, K., Pransky, G. S., Besen, E., Fassier, J. B., Feuerstein, M., Munir, F., & Blanck, P. (2016). New business structures creating organizational opportunities and challenges for work disability prevention. *Journal of Occupational Rehabilitation, 26*(4), 480–489.

Emens, E. F. (2008). Integrating accommodation. *University of Pennsylvania Law Review*, 839–922.

Erevelles, N. (2014). Thinking with disability studies. *Disability Studies Quarterly, 34*(2), 1–16.

Feingold, L. (2017). The gig economy: Making it available to everyone. *Scitech Lawyer, 13*(2), 8.

Fichten, C. S., & Amsel, R. (1986). Trait attributions about college students with a physical disability: Circumplex analyses and methodological issues 1. *Journal of Applied Social Psychology, 16*(5), 410–427.

Fuqua, D. R., Rathbun, M., & Gade, E. M. (1984). A comparison of employer attitudes toward the worker problems of eight types of disabled workers. *Journal of Applied Rehabilitation Counseling, 15*(1), 40–43.

Gayle, A., & Palmer, D. (2005). The activism of persons with disabilities in Jamaica: An evaluation of the impact. *Social and Economic Studies*, 122–142.

Gjertsen, H., Hardonk, S., & Ineland, J. (2021). Work Inclusion for People with Intellectual Disabilities in Three Nordic Countries: The Current Policy and Challenges. *Scandinavian Journal of Disability Research, 23*(1).

Goodman, J. H. (2008). Influences of maternal postpartum depression on fathers and on father–infant interaction. *Infant Mental Health Journal: Official Publication of The World Association for Infant Mental Health, 29*(6), 624–643.

Grünke, M., & Cavendish, W. M. (2016). Learning disabilities around the globe: Making sense of the heterogeneity of the different viewpoints. *Learning Disabilities: A Contemporary Journal, 14*(1), 1–8.

Harpur, P., & Blanck, P. (2020). Gig workers with disabilities: Opportunities, challenges, and regulatory response. *Journal of Occupational Rehabilitation, 30*(4), 511–520.

Hartnett, H. P., Stuart, H., Thurman, H., Loy, B., & Batiste, L. C. (2011). Employers' perceptions of the benefits of workplace accommodations: Reasons to hire, retain and promote people with disabilities. *Journal of Vocational Rehabilitation, 34*(1), 17–23.

Hebl, M. R., & Kleck, R. E. (2002). Acknowledging one's stigma in the interview setting: Effective strategy or liability? *Journal of Applied Social Psychology, 32*(2), 223–249.

Hebl, M. R., & Skorinko, J. L. (2005). Acknowledging one's physical disability in the interview: Does "when" make a difference? *Journal of Applied Social Psychology, 35*(12), 2477–2492.

Hendricks, D. (2010). Employment and adults with autism spectrum disorders: Challenges and strategies for success. *Journal of Vocational Rehabilitation, 32*(2), 125–134.

Hennis, A., Wu, S., Nemesure, B., Li, X., & Leske, M. (2002). Diabetes in a Caribbean population: Epidemiological profile and implications. *International Journal of Epidemiology, 31*(1), 234–239.

Hernandez, B., Keys, C., & Balcazar, F. (2000). Employer attitudes toward workers with disabilities and their ADA employment rights: A literature review. *Journal of Rehabilitation, 66*(4), 4–16.

Jans, L. H., Kaye, H. S., & Jones, E. C. (2012). Getting hired: Successfully employed people with disabilities offer advice on disclosure, interviewing, and job search. *Journal of Occupational Rehabilitation, 22*(2), 155–165.

Jasper, C. R., & Waldhart, P. (2013). Employer attitudes on hiring employees with disabilities in the leisure and hospitality industry: Practical and theoretical implications. *International Journal of Contemporary Hospitality Management, 25*(4), 577–594.

Johnson, W. G., & Baldwin, M. (1993). The Americans with disabilities act: Will it make a difference? *Policy Studies Journal, 21*(4), 775–788.

Kotter, J. P. (2012). *Leading change*. Boston, U.S.A: Harvard Business Press.

Kaye, H. S., Jans, L. H., & Jones, E. C. (2011). Why don't employers hire and retain workers with disabilities? *Journal of Occupational Rehabilitation, 21*(4), 526–536.

Krzeminskà, A., Austin, R. D., Bruyère, S. M., & Hedley, D. (2019). The advantages and challenges of neurodiversity employment in organizations. *Journal of Management & Organization, 25*(4), 453–463.

Kulkarni, M. (2022). Hiding but hoping to be found: Workplace disclosure dilemmas of individuals with hidden disabilities. *Equality, Diversity and Inclusion: An International Journal, 41*(3), 491–507.

Landau, D. A. (1993). Employment discrimination against lesbians and gays: The incomplete legal responses of the United States and the European Union. *Duke J. Comp. & Int'l l., 4*, 335.

Laughlin, R. (1991). Enviornmental disturbances and organisational transitions and transformations – Some alternative models. *Organisational Studies, 12*(2), 209–232.

Lewin, K. (1947). Group decision and social change. *Readings in Social Psychology, 3*(1), 197–211.

Lingsom, S. (2008). Invisible impairments: Dilemmas of concealment and disclosure. *Scandinavian Journal of Disability Research, 10*(1), 2–16.

Lipow, V. (2015). Don't let disabilities get in the way of getting the job. Retrieved from http://career-advice.monster.com/job-search/Getting-Started/Job-Hunting-with-a-Disability/article.aspx

Lyons, B. J., Martinez, L. R., Ruggs, E. N., Hebl, M. R., Ryan, A. M., O'Brien, K. R., & Roebuck, A. (2018). To say or not to say: Different strategies of acknowledging a visible disability. *Journal of Management, 44*(5), 1980–2007.

MacDonald-Wilson, K. L., Russinova, Z., Rogers, E. S., Lin, C. H., Ferguson, T., Dong, S., & MacDonald, M. K. (2011). Disclosure of mental health disabilities in the workplace: Work accommodation and retention. In Izabela Z. Schultz & E. Sally Rogers (Eds.), *Work Accommodation and Retention in Mental Health* (pp. 191–218). New York: Springer.

Martinez-Marrero, I. (2007). Assistive technology: An instructional tool to assist college students with written language disabilities. Unpublished doctoral dissertation. University of Northern Iowa.

Martz, E. (2003). Invisibility of disability and work experience as predictors of employment among community college students with disabilities. *Journal of Vocational Rehabilitation, 18*(3), 153–161.

McDonald, K. E., Keys, C. B., & Balcazar, F. E. (2007). Disability, race/ethnicity and gender: Themes of cultural oppression, acts of individual resistance. *American Journal of Community Psychology, 39*(1), 145–161.

Mik-Meyer, N. (2016). Othering, ableism and disability: A discursive analysis of co-workers' construction of colleagues with visible impairments. *Human Relations, 69*(6), 1341–1363.

Mizunoya, S., & Mitra, S. (2013). Is there a disability gap in employment rates in developing countries? *World Development, 42*, 28–43.

Newton, D. C., Tomyn, A., & LaMontagne, A. (2021). Exploring the challenges and opportunities for improving the health and wellbeing of international students: Perspectives of professional staff at an Australian University. *JANZSSA-Journal of the Australian and New Zealand Student Services Association, 29*(1), 74–92.

Norstedt, M. (2019). Work and invisible disabilities: Practices experiences and understandings of nondisclosure. *Scandinavian Journal of Disability Research, 21*(1), 14–24.

Ozturk, M. B., & Tatli, A. (2018). Sexuality, gender identity and career journeys. In *Research Handbook of Diversity and Careers*. Edward Elgar Publishing.

Pan American Health Organization (PAHO). (2021). Leading causes of mortality and health loss at regional, subregional, and country levels in the Region of the Americas, 2000–2019. ENLACE data portal. Pan American Health Organization. https://www.paho.org/en/enlace/leading-causes-death-and-disability

Perry, E. L., Hendricks, W., & Broadbent, E. (2000). An exploration of access and treatment discrimination and job satisfaction among college graduates with and without physical disabilities. *Human Relations, 53*(7), 923–955.

Pinilla-Roncancio, M., & Gallardo, M. (2022). Inequality in labour market opportunities for people with disabilities: Evidence for six Latin American countries. *Global Social Policy*, 14680181211070201.

Pollard, N., & Block, P. (2017). Who occupies disability? Cadernos Brasileiros de Terapia Ocupacional. *Brazilian Journal of Occupational Therpy, 25*(2), 417–426.

Prince, M. J. (2017). Persons with invisible disabilities and workplace accommodation: Findings from a scoping literature review. *Journal of Vocational Rehabilitation, 46*(1), 75–86.

Purc-Stephenson, R. J., Jones, S. K., & Ferguson, C. L. (2017). "Forget about the glass ceiling, I'm stuck in a glass box": A meta-ethnography of work participation for persons with physical disabilities. *Journal of Vocational Rehabilitation, 46*(1), 49–65.

Roberts, S. (2005, April). The inequality of treating unequals equally: the future of direct discrimination under the Disability Discrimination Act 1992 (Cth)? [Paper presented at ANU Public Law Weekend, Canberra, 6 November (2004).]. In AIAL Forum (No. 45, pp. 20–38).

Sabat, I. E., Lindsey, A. P., Membere, A., Anderson, A., Ahmad, A., King, E., & Bolunmez, B. (2014). Invisible disabilities: Unique strategies for workplace allies. *Industrial and Organizational Psychology, 7*(2), 259–265.

Samuels, E. (2017). Passing, coming out, and other magical acts. *Negotiating Disability: Disclosure and Higher Education*, 15–24.

Samuels, E. J. (2003). My body, my closet: Invisible disability and the limits of coming-out discourse. *GLQ: A Journal of Lesbian and Gay Studies, 9*(1), 233–255.

Santuzzi, A. M., Waltz, P. R., Finkelstein, L. M., & Rupp, D. E. (2014). Invisible disabilities: Unique challenges for employees and organizations. *Industrial and Organizational Psychology, 7*(2), 204–219.

Schartz, H. A., Hendricks, D. J., & Blanck, P. (2006). Workplace accommodations: Evidence based outcomes. *Work, 27*(4), 345–354.

Schroeder, A. N., Bricka, T. M., & Whitaker, J. H. (2021). Work design in a digitized gig economy. *Human Resource Management Review*.

Schur, L., Kruse, D., & Blanck, P. (2005). Corporate culture and the employment of persons with disabilities. *Behavioral Sciences & the Law, 23*(1), 3–20.

Schur, L. A., Ameri, M., & Kruse, D. (2020). Telework after COVID: A "silver lining" for workers with disabilities? *Journal of Occupational Rehabilitation, 30*(4), 521–536.

Scott, M., Jacob, A., Hendrie, D., Parsons, R., Girdler, S., Falkmer, T., & Falkmer, M. (2017). Employers' perception of the costs and the benefits of hiring individuals with autism spectrum disorder in open employment in Australia. *PLoS ONE, 12*(5), e0177607.

Shier, M., Graham, J. R., & Jones, M. E. (2009). Barriers to employment as experienced by disabled people: A qualitative analysis in Calgary and Regina, Canada. *Disability & Society, 24*(1), 63–75.

Shih, M., Young, M. J., & Bucher, A. (2013). Working to reduce the effects of discrimination: Identity management strategies in organizations. *The American Psychologist, 68*(3), 145–157.

Siebers, T. (2019). Returning the social to the social model. *The Matter of Disability*, 39–47.

Solomon, C. (2020). Autism and employment: Implications for employers and adults with ASD. *Journal of Autism & Developmental Disorders, 50*(11).

Solovieva, T. I., Dowler, D. L., & Walls, R. T. (2011). Employer benefits from making workplace accommodations. *Disability and Health Journal, 4*(1), 39–45.

Stone, D. L., & Colella, A. (1996). A model of factors affecting the treatment of disabled individuals in organizations. *Academy of Management Review, 21*(2), 352–401.

Stone, S. D. (2005). Reactions to invisible disability: The experiences of young women survivors of hemorrhagic stroke. *Disability and Rehabilitation, 27*, 293–304.

Suresh, V., & Dyaram, L. (2020). Workplace disability inclusion in India: Review and directions. *Management Research Review, 43*(12). https://doi.org/10.1108/MRR-11-2019-0479

Svinndal, E. V., Jensen, C., & Rise, M. B. (2020). Working life trajectories with hearing impairment. *Disability and Rehabilitation, 42*(2), 190–200.

Taub, D. E., Blinde, E. M., & Greer, K. R. (1999). Stigma management through participation in sport and physical activity: Experiences of male college students with physical disabilities. *Human Relations, 52*(11), 1469–1484.

Thornicroft, G., Brohan, E., Kassam, A., & Lewis-Holmes, E. (2008). Reducing stigma and discrimination: Candidate interventions. *International Journal of Mental Health Systems, 2*(1), 1–7.

Tompa, E., Buettgen, A., Mahood, Q., Padkapayeva, K., Posen, A., & Yazdani, A. (2015). Evidence synthesis of workplace accommodation policies and practices for persons with visible disabilities: Final report. *October 22*, 2015.

Tregaskis, C. (2000). Interviewing non-disabled people about their disability-related attitudes: Seeking methodologies. *Disability & Society, 15*(2), 343.

Tringo, J. L. (1970). The hierarchy of preference toward disability groups. *The Journal of Special Education, 4*(3), 295–306.

Vallas, S., & Schor, J. B. (2020). What do platforms do? Understanding the gig economy. *Annual Review of Sociology, 46*(1), 273–294.

Von Schrader, S., Malzer, V., & Bruyère, S. (2014). Perspectives on disability disclosure: The importance of employer practices and workplace climate. *Employee Responsibilities and Rights Journal, 26*(4), 237–255.

Wilton, R. D. (2006). Disability Disclosure in the Workplace. *Just Labour, 8.*

Woodcock, J., & Graham, M. (2019). *The gig economy*. Polity Press.

World Bank. (2019). World Report on Disabilities. World Bank Group, Washington, D.C. Retrieved from: http://documents.worldbank.org/curated/en/665131468331271288/Main-report

World Health Organisation (WHO). (2011). World Report on Disability—WHO.

World Health Organisation (WHO). (2019). Global Health Estimates, 2019. Published by the World Health Organisation. Retrieved from: https://www.paho.org/en/enlace/leading-causes-death-and-disability

World Health Organisation (WHO). (2020). World Report on Disability, 2020. Published by the World Health Organisation. Retrieved from: https://www.paho.org/en/enlace/leading-causes-death-and-disability

Yap, M., & Konrad, A. (2009). Gender and racial differentials in promotions: Is there a sticky floor, a mid-level bottleneck, or a glass ceiling? *Relations Industrielles/industrial Relations, 64*(4), 593–619. https://doi.org/10.7202/038875ar

Ysasi, N., Becton, A., & Chen, R. (2018). Stigmatizing effects of visible versus invisible disabilities. *Journal of Disability Studies, 4*(1), 22–29.

CHAPTER 3

Education and Persons with Disabilities in the Caribbean: A Law and Policy Perspective

Introduction

Many people with disabilities face barriers which prevent their full and equal participation in society (Jones & Serieux-Lubin, 2018). Issues that many take for granted, such as access to physical, as well as digital, spaces, can disproportionally affect persons with disabilities. This is especially true of educational opportunities. In this regard, UNICEF (n.d.) has noted that disability is one of the most serious barriers to education across the globe; this is important given the organisation's mandate is to ensure each child's right to quality education and learning is realised. This, of course, has a ripple effect throughout the life of a person with disabilities, as it restricts personal development early on and then job prospects and autonomy in adulthood (Gayle-Geddes, 2016; Morris, 2018). These challenges have a cumulative effect, making it significantly more difficult for persons with disabilities to find employment or generate an income (Jones & Serieux-Lubin, 2018; Peters, 2008; Terrana et al., 2016). Noteworthy, however, is the fact that it is not the disability itself that is the barrier, but rather the paucity or absence of accommodating physical and electronic infrastructure, funding, technology and teacher training, among other issues (Pandey, 2021).

Persons with disabilities face very similar issues in Caribbean countries, where legal and policy approaches concerning this group are nascent and

J. H. Stephenson and N. Persadie, *Disability in the Workplace*, Palgrave Explorations in Workplace Stigma,
https://doi.org/10.1007/978-3-031-19340-8_3

only now being developed. As an emerging area of interest, this chapter provides an examination of the legal and policy approaches of the English-speaking Caribbean countries in addressing disability and education. This overview is done primarily on the basis of international legal obligations and existing domestic statute and policy that address the education of persons with disabilities in some way.

Disability and Education

Education and training provide the single most important tool in facilitating the full participation of persons with disabilities in society; the provision of quality education and training can be seen as key indicators of equal treatment of persons with disabilities (Gayle-Geddes, 2015). These principles are certainly widely applicable to any country's educational system, as education empowers the vulnerable, shapes a capable workforce and has a major influence on a country's standard of living (Jacob & Holsinger, 2008; UNICEF, 2017a–f). UNICEF (2017a–f) further notes that persons regardless of their (dis)ability have the right to lifelong opportunities that equip them with skills and knowledge to fully participate in society. It is therefore important to ensure that children with disabilities have access to quality education and to educators who are trained to teach such children (UNICEF, 2019). Children with disabilities, however, are often marginalised or excluded from accessing educational opportunities and, even when provisions are made for them, they are often isolated in institutions, special schools (Schmid et al., 2008) or separate classes. Limited access to educational opportunities is a fundamental concern for children with disabilities, as they are likely to face limited access to employment opportunities as adults (Aron & Loprest, 2012; Connor et al., 2008; Lavia, 2007) and remain dependent on caregivers. Children with disabilities generally have a lower rate of success in their educational achievements in relation to their other classmates and are likely to withdraw from established education (Aron & Loprest, 2012) or even be kept away from attending by caregivers. Stigma and discrimination from school administrators, teachers, parents or other students are some of the causal factors that contribute to this low success rate; this is compounded by low societal expectations of success, an absence of an adequate support structure to realise outstanding academic outcomes, namely, insufficient resources, access, facilities and trained teachers (Armstrong et al., 2005;

Charran, 2018; Charran & Seetahal, 2018; Lavia, 2007). Such a support structure necessarily includes well-trained and qualified teachers, support within the schools from colleagues and administrators, and the provision of appropriate access and accommodations, with a view to facilitating the optimal educational outcomes of students with disabilities (Ajodhia-Andrews & Frankel, 2010; Bines & Lei, 2011; Conrad & Brown, 2011). Needless to say, adequate resources—financial, human, infrastructural/architectural, technical, and educational (as it relates to teacher and support staff training)—are key to facilitating the education of children with disabilities.

Fortunately, this situation is changing, albeit very slowly, in the Caribbean where some countries are discussing or adopting education policies that focus on inclusion, mainstreaming, integration and special education, or any combination thereof, in an attempt to mainstream special education and no longer relegate it to the periphery of the educational system. It has been shown that persons with disabilities with access to mainstream and combined access to mainstream and special education obtain better educational outcomes than special education only (Gayle-Geddes, 2020); the social interaction makes for better socially adapted students, regardless of (dis)ability. Learner-centred approaches to teaching, learning and assessment, addressing the needs of learners, regardless of (dis)ability, become imperative in order to address inequality, improve achievement and meet the economic and social needs of Caribbean countries (OECS, 2012). In so doing, education systems will be revolutionised, allowing children with disabilities to be able to participate on a full and equal basis with non-disabled children (Jones & Serieux-Lubin, 2018) and, consequently, help to change attitudes towards disability by removing the stigma often associated with it. This chapter provides a review of the Anglophone Caribbean countries' policy and legal commitment to dealing with disability and education. It will first review their commitment at the international and regional levels, followed by the legal and policy activities undertaken within each respective jurisdiction to illustrate how this commitment translates at the domestic level.

Disability, Education and the Law in the Anglophone Caribbean

There are twelve independent English-speaking Caribbean countries which form the basis of this study: Antigua and Barbuda, The Bahamas, Barbados, Belize, Dominica, Grenada, Guyana, Jamaica, St Kitts and

Table 3.1 Signatory/Accession Status of Anglophone Caribbean Countries to three Conventions addressing Disability and Education

	CRC	*CRPD*	*IAC*
	Date of signature/accession (a)		
Antigua and Barbuda	1991	2007	–
Barbados	1990	2007	–
Belize	1990	2011	–
Dominica	1990	2007	1999
Grenada	1990	2010	–
Guyana	1990	2007	–
Jamaica	1990	2007	1999
St Kitts and Nevis	1990(a)	2019	–
St Lucia	1993(a)	2011	–
St Vincent and the Grenadines	1993(a)	2010(a)	–
The Bahamas	1990	2013	–
Trinidad and Tobago	1990	2007	–

CRC: Convention on the Rights of the Child
CRPD: Convention on the Rights of Persons with Disabilities
IAC: Inter-American Convention on the Elimination of All Forms of Discrimination against Persons with Disabilities
Source Compiled by author from United Nations (1960, 1966, 1989, 2008, 2014); Organisation of American States (n.d.; 2001)

Nevis, St Lucia, St Vincent and the Grenadines and Trinidad and Tobago. As illustrated in Table 3.1, all these countries are either signatories or have acceded to two of the main international conventions that address the education of persons with disabilities. Only two countries of the group—Dominica and Jamaica—signed the regional Inter-American Convention on the Elimination of All Forms of Discrimination against Persons with Disabilities; the reason for such poor participation among the English-speaking Caribbean countries is not clear, except to surmise that already being a signatory to the international conventions might make it feel redundant to do so again at a more localised level. Despite this show of international commitment, it is often the case that countries show enthusiasm to become a State Party to an international or regional convention, however, it should be noted that international legal instruments are not automatically applicable in the domestic law of many of the Anglophone Caribbean countries, as they must first be enacted by Parliament; there exists no real mandate to force the country to enact such legislation (Persadie, 2012: 44). The section below reviews the relevant content of each of the instruments as they relate to the education of persons with disabilities, including two that address education only.

International and Regional Legal Instruments Addressing Disability and Education

There are several international and regional legal instruments which deal with disability in children and education, either as separate subject matters or combined. This section will provide a cursory review of the relevant content of the instruments listed below and provide a country status per Caribbean country, as shown in Table 3.1, but only of the instruments that address both disability and education. In doing so, it highlights the commitment shown by each country towards addressing the education of persons with disabilities at the international level which will then be supported by legal and policy development activity at the domestic level. The following list of conventions[1] addresses education and disability in children:

- Convention on the Rights of the Child, 20 November 1989;
- Convention against Discrimination in Education, 14 December 1960;
- Convention on the Rights of Persons with Disabilities, 03 May 2008;
- International Covenant on Economic, Social and Cultural Rights, 16 December 1966;
- Inter-American Convention on the Elimination of All Forms of Discrimination against Persons with Disabilities, 2001.

Convention on the Rights of the Child

As the name suggests, this convention enshrines the rights of children in all aspects of life. Article 2 notes the general protection of each child's rights without discrimination of any kind with respect to various characteristics, including disability. Article 23 specifically addresses the rights of "mentally or physically disabled" children and recognises the need

[1] For the purposes of the following section, the only type of international and regional legal instruments under review are conventions. There is no focus on any agreement, declaration, treaty, charter, statement, protocol or any other type, notwithstanding the extremely important, but non-binding, Salamanca Statement and Framework for Action on Special Needs Education, 1994.

to ensure their effective access to education and training, among other services, to ensure their "fullest possible social integration and individual development".

Convention Against Discrimination in Education

The Convention against Discrimination in Education recognises education as a fundamental human right, any breach of which can lead to inequality of opportunity and treatment for all. Interestingly, in the definition of "discrimination" in Article 1, there is no mention of disability as a possible ground for discrimination. In fact, there is no mention whatsoever of disability throughout the text of the entire convention and it would be inappropriate to infer it.

Convention on the Rights of Persons with Disabilities

Like the Convention on the Rights of the Child, the Convention on the Rights of Persons with Disabilities enshrines the rights of persons with disabilities in all spheres of life. It addresses education in a few of the articles of the convention with a view to ensuring that education is key to raising awareness (article 8) and mitigating (and ending, where possible) stigma, violence and abuse (article 16) against persons with disabilities. Article 24 is dedicated to education, particularly inclusive education, recognising the right of persons with disabilities to education and promoting inclusive education systems at all levels of learning in all States Parties from primary education up to tertiary and adult education, vocational training and general lifelong learning without discrimination. The Convention also recognises the importance of teacher training and the provision of reasonable accommodation to assist in this regard.

International Covenant on Economic, Social and Cultural Rights

As a social right, the International Covenant on Economic, Social and Cultural Rights deals with education as a right available to everyone in Article 13 but does not specify the rights of persons with disabilities to education. It enshrines the right of compulsory education at the primary education level free of charge for all as well as the availability and accessibility of secondary and tertiary education with a view to such education ultimately being available free of charge.

Inter-American Convention on the Elimination of All Forms of Discrimination Against Persons with Disabilities

The focus of this convention is similar to the focus of the Convention on the Rights of Persons with Disabilities, which enshrines the rights of persons with disabilities in all spheres of life by seeking to "prevent and eliminate all forms of discrimination against persons with disabilities and to promote their full integration into society" (Article II). While not as comprehensive as the Convention on the Rights of Persons with Disabilities in its approach, this Convention addresses education in Article III with a view to ensuring the adoption of legislative and educational measures, among others, to eliminate discrimination against persons with disabilities. Education is to be used to ensure the independence and quality of life of persons with disabilities as well as to raise awareness with a view to eliminating prejudice against this group.

As this very brief and inexhaustive review shows, English-speaking Caribbean countries are State Parties to regional and international legal instruments that address disability and education, two of which do so comprehensively.

Domestic Legal and Policy Approaches for Addressing Disability and Education: The Country Level

Each country under study has illustrated its commitment at the international level to addressing the issues of disability and education, but how has this translated at the country level? UNESCO (n.d.) provides a comprehensive online database, known as PEER, on all countries and their legal and policy approaches to education. This is complemented by their Global Education Monitoring Reports (UNESCO, 2020). This section will rely, in part, on these resources and review the legal and policy approaches of each of the twelve countries under study as it relates to dealing with disability and education.[2]

[2] Key terms related to disability and education, such as special (needs) education, mainstreaming, integration, and inclusion, are used sometimes interchangeably in the various country documents reviewed, but it should be noted that they have different meanings and are defined according to the user, which is not without its challenges. Bergsma (2000), for example, aligns integration with mainstreaming as a means of placing students with special needs in the mainstream of regular education. Inclusion and special needs

Antigua and Barbuda

Antigua and Barbuda's educational system is challenged by poor resources and a lack of specialised teacher training to assist persons with disabilities. In recognition of these challenges, a priority for the government was to address early diagnosis and intervention for students with special needs and providing "appropriate school facilities, teaching staff and school management support to adequately address their learning and developmental challenges" (UWI Consulting Inc., 2012: 11). Adequate access to education, lifelong learning plans, and a mainstreaming strategy for children with disabilities are key foci of the government (UNICEF, 2017b: 43).

Its mainstreaming strategy is reflected in its Special Educational Needs Policy, which focuses on "inclusion" (Harrigan, 2013) by providing educational services for children with disabilities in the general school system. Key areas of focus of the policy include identification and assessment of students with special needs and provision for them; monitoring children's progress; teacher training; school action, where the teacher who identifies a student with special needs provides educational interventions; the development of individual education plans (see s 83, *The Education Act*); statutory assessments of special educational needs (see The *Education Act*); and annual reviews of a statement of special educational needs (Harrigan, 2013). Nevertheless, separate schools serve the needs of those requiring special education. There is also an ICT in Education Policy which notes that the Ministry will prioritise the procurement of assistive technologies for students with special educational needs (Ministry of Education, Antigua and Barbuda, 2013).

education are synonymous for Bergsma (2000) and reflect meeting the needs of a diversity of student and meeting individual student needs in a general setting. Disability Rights California (2022) defines "mainstreaming" similarly to Bergsma (2000) where students with disabilities are placed in regular classrooms but may receive special attention if required; "integration" is similar to mainstreaming but refers to integrated school sites where students with disabilities may receive special education classes separately, but interaction between both groups can still occur. "Inclusion" means the total integration of a student with disabilities into the regular education program and classes with special support and no separate special education assignments (Disability Rights California, 2022). "Special education" refers to specially designed instruction, such as individual education plans, often legislated as seen in the case of six countries below, to meet the unique needs of a child with disabilities whether in the classroom setting or other settings (Disability Rights California, 2022).

In terms of its legal obligations, Antigua and Barbuda has separate pieces of legislation dealing with education and disability. In the *Education Act*, 2008, a child of compulsory school age is exempt from attendance in the case of certified mental or physical disability (s 38). Sections 81–84 address special education for students of various "exceptionalities" (s 83 (1)) to be provided in the "least restrictive and most enabling environment" (s 83(2)) at the shared expense of the parent (for minors) and the Ministry of Education (s 83 (4)). Customised individual education plans comprise a special education programme (83(3)) for which an assessment is required to determine individual student needs (s 84).

Part V of the *Disabilities & Equal Opportunities Act*, 2017 deals with access to education and training for persons with a disability as one of several matters of importance. The Act does not specify the age of persons to whom this Act applies, but it can reasonably be inferred that it should apply to minors and adults equally. Part V of the Act protects the right of a person with a disability to an education without discrimination and on the basis of equal opportunity (s 17 (1)) and is further entitled to be facilitated by special arrangements by the Minister responsible for education as necessary (s 17 (2)). Educational and training institutions are required to provide reasonable access to persons with disabilities in the least restrictive environment such that they are not placed at a disadvantage relative to others (s 17 (4)). The Minister is responsible for providing the relevant teacher training and adequate staff for the education and training of persons with disabilities (s 19).

Barbados

There does not seem to be much in the way of specific policy developments in Barbados as it relates to disability and education, but rather generic statements of intent. In its National Strategic Plan, it seeks to work towards the removal of discrimination against and stigma towards persons with disabilities and further aims to provide appropriate teaching aids and support; teacher training and support for special education teachers; and "educational infrastructure that will support persons who are physically or intellectually challenged" (Ministry of Economic Affairs and Development, 2007; Ministry of Education, Youth Affairs & Culture, 2000; Ministry of Education, Youth Affairs & Culture, 2002). The government has attempted to cater for as many children with special needs as possible in ordinary schools, while maintaining special schools and units for those with the most severe disabilities (Hornby, 2001), described as a "bifurcated system" (Gregory, 2018). Strident calls have been made for a special needs policy (in draft form for two years) to be approved to allow for educational system reforms (The Barbados Advocate, 2017) as well as legislation to protect the rights of the disabled (Carrington, 2021).

The *Education Act*, 2008 addresses special education at s 53. It deals with assessing and providing for students either at special educational facilities or within existing schools through the implementation of special education programmes, among other matters. Section 42(1)(a) exempts a child of compulsory school age from attending school if the child is receiving special education. There is currently no law that addresses disability as the main issue.

Belize

Belize's Ministry of Education has adopted a policy of assimilating children with disabilities into schools but they are challenged by inadequate human and financial resources; inaccessible buildings; an outdated curriculum; lack of transportation, particularly for students with mobility impairments; lack of parental involvement; and limited experienced, qualified, motivated and trained teachers (UNICEF, 2011, 2013). The Ministry has created a special unit, the National Resource Centre for Inclusive Education (NaRCIE), formerly the Special Education Unit, which has the task of ensuring that the special learning needs of students are properly addressed within the existing education system (UNESCO, 2007a). Each of the education plans and strategies has highlighted a focus on inclusive education and attempted to chart ways forward for the educational needs of children with disabilities while recognising that there continues to be no policy or legal framework to promote this thrust (Cambridge Education, 2012; Government of Belize, 2004; Ministry of Education, Youth and Sports, 2012; Ministry of Education, Culture, Science and Technology, 2021). Nevertheless, they all note the country's international legal obligations to provide the means to achieving these goals and ensuring that the rights of children with disabilities to a quality education are met.

The *Education Act*, Cap 36 and the *Education and Training Act*, Cap 36.01 both make very broad statements about catering to the special needs of challenged pupils (s 25; s 49) and that schools shall be free of "gender, racial and other biases" but do not specify disability as a particular bias. The *Families and Children Act*, Cap 173 places the onus on the

State to "take appropriate steps to ensure that children with disabilities are afforded equal opportunities to education" (s 8(2)). Legislatively, there is no separate law that provides for the protection or promotion of the rights of persons with disabilities, although a draft bill made it to Parliament but did not proceed further due to procedural issues (Government of Belize, Press Office, 2020). The Government nevertheless restated its commitment to fight for the rights of all.

Dominica

Dominica currently has no legal or policy framework to address disability but does address the education of children with special needs in its *Education Act*. There is a hybrid system for educating children with disabilities: children with intellectual disabilities are placed in special schools while children with physical disabilities are mainstreamed but are often stigmatised (UNICEF, 2017a). Challenges similar to those experienced by other countries related to special needs education arise with respect to the lack of specialised teacher training (Thomas-Jeremy, n.d.) and staff for detection, diagnosis and treatment (UNICEF, 2017a). The Government indicated its commitment to teacher training in special education (Caribbean Monitoring, 2017), although training is also offered in partnership with non-governmental organisations (Hackett, 2019). An education sector plan is currently being developed (The Chronicle, 2020).

The only piece of legislation addressing the education of children with disabilities is the *Education Act*, 1997 and the regulations made thereunder. It makes provisions for the referral of children with learning difficulties to appropriate education services where they exist (s 4(3)(i)) and the designation of special programmes to be offered in public schools (5(d)). Section 14 enshrines the right of all persons to receive an educational programme appropriate to their needs. Each student has the right to be treated with respect and dignity, fairly and reasonably (s 19). A child of compulsory school age is exempt from attendance in the case of certified mental or physical disability (s 37(1)(d)). Sections 81–84 address special education for students of various "exceptionalities" to be provided in the "least restrictive and most enabling environment" (s 83(2)) at the shared expense of the parent (for minors) and the Ministry of Education (s 83 (4)). Customised individual education plans comprise a special education programme (83(3)) for which an assessment is required to determine individual student needs (s 84). Teachers have the right to appropriate equipment, adequate physical facilities, and training and development (s 132). While this section does not specify this, it can be inferred to apply to special education needs as well. Regulations made pursuant to the Education Act provide for students requiring special education, with the Chief Education Officer having responsibility for ensuring that such children are provided with special education programmes. As mentioned above, there is no law which specifically addresses disability, but advocacy groups continue to lobby for the enactment of legislation to address disability (Dominica News Online, 2020).

Grenada

Much like some of its Caribbean neighbours, Grenada has no policy or legal framework to address disability, but special educational needs are addressed in its Education and Child (Protection and Adoption) Acts. Different reports highlight various challenges in meeting the needs of children with disability, such as lack of specialised staff for detection, diagnosis and treatment, lack of specialised teacher training, and disability-unfriendly educational facilities (UNICEF, 2017c: 45; The Saving Brains Grenada Team, 2020: 12–13, 57). This is compounded by the stigma faced by children with disabilities who are mainstreamed in the public school system (UNICEF, 2017c: 49). As part of its hybrid system, the Ministry of Education (2006) proposed the provision of school facilities for special needs students at all levels, whether in mainstream or specialised schools, however, these recommendations have only been partially met (The Saving Brains Grenada Team, 2020) due to limited resources. While separate facilities exist, children with disabilities are mainstreamed where possible. The need for a Special Needs Education Policy has been recognised by the Government (see Antoine & EconoTech, 2014) and there is a draft policy currently under review by the Ministry of Education (The Saving Brains Grenada Team, 2020).

Two laws address children with disabilities. Under the *Education Act*, Cap. 86, a child of compulsory school age is exempt from attendance in the case of certified mental or physical disability (s 41(2)(d)). Sections 114–117 address special education for students of various "exceptionalities" to be provided in the "least restrictive and most enabling environment" (s 114(2)) at the shared expense of the parent (for minors) and the Ministry of Education (s 114(4)). Customised individual education plans comprise a special education programme (114(3)) for which an assessment is required to determine individual student needs (s 115). While not specific, the *Child (Protection and Adoption) Act*, Cap. 44A makes provisions for the educational welfare of children, including those with disabilities.

Guyana

Stigma, lack of specialised teachers and teacher training, lack of support staff, lack of financial resources, lack of equipment, teachers' attitudes and resistance to mainstreaming children with disabilities and disability-unfriendly infrastructure create serious challenges for children with disabilities to access educational opportunities in Guyana (Ajodhia-Andrews, 2007; Ajodhia-Andrews & Frankel, 2010; Cheong et al., 2018; Frankel et al., 2010; UNICEF, 2016). Much like Belize, due to its vast geography, these issues are compounded by the cost of transportation of students with special needs, particularly those who live in the hinterland and need to access special services which are only available in the capital. Despite these many challenges, and in the absence of a specific special needs educational policy which is being finalised (Commonwealth Foundation, 2018; Department of Public Information, 2021), the Government's general educational policy approach commits to providing equal access to quality education and lifelong learning for all, with special mention of children with disabilities (Ministry of Education, Guyana, n.d.: 3, 4, 16). Mainstreaming students with disabilities into the general educational system is the desired approach, but separate schools do exist for those requiring special education as well, and the Government works with the NGO sector in some cases (Ministry of Education, Guyana, n.d.). The plan highlights the need for a relevant curriculum that is inclusive and student-focused (Ministry of Education, Guyana, n.d.). A Special Education Needs Unit (SEN Unit) has been established by the ministry to work towards the national education policy on inclusion (Ministry of Education, Guyana, n.d.). The Ministry's Education for Sustainable Development Plan highlights key action areas for persons with special educational needs which include disability-friendly facilities; alternative learning paths; public sensitisation and teacher training, among other areas (Ministry of Education, Guyana, 2021).

Guyana is one of a handful of Caribbean countries with legislation that protects the rights of and prohibits discrimination against persons with disabilities. Laws also protect equal rights (of men and women: *Equal Rights Act*, Cap. 38:01) and children's rights. Nevertheless, the *Education Act*, Cap. 39:01 does not in any way address children with disabilities and, while not specific, the *Protection of Children Act*, Cap. 44:06 makes provisions for the educational welfare of children, including those with disabilities. The *Persons with Disabilities Act*, Cap. 36:05, however, makes integration of students with disabilities into the general education system, quality education for all, the establishment of special schools, support services for special education, financial assistance to adult students with disabilities, teacher training and research into the needs of persons with disabilities legally enshrined rights to ensure equal opportunities in education (ss 14–19). Parliament is tasked with ensuring that the necessary funds are available to implement the special education facilities (s 18(3)). While the *Prevention of Discrimination Act*, Cap. 99:08 prohibits discrimination in training as it relates to employment, with disability being a key ground of discrimination, it does not address discrimination in education.

Jamaica

Inclusive education is a goal of the Jamaican education system but special needs students are underserved and marginalised (Gayle-Geddes, 2020; Ministry of Education, Jamaica, 2012). In its draft special education policy, several challenges in dealing with special needs students were highlighted: limited teacher, parent and support staff training; insufficient financial resources; administrator reluctance in admitting students with certain disabilities in mainstream schools; and no legislative framework, among other challenges (Ministry of Education, Jamaica, 2017). The draft policy identifies the actions needed to be taken to accommodate children with disabilities at each level of schooling from early childhood to secondary school, focusing on the role of the Ministry's Special Education Unit in providing support in the mainstream educational system (Ministry of Education, Jamaica, 2017). It also emphasises the need for continued support at the post-secondary or tertiary levels, teacher training, support for caregivers, and partnerships with non-state entities to provide and deliver special education programmes and services to ensure that all children perform maximally (Ministry of Education, Jamaica, 2017). It is a comprehensive document that seeks to ensure equity and access to educational opportunities and to promote inclusive education where possible (Ministry of Education and Youth, 2018). A recently published report by the Jamaica Education Transformation Commission noted that "[e]xisting efforts by the Government of Jamaica were considered insufficient to adequately provide for the needs of PWD in general and more specifically, children, particularly in accessing information, educational and support services" (2021: 210). The report identified numerous challenges related to the education of children with disabilities in a number of spheres: legal, financial, medical, educational, training and support, data collection, monitoring, and inclusion and accessibility, among others. Recommendations to address these shortcomings include legislative/policy effectiveness and governance coherence; assessing and financing equitable educational provisions for persons with disabilities; strengthening public education to create an inclusive society; and promoting research to inform evidence-based programming, monitoring and evaluation (Gayle-Geddes, 2020).

Jamaica is one of the Caribbean countries that promotes and protects the rights of and prohibits discrimination against persons with disabilities on an equal basis with others. The *Disabilities Act* of 2014 enshrines these rights and also makes specific provisions for access to education and training in the least restrictive environment and for persons to be reasonably accommodated (s 26). The *Education Act* addresses children with disability of compulsory school age only inasmuch as they require special education treatment (s 24) and for making regulations to address the various categories of students requiring such treatment (s43(1)(k)). While not specific, the *Child Care and Protection Act* makes provisions for the educational welfare of children, including those with disabilities (s 28). This piecemeal framework has led to calls for ensuring that there is a legal and policy framework in place to address the rights of children with disabilities by finalising and/or operationalising all relevant laws (Jamaica Education Transformation Commission, 2021).

St Kitts and Nevis

The situation with respect to the education of children with disabilities reflects much of what is experienced in some of the other Caribbean states. There is no legal or policy framework for dealing with disability or the education of children with disabilities (UNICEF, 2017d). While many children with disabilities are placed in mainstream schools, there are special schools for children who cannot be integrated into the main system (UNICEF, 2017d). Mainstreaming remains the responsibility of the Office for Special Education in the Ministry of Education which is responsible for assessments and interventions and teaching students with moderate to severe mental challenges. Nevertheless, mainstreaming is problematic given that most education and training institutions are disability-unfriendly and restrict physical access (Ministry of Education, St Kitts and Nevis, 2017). Stigma, too, affects students with disabilities who are mainstreamed (UNICEF, 2017d) as well as caregivers' willingness to have children assessed for special education needs (Ministry of Education, St Kitts and Nevis, 2017). Other challenges include inadequate diagnostic testing, teacher training and support services (Ministry of Education, St Kitts and Nevis, 2017; UNESCO, 2016). Public awareness, parent training and NGO involvement, teacher training and early intervention were identified as some of the ways of addressing challenges in delivering education to children with disabilities in earlier policy approaches (Ministry of Education, St Kitts and Nevis, 2009).

In terms of its legal obligations, St Kitts and Nevis has legislation dealing with education but none with disability. Under the *Education Act*, Cap 13:01 a child of compulsory school age is exempt from attendance in the case of certified mental or physical disability (s 37). Sections 82–85 address special education for students of various "exceptionalities" to be provided in the "least restrictive and most enabling environment" (s 82(2)) at the shared expense of the parent (for minors) and the Ministry of Education (s 82(4)). Customised individual education plans comprise a special education programme (82(3)) for which an assessment is required to determine individual student needs (s 83). While not specific, the *Child (Care and Adoption) Act*, Cap. 12.01 makes provisions for the educational welfare of children, including those with disabilities.

St Lucia

Inequitable access; limited support services; inadequate physical spaces for special education; the need for specialised staff for early detection, diagnoses and treatment of non-physical disabilities; lack of teaching and learning resources and materials; unadapted curricula; unclear roles of special educators; lack of human and financial resources; and stigma and discrimination adversely affect the education of children with disabilities in this country (Lubin, 2020; UNICEF, 2017e). St Lucia also has a hybrid system of mainstreaming those who can be facilitated as well as Special Education Centres for those who cannot. Initiatives under the Education Sector Development Plan seek to ensure affordable transportation, assessments, student support services, seamless transition through the education system, programme development, teacher training and increased capacity of special education centres were made available to children requiring special education (Ministry of Education, St Lucia, n.d.). There is a draft policy on persons with disabilities that needs to be adopted and implemented (Child Rights International Network, 2015).

Under the *Education Act*, Cap. 18:01, a child of compulsory school age is exempt from attendance in the case of certified mental or physical disability (s 38). Sections 83–86 address special education for students of various "exceptionalities" to be provided in the "least restrictive and most enabling environment" (s 83(2)) at the shared expense of the parent (for minors) and the Ministry of Education (s 83(4)). Customised individual education plans comprise a special education programme (83(3)) for which an assessment is required to determine individual student needs (s 84). While not specific, the *Child Justice Act* of 2018 makes provisions for the educational welfare of children, including those with differing cognitive abilities.

St Vincent and the Grenadines

In 2016, the Government of St Vincent and the Grenadines approved a National Policy Framework for Child Protection which promotes inclusive education and integration of students with disabilities into the general education system (Committee on the Rights of the Child, 2017). Inclusiveness and equity are central to the educational legal and policy framework of the country (UNICEF, 2017f), nevertheless, multiple challenges affect this aspiration. These include no early intervention programme, lack of teacher training, lack of assistive devices, insufficient human and financial resources, lack of support services, physically disability-unfriendly educational infrastructure, stigma and discrimination, poor access to educational opportunities by students from rural areas, limited access to transportation, insufficient integration of children with disabilities into the mainstream educational system, lack of adequate resources/learning materials, and inability of teachers to adapt the curriculum to cater to individual student needs, among other issues (Ministry of Education, St Vincent & the Grenadines, 2015; UNESCO, 2007b; UNICEF, 2017f). There exists a hybrid system of mainstreaming those who can be facilitated as well as special education facilities for those who cannot. There is no law that addresses disability.

Under the *Education Act*, Cap. 225, a child of compulsory school age is exempt from attendance in the case of certified mental or physical disability (s 40). Sections 112–115 address special education for students of various "exceptionalities" to be provided in the "least restrictive and most enabling environment" (s 112(2)) at the shared expense of the parent (for minors) and the Ministry of Education (s 112(4)). Customised individual education plans comprise a special education programme (112(3)) for which an assessment is required to determine individual student needs (s 113). While not specific, the *Child (Care and Adoption) Act*, Cap. 225 makes provisions for the educational welfare of children, including those with disabilities.

The Bahamas

In its ten-year Education Plan, the Government of The Bahamas made the move towards the development of a realistic and effective inclusion policy (Ministry of Education, Bahamas, 2009). The Plan notes several long-term objectives as they relate to special needs which focus on teacher training, integration of special needs students into mainstream classes, outfitting schools with the necessary facilities and equipment, dedicating sufficient tuition resources to meet the needs of special students, technology upgrades, and accessibility. Policy development, student screening, intervention and transitional programmes are among some of the short-term objectives (Ministry of Education, Bahamas, 2009). The Government's Shared Vision for Education reinforces what was in the previous plan and continues to support inclusion, teacher training, screening, public awareness-raising and education, and provision of necessary resources at mainstream and specialised schools; it has also added the component of conducting research to further understand the special needs requirements of children and assess the effectiveness of intervention programmes (National Education Committee, 2015). The plan acknowledges that a hybrid system of separate facilities may be required for those who cannot cope with the mainstream system. In its Vision 2040 document, the Government commits itself to enhancing the provision of special education to ensure equity in education through mandatory screening to identify students with learning disabilities, teacher training, and providing opportunities to students with special needs to develop their full potential (NDP Secretariat, 2017).

While there is no dedicated special needs or disability policy, The National Commission for Persons with Disabilities advises persons with disabilities of their right to equal access to training and education, among other rights (The National Commission for Persons with Disabilities, n.d.).

The *Education Act*, 2001 deals with the education of students requiring special educational treatment in . ss 20–21. These sections allow for regulations to be made for the provision of special educational treatment and assessments of students. The Minister is obligated to ensure the provision of special educational treatment whether in special schools or mainstream schools for students who require this (s 12(2)(c)), reflecting the hybrid approach in the Vision for Education plan. Part V of the *Persons with Disabilities (Equal Opportunities) Act*, 2014 addresses education and reflects the policy approach taken by the government. The law provides for teacher training, access to quality education, and integration of persons with disabilities in schools as well as the establishment of special schools as required. The Act also provides for vocational training skills, development and training programmes for persons with disabilities of age for employment. The *Child Protection Act*, 2010 also seeks the interests of children with disabilities by placing the onus on the Minister responsible for education to take appropriate steps to ensure that such children are afforded equal opportunities to education (s 8(2)).

Trinidad and Tobago

Trinidad and Tobago has a policy and legislative framework for disability, education and inclusive education. The Ministry of Education has noted various challenges that arise in educating students with disabilities: inequality, inequity, lack of inclusivity, inadequate stakeholder collaboration, discrimination in enrolment practices, inaccessibility, inadaptability of curriculum to special needs students and inadequate teacher training (n.d.; Charran, 2018; Persons, 2018). In noting these challenges, it proposes solutions to address each one. The Inclusive Education Policy states that the Ministry "is committed to a seamless education system of which inclusive education is a major component. It shall provide support and services to all learners by taking appropriate steps to make education available, accessible acceptable and adaptable" (Ministry of Education, Trinidad and Tobago, 2009). It promotes a hybrid system where students can enrol in the general education system or in special schools which might better suit their needs and where they are expected to receive a quality education from adequately trained and qualified staff as well as adequate support services (Ministry of Education, Trinidad and Tobago, 2009). As required, they may benefit from tailored education programmes. The Policy also provides for continuous administrator and teacher training, research, adapted curricula and assessment, funding, school management, support services, support for parents, physical access, alternative forms of education delivery, and access to transport (Ministry of Education, Trinidad and Tobago, 2009: 8–12). There is a higher education policy as well which strives for inclusion to allow persons with disabilities to develop to their fullest potential and become contributing members of society (Ministry of Science, Technology and Tertiary Education, 2010). Moreover, there is a national policy framework that addresses tertiary education and skills training which seeks to "[p]rovide opportunities for lifelong learning and ensuring equity and inclusiveness by expanding tertiary education and skills training to all citizens, and in particular, disadvantaged groups such as the disabled" (Ministry of Tertiary Education and Skills Training, 2015). These are all supported by an ICT policy which promotes inclusivity for special education through the use of assistive technologies, educating stakeholders, programme development and delivery, and teacher training (Ministry of Education, Trinidad and Tobago, 2005). The National Child Policy reiterates the need for education that is "inclusive and accessible, including meeting the requirements of special needs students and children with learning disabilities" (Office of the Prime Minister, 2020: 13) which is also highlighted in the National Development Strategy (Ministry of Planning and Development, 2017).

Disability is addressed in a separate policy document which also promotes inclusive education and identified 14 measures to support this (Ministry of Social Development and Family Services, Government of Trinidad and Tobago, 2019). Among the measures targeting children with disabilities is the creation of educational and training opportunities; the provision of adequate support services, teaching aids and supports, and special education teachers and resource personnel; sensitisation of children and public officers; employment programmes; special facilities for persons who cannot be integrated; accessible educational and training materials; counselling programmes for parents and students and stakeholder collaboration (Ministry of Social Development and Family Services, Government of Trinidad and Tobago, 2019).

On the legal side, the *Education Act*, Ch. 39:01 and the *Equal Opportunity Act*, Ch. 22:03 address disability, special education and non-discrimination; there is no law that addresses disability as the main subject. Sections 39–40 of the *Education Act* deal with the establishment of special schools or classes, whether separately or not; special schools may become part of the public school system (12(1)(h)). The Act carries wide regulatory powers for categorising children requiring special education; creating eligibility criteria for institutional funding; providing for the expenditure of such funds; staffing; management and inspection of special educational facilities; and teacher training. The *Equal Opportunity Act* includes disability as a status against which discrimination in relation to education is prohibited and further prohibits discrimination against applicants to and students of educational establishments (s 15) except where unjustifiable hardship would arise for the institution (s 18A(2)). It has been reported that the "disabilities legislation" is to be reviewed with a view to ensuring there are stronger provisions for equality and non-discrimination in the school system (LOOP News, 2022).

Discussion

Anglophone Caribbean countries find themselves at very different stages in their policy, legal and practical approaches to dealing with the education of persons with disabilities. As illustrated in Table 3.2, some policies and laws are nascent (in draft form) while some are quite advanced. Only two countries (Antigua and Barbuda and Trinidad and Tobago) have policies specific to special education/inclusive education/mainstreaming, with four countries (Barbados, Grenada, Guyana, Jamaica) having draft forms. Seven of the countries have education/development and strategic plans which address these issues but not as a central theme; St Vincent and the Grenadines has an overarching policy framework that includes issues affecting children. Two countries (Antigua and Barbuda and Trinidad and Tobago) have ICT policies geared towards assisting children with disabilities. Trinidad and Tobago is the only country to have a separate policy dealing with disability, with St Lucia having one in draft form. Further, Trinidad and Tobago is also the only country to have a separate policy dealing with higher education and vocational training that includes the development of persons with disabilities; Jamaica's draft policy on special education does address this and The Bahamas' Education Plan includes transitional programmes. This is a relatively new thrust, as the emphasis was originally placed on early childhood, primary and secondary school students (Wolanin & Steele, 2004).

All countries—except for Guyana—have Education Acts which address special educational needs in some way, some more comprehensively than others. Guyana, however, is only one of four countries (Antigua and Barbuda, Guyana, Jamaica, The Bahamas) with a law on disability and one

Table 3.2 Policy, Plans and Laws in Anglophone Caribbean Countries related to Education and Disability

	PLANS	*POLICY*				*LAW*		
	Education/ Development/ Strategic	*Special Ed/Incl/Main**	*Higher Ed/Voc Training⁺*	*ICT*	*Disability*	*Education*	*Disability*	*Non-Discrimination*
Antigua and Barbuda		✓		✓		✓	✓	✓
Barbados	✓	■				✓		
Belize	✓					✓	■	
Dominica	■					✓		
Grenada		■				✓		
Guyana	✓	■					✓	✓
Jamaica	✓	■			✓^	✓	✓	
St Kitts and Nevis						✓		

	PLANS	POLICY				LAW		
	Education/ Development/ Strategic	*Special Ed/Incl/Main**	*Higher Ed/Voc Training+*	*ICT*	*Disability*	*Education*	*Disability*	*Non-Discrimination*
St Lucia	✓				■	✓		
St Vincent and the Grenadines		◆				✓		
The Bahamas	✓					✓	✓	✓
Trinidad and Tobago	✓	✓	✓	✓	✓	✓		✓

✓ Approved and in use
■ Draft policy or law
◆ Policy framework
^ Unavailable for review
* Policies dealing with Special Education, Inclusion or Mainstreaming
+ Policies dealing with Higher Education and Vocational Training
Source Compiled by author from the various plans, policies and laws of each country

of four countries (Antigua and Barbuda, Guyana, The Bahamas, Trinidad and Tobago) with legislation that promotes equal opportunities or non-discrimination in education, among other areas. All disability legislation makes specific provisions for education and children with disabilities, hence their inclusion. While not included in the table and not specifically mentioned in the law, seven countries (Grenada, Guyana, Jamaica, St Kitts and Nevis, St Lucia, St Vincent and the Grenadines and The Bahamas) have some form of child protection or childcare law that makes provisions for the educational welfare of children, including those with disabilities. As can be seen from the country reviews, seven of them (Antigua and Barbuda, Barbados, Dominica, Grenada, St Kitts and Nevis, St Lucia, and St Vincent and the Grenadines) have very similar legislation dealing with education, presumably modelled on OECS or CARICOM model education legislation or drafted by the same person.

Nevertheless, no country in the study finds itself being able to optimally address the situation of educating children with disabilities. Cross-cutting challenges for all countries include insufficient human, financial and technical resources; inaccessible physical infrastructure; inadequately trained teaching and support staff for the purposes of assessment, diagnosis, intervention and treatment; stigma and discrimination; inadequate support staff and services; unavailable support for caregivers; and prohibitive transportation costs in countries with larger land masses and centralised services (Hincapié et al., 2019). Many ministries responsible for education have special units dedicated to providing for students with special needs. Often, however, governments partner with or depend on supplementary support from NGOs and the private sector to deliver services to children with disabilities (UNESCO, 2010).

In studies conducted in five countries (Belize, Barbados, Guyana, The Bahamas, Trinidad and Tobago), teacher attitudes towards children with disabilities have been highlighted as a major challenge to the education of this group. This is important only because teachers are at the front line of service delivery. Teachers' feelings of ambivalence (Blackman et al., 2012, 2017), reticence (Jones, 2020; Maynard & Jules, 2017), resistance or negativity (Ajodhia-Andrews, 2007; Ajodhia-Andrews & Frankel, 2010; Cambridge-Johnson et al., 2014; Frankel et al., 2010; Johnson & Harris, 2014) about teaching children with disabilities stem from key concerns they have including lack of training, knowledge, support, resources and facilities, unadapted curricula (McIntosh et al., 1993), funding, and large class sizes. Once the necessary resources are provided to upskill these teachers, it can positively transform their attitudes about teaching children with disabilities and help make educational systems successes in this regard.

Contrary to the belief that children with disabilities perform more poorly than their other classmates, it has been reported in a country study of Jamaica that persons with disabilities with "access to *mainstream* and combined access to *mainstream and special education* obtain better educational outcomes than *special education only*" (Gayle-Geddes, 2015; emphasis in original). The study also found that, given the necessary assistive supports and opportunities, persons with disabilities are able to excel educationally (Gayle-Geddes, 2015). This is very important to note so that the necessary policy and legal approaches can be taken and resources provided to make better provisions for positive educational outcomes for persons with disabilities.

While full inclusion is ideal and will help with the social development of children with disabilities in schools, it is simply not practical due to the diverse needs present among this group. Consequently, inclusive education is more readily evidenced through policy development and rhetoric rather than legislation (Blackman et al., 2012) and actual implementation. Lubin (2020) notes that exclusionary practices are needed to supplement or complement inclusionary practices based on the unique needs of students with disabilities; this concept is explicitly recognised in the Draft Policy on Special Education for Jamaica (Ministry of Education, Jamaica, 2017) and implicitly addressed by the other countries as evidenced by the need for and existence of hybrid systems. Children with disabilities form a heterogeneous group, with different types and varying degrees of physical and/or intellectual disabilities. Inclusive education therefore cannot be a one-size-fits-all solution, which explains why every country has taken a hybrid approach to special education, legislating, in some cases, individual education/intervention plans in an attempt to provide customised learning to meet individual needs.

Conclusion

In terms of translating commitment at the international and regional levels to policy and legal activities at the domestic level, measurement is difficult and subjective. Often, the policy and legal commitment to dealing with disability and education is not afforded the priority that it deserves due to insufficient availability and allocation of resources and lack of political will. The enactment of laws would create the regulatory framework required to provide the necessary support and protections for this vulnerable group. Few Caribbean countries, if any, have a single, comprehensive policy and legal framework to address the education of children with disabilities. Rather, different policies, plans and legislative provisions exist in varying degrees that comprise the approach adopted by the various countries. Even where policy and legal approaches are inadequate or partially implemented, they are often complemented by practical approaches, although themselves insufficient based on limited resources, where feasible. In many cases, the ministries responsible for education have specialised units dedicated to dealing with special educational needs and their work is often supplemented by the private sector and non-governmental organisations in providing for children with disabilities due to limited resources. Nevertheless, unless and until sufficient resources are allocated to providing quality education, equitable access and equal opportunities to children with disabilities, they will continue to be marginalised, prevented from realising their full potential and contributing to society.

References

Ajodhia-Andrews, A. (2007). Inclusive education in Guyana: Perspectives of policy makers, teachers, and parents of children with special needs. Unpublished dissertation submitted at the University of Ryerson, Paper 466. Available from http://digitalcommons.ryerson.ca/dissertations

Ajodhia-Andrews, A., & Frankel, E. (2010). Inclusive education in Guyana: A call for change. *International Journal of Special Education, 25*(1), 126–144.

Antoine, P., & EconoTech. (2014). *Grenada's Growth and Poverty Reduction Strategy (GPRS) 2014–2018*. Ministry of Finance.

Armstrong, A. C., Armstrong, D., Lynch, C., & Severin, S. (2005). Special and inclusive education in the Eastern Caribbean: Policy practice and provision. *International Journal of Inclusive Education, 9*(1), 71–87. https://doi.org/10.1080/1360311042000302905

Aron, L., & Loprest, P. (2012). Disability and the education system. *The Future of Children, 22*(1), 97–122.

Bergsma, S. (2000). *The regular classroom as battleground for inclusive special needs education: An assessment of options of special needs education in the commonwealth Caribbean*. Education for All in the Caribbean: Assessment 2000. Caribbean Monograph Series. Jamaica: UNESCO.

Bines, H., & Lei, P. (2011). Disability and education: The longest road to inclusion. *International Journal of Educational Development, 31*, 419–424.

Blackman, S., Conrad, D., & Brown, L. (2012). The Attitude of Barbadian And Trinidadian teachers to integration. *International Journal of Special Education, 27*(3), 158–168.

Blackman, S., Conrad, D., & Philip, L. (2017). The pre-university experiences of students with disabilities in Barbados and Trinidad. *International Journal of Special Education, 32*(2), 238–270.

Cambridge Education. (2012). *Improving access, quality and governance of education in Belize Education Sector Strategy 2011–2016*. Ministry of Education.

Cambridge-Johnson, J., Hunter-Johnson, Y., & Newton, N. (2014). Breaking the silence of mainstream teachers' attitude towards inclusive education in the Bahamas: High school teachers' perceptions. *The Qualitative Report, 19*(42): 1–20. https://doi.org/10.46743/2160-3715/2014.1099

Caribbean Monitoring. (2017). Dominica government to boost special education teachers. *WIC News*. Available from https://wicnews.com/caribbean/dominica-government-boost-special-education-teachers-20425530/

Carrington, J. (2021). Negative attitudes towards the disabled need to be addressed. Barbados Government Information Service. Retrieved 18 May 2022, from https://gisbarbados.gov.bb/blog/negative-attitudes-towards-the-disabled-need-to-be-addressed/

Charran, C. (2018). Inclusion in Trinidad and Tobago: A dream in progress. *Texas Education Review* 7(1), 102–106. https://doi.org/10.26153/tsw/16

Charran, C., & Seetahal, K. (2018). Education for some? The exploration of inclusive education in Trinidad and Tobago. *Texas Education Review* 7(1), 107–115. https://doi.org/10.26153/tsw/17

Cheong, K., Kellems, R., Andersen, M., & Steed, K. (2018). The education of individuals with disabilities in Guyana: An overview (pp. 1–5). Hammill Institute on Disabilities, https://doi.org/10.1177/1053451218782435

Child Rights International Network. (2015). *Saint Lucia: Children's Rights References in the Universal Periodic Review*. Available from https://archive.crin.org/en/library/publications/saint-lucia-childrens-rights-references-universal-periodic-review.html

Committee on the Rights of the Child. (2017). List of issues in relation to the combined second and third periodic report of Saint Vincent and the Grenadines, CRC/C/VCT/Q/2–3/Add.1. Available from https://tbinternet.ohchr.org/Treaties/CRC/Shared%20Documents/VCT/INT_CRC_RLI_VCT_26390_E.docx

Commonwealth Foundation. (2018). Ensuring the inclusive education of children with disabilities in Guyana and Jamaica. Available from https://commonwealthfoundation.com/project/ensuring-the-inclusive-education-of-children-with-disabilities-in-guyana-and-jamaica/#:~:text=In%20Guyana%2C%20the%20lack%20of,as%20those%20with%20mild%20autism

Connor, D., Gabel, S., Gallagher, D., & Morton, M. (2008). Disability studies and inclusive education—Implications for theory, research, and practice. *International Journal of Inclusive Education, 12*(5–6), 441–457. https://doi.org/10.1080/13603110802377

Department of Public Information, Guyana. (2021, September 29). *MoE host final consultation on SEND Strategic Action Plan.* Available from https://dpi.gov.gy/moe-hosts-final-consultation-on-send-strategic-action-plan/

Disability Rights California. (2022). *Special Education Rights and Responsibilities (SERR).* Available from https://serr.disabilityrightsca.org/

Dominica News Online. (2020). *DAPD says 'Dominican with Disability Act' is needed.* Available from https://dominicanewsonline.com/news/homepage/news/dapd-says-dominicans-with-disability-act-is-needed/

Frankel, E., Gold, S., & Ajodhia-Andrews, A. (2010). International preschool inclusion: Bridging the gap between vision and practices. *Young Exceptional Children, 13*(5), 2–16. https://doi.org/10.1177/1096250610379983

Gayle-Geddes, A. (2015). *Disability and inequality: Socioeconomic imperatives and public policy in Jamaica.* Palgrave MacMillan.

Gayle-Geddes, A. (2016). A situational analysis of persons with disabilities in Jamaica and Trinidad and Tobago: Education and employment policy imperatives. *Occupying disability: Critical approaches to community, justice, and decolonizing disability* (pp. 127–141). Springer, Dordrecht.

Gayle-Geddes, A. (2020). *Disability and education in Jamaica: Analysis of Policy and Praxis.* ED/GEMR/MRT/2020/LAC/10. UNESCO.

Government of Belize. (2004). *The National Plan of Action for children and adolescents in Belize 2004–2015.* UNICEF.

Government of Belize, Press Office. (2020). *Cabinet will not table equal opportunities bill.* Available from https://www.pressoffice.gov.bz/cabinet-will-not-table-equal-opportunities-bill/

Gregory, J. (2018). Not my responsibility: The impact of separate special education systems on educators' attitudes toward inclusion. *Educational Policy Analysis and Strategic Research, 13*(1), 127–148.

Grigal, M., Hart, D., & Migliore, A. (2011). Comparing the transition planning, postsecondary education, and employment outcomes of students with intellectual and other disabilities. *Career Development for Exceptional Individuals, 34*(1), 4–17.

Hackett, V. (2019). Teachers from Dominica receive special education training in Barbados. *CARICOM Today*. Available from https://today.caricom.org/2019/09/04/teachers-from-dominica-receive-special-education-training-in-barbados/

Harrigan, J. (2013). *Special Educational Needs (SEN) Policy: Antigua and Barbuda*. Ministry of Education, Sports, Youth and Gender Affairs: St John's.

Hincapié, D., Duryea, S., & Hincapié, I. (2019). *Education for All: Advancing Disability Inclusion in Latin America and the Caribbean*. Education Division, Social Sector. Policy Brief No. IDB-PB-299. Inter-American Development Bank. Retrieved 24 November 2021, from https://publications.iadb.org/publications/english/document/Education_for_All_Advancing_Disability_Inclusion_in_Latin_America_and_the_Caribbean_en_en.pdf

Hornby, G. (2001). *Children with special needs: Parents' handbook*. Ministry of Education, Youth Affairs & Culture.

Jacob, W., & Holsinger, D. (2008). Inequality in education: A critical analysis. In W. Jacob, & D. Holsinger (Eds.), *Inequality in education: Comparative and international perspectives* (pp. 1–33). CERC Studies in Comparative Education 24. The University of Hong Kong: Comparative Education Research Centre.

Johnson, S., & Harris, O. (2014). Special educator attitudes toward children with communication disorders in the Caribbean. *Caribbean Educational Research Journal, 2*(2), 133–148.

Jones, F., & Serieux-Lubin, L. (2018). *Disability, human rights and public policy in the Caribbean: A situation analysis*. Studies and Perspectives Series: The Caribbean: No. 64. Santiago: UNECLAC.

Jones, J. (2020). Attitudes of primary school teachers towards inclusive education in Belize: A systematic review. Unpublished dissertation submitted at the University of South Wales. Available from https://files.eric.ed.gov/fulltext/ED612707.pdf

Lavia, J. (2007). Girls and special education in the Caribbean. *Support for Learning, 22*(4), 189–196.

LOOP News. (2022, February 14). *T&T's disabilities legislation to be reviewed*. Available from https://tt.loopnews.com/content/tts-disabilities-legislation-be-reviewed

Lubin, J. (2020). Roles of special educators in St. Lucia: Implications of policy and practice on inclusion. *Journal of International Special Needs Education, 23*(1), 33–44.

McIntosh, R., Vaughn, S., Schumm, J., Haager, D., & Lee, O. (1993). Observations of students with learning disabilities in general education classrooms. *Exceptional Children, 60*(3), 249–257.

Ministry of Economic Affairs and Development, Barbados. (2007). *The National Strategic Plan of Barbados, 2006–2025*. Bridgetown: Ministry of Economic Affairs & Development.

Ministry of Education, Guyana. (n.d.). *Education Sector Plan 2021–2025*. Ministry of Education.

Ministry of Education, St Lucia. (n.d.). *Education Sector Development Plan: Priorities and Strategies 2015–2020*. Ministry of Education.

Ministry of Education, Trinidad and Tobago. (n.d.). *Draft education policy paper 2017–2022*. Ministry of Education.

Ministry of Education, Youth Affairs & Culture, Barbados. (2000). *Education in Barbados information handbook*. Ministry of Education, Youth Affairs & Culture.

Ministry of Education, Youth Affairs & Culture, Barbados. (2002). *Strategic Plan 2002–2012*. Ministry of Education, Youth Affairs & Culture.

Ministry of Education, Trinidad and Tobago. (2005). *Draft policy for information and communications technology in education*. Ministry of Education.

Ministry of Education, Grenada. (2006). *Strategic Plan for Educational Enhancement and Development 2006 -2015*. Ministry of Education.

Ministry of Education, Bahamas. (2009). *10 Year Education Plan*. Ministry of Education.

Ministry of Education, St Kitts and Nevis. (2009). *White Paper on Education Development and Policy 2009–2019*. Ministry of Education.

Ministry of Education, Trinidad and Tobago. (2009). *Inclusive education policy*. Ministry of Education.

Ministry of Education, Jamaica. (2012). *National Education Strategic Plan: 2011–2020*. Ministry of Education.

Ministry of Education, Youth and Sports, Belize. (2012). *National youth development policy of Belize*. Ministry of Education, Youth and Sports.

Ministry of Education, Antigua and Barbuda. (2013). *ICT in Education Policy for Antigua and Barbuda*. Ministry of Education, Antigua and Barbuda: St John's.

Ministry of Education, St Vincent & the Grenadines. (2015). *Education for All 2015 National Review Report: Saint Vincent and the Grenadines*. Ministry of Education.

Ministry of Education, Jamaica. (2017). *Draft policy on special education: Access, equity and relevance*. Ministry of Education.

Ministry of Education, St Kitts and Nevis. (2017). *The Government of St. Kitts and Nevis Ministry of Education 2017–2021 Education Sector Plan Education for All: Embracing Change, Securing the Future*. Ministry of Education.

Ministry of Education and Youth, Jamaica. (2018). *Special education policy before cabinet*. Available from https://moey.gov.jm/special-education-policy-before-cabinet/

Ministry of Education, Culture, Science and Technology, Belize. (2021). *Belize Education Sector Plan 2021–2025*. Ministry of Education, Culture, Science and Technology.

Ministry of Education, Guyana. (2021). *Education for Sustainable Development*. Available from https://education.gov.gy/en/index.php/policies/78-education-for-sustainable-development/1489-education-for-sustainable-development#gsc.tab=0

Ministry of Planning and Development. (2017). *Draft national development strategy 2016–2030 (Vision 2030)*. Ministry of Planning and Development.

Ministry of Science, Technology and Tertiary Education. (2010). *Policy on Tertiary education, technical vocational education and training, and life-long learning in Trinidad and Tobago*. Ministry of Science, Technology and Tertiary Education.

Ministry of Social Development and Family Services, Government of Trinidad and Tobago. (2019). *National policy on persons with disabilities*. Ministry of Social Development and Family Services.

Ministry of Tertiary Education and Skills Training. (2015). *The future of tertiary education and skills training 2015–2025: A national policy framework*. Ministry of Tertiary Education and Skills Training.

Morris, F. (2018). An inclusive, equitable and prosperous Caribbean: The case of persons with disabilities. *Social and Economic Studies, 67*(4), 95–119.

National Education Committee, Bahamas. (2015). *Vision 2030: A shared vision for education*. National Education Committee.

NDP Secretariat. (2017). *Vision 2040: National development plan of the Bahamas*. NDP Secretariat.

OECS. (2012). *OECS Education Sector Strategy: 2012–2026*. OECS: Castries.

Office of the Prime Minister (Gender and Child Affairs), Trinidad and Tobago. (2020). *The National Child Policy: Our Children…Our Treasure*. Office of the Prime Minister (Gender and Child Affairs). Retrieved 03 April 2021, from http://opm-gca.gov.tt/National-Child-Policy

Organisation of American States. (2001). Inter-American Convention on the Elimination of All Forms of Discrimination against Persons with Disabilities, 14 September 2001. Available from https://www.oas.org/juridico/english/treaties/a-65.html

Organisation of American States. (n.d.). *Multilateral treaties: Signatories and ratifications*. Available from https://www.oas.org/juridico/english/sigs/a-65.html

Pandey, S. (2021, October 13). Four ways India could help students with disabilities continue their education during the pandemic. *Scroll.in*. Retrieved 23 December 2021, from https://scroll.in/article/1007571/four-ways-india-could-help-students-with-disabilities-continue-their-education-during-the-pandemic

Persadie, N. (2012). *A critical analysis of the efficacy of law as a tool to achieve gender equality*. University Press of America.

Persons, H. (2018). *Persons with disabilities in Trinidad & Tobago: A situational analysis*. Commonwealth of Learning.

Peters, S. (2008). Inequalities in education for people with disabilities. In W. Jacob, & D. Holsinger (Eds.), *Inequality in education: Comparative and international perspectives* (pp. 149–171). CERC Studies in Comparative Education 24. The University of Hong Kong: Comparative Education Research Centre.

Schmid, K., Vézina, S., & Ebbeson, L. (2008). *Disability in the Caribbean. A study of four countries: a sociodemographic analysis of the disabled*. ECLAC – Studies and Perspectives series – The Caribbean – No. 7. UN ECLAC: Port of Spain.

Seetahal, K., & Charran, C. (2018). The unknown and unemployed masses with disabilities in Trinidad and Tobago. *Texas Education Review, 7*(1), 130–139. https://doi.org/10.26153/tsw/20

Terrana, A., Dowdell, J., Edwards, B., Tahsin, F., Cacciacarro, L., & Cameron, D. (2016). Perspectives of key stakeholders about vocational training and rehabilitation in Trinidad and Tobago. *British Journal of Occupational Therapy, 79*(11), 703–712. https://doi.org/10.1177/0308022616669380

The Barbados Advocate. (2017). *Special needs policy lacking*. Retrieved 18 May 2022, from https://www.barbadosadvocate.com/news/special-needs-policy-lacking

The Chronicle. (2020). *DA's new education sector plan initiated*. Available from https://thedominicachronicle.com/das-new-education-sector-plan-initiated/

The National Commission for Persons with Disabilities. (n.d.). *Know your rights*. Available from https://disabilitiescommissionbahamas.org/disabled-persons.html

The Saving Brains Grenada Team, Caribbean Center for Child Neurodevelopment, Windward Islands Research and Education Foundation. (2020). *Grenada landscape assessment: Mapping existing systems to address developmental delays in 0–5-year-olds*. UNICEF: Eastern Caribbean Office.

Thomas-Jeremy, J. (n.d.). Facilitating successful inclusion at secondary schools in Dominica: A study of teachers' perspectives. Available from https://www.lynchburg.edu/wp-content/uploads/volume-6-2012/ThomasJeremyJ-Facilitating-Successful-Inclusion-Dominca.pdf

UNESCO. (2007a). *Belize*. Caribbean Symposium on Inclusive Education, Kington, Jamaica.

UNESCO. (2007b). *St Vincent & the Grenadines*. Caribbean Symposium on Inclusive Education, Kington, Jamaica.

UNESCO. (2010). *World Data on Education: Grenada*. Available from http://www.ibe.unesco.org/fileadmin/user_upload/Publications/WDE/2010/pdf-versions/Grenada.pdf

UNESCO. (2016). *Education policy review: Saint Kitts and Nevis*. ED-2016/WS/13. Available from https://unesdoc.unesco.org/ark:/48223/pf0000245170

UNESCO. (2020). *Global education monitoring report 2020 – Latin America and the Caribbean – Inclusion and education: All means all*. UNESCO.

UNESCO. (n.d.). PEER. Available from https://education-profiles.org/

UNICEF. (2011). *The situation analysis of children and women in Belize 2011: An Ecological Review*. UNICEF.

UNICEF. (2013). *The situation analysis of children with disabilities*. UNICEF.

UNICEF. (2016). *The situation analysis of children and women in Guyana*. UNICEF.

UNICEF. (2017a). *Situation analysis of children: Commonwealth of Dominica*. UNICEF.

UNICEF. (2017b). *Situation analysis of children in Antigua and Barbuda*. UNICEF.

UNICEF. (2017c). *Situation analysis of children in Grenada*. UNICEF.

UNICEF. (2017d). *Situation analysis of children in Saint Kitts and Nevis*. UNICEF.

UNICEF. (2017e). *Situation analysis of children in St Lucia*. UNICEF.

UNICEF. (2017f). *Situation analysis of children in St Vincent and the Grenadines*. UNICEF.

UNICEF. (2019). *Situation analysis of children in the Eastern Caribbean*. UNICEF.

UNICEF. (n.d.). *Inclusive education*. Retrieved 23 December 2021, from https://www.unicef.org/education/inclusive-education

United Nations. (1960). Convention against Discrimination in Education, 14 December 1960. Available from https://www.ohchr.org/en/instruments-mechanisms/instruments/convention-against-discrimination-education

United Nations. (1966). International Covenant on Economic, Social and Cultural Rights, 16 December 1966. General Assembly Resolution 2200A (XXI). Available from https://www.ohchr.org/en/instruments-mechanisms/instruments/international-covenant-economic-social-and-cultural-rights

United Nations. (1989). Convention on the Rights of the Child, 20 November 1989. General Assembly resolution 44/25. Available from https://www.ohchr.org/en/instruments-mechanisms/instruments/convention-rights-child

United Nations. (2008). Convention on the Rights of Persons with Disabilities, 03 May 2008. Available from https://www.un.org/disabilities/documents/convention/convoptprot-e.pdf

United Nations. (2014). *Status of ratification interactive dashboard*. United Nations Human Rights, Office of the High Commissioner. Available from https://indicators.ohchr.org/

UWI Consulting Inc., Profiles Antigua Inc. Consortium. (2012). *Draft Education Sector Plan 2013–2018*. UWI.

Wolanin, T., & Steele, P. (2004). *Higher education opportunities for students with disabilities: A primer for policymakers*. The Institute for Higher Education Policy.

Laws

Antigua and Barbuda

Disabilities and Equal Opportunities Act, 2017. Available from http://laws.gov.ag/wp-content/uploads/2019/04/No.-32-of-2017-Disabilities-and-Equal-Opportunities-Act-2017.pdf

The Education Act, 2008. Available from http://laws.gov.ag/wp-content/uploads/2019/02/a2008-21.pdf

The Social Protection Bill, 2020. Available from http://laws.gov.ag/wp-content/uploads/2020/07/Social-Protection-Bill-2020.pdf

Barbados

Education Act, 2008. Available from http://www.barbadosparliament-laws.com/en/ShowPdf/41.pdf

Belize

Education Act, Cap. 36, Revised Edition 2020. Available from http://www.belizelaw.org/web/lawadmin/PDF%20files/cap036.pdf

Education and Training Act, Cap. 36:01, Revised Edition 2020. Available from https://www.agm.gov.bz/wp-content/uploads/2021/11/Cap-36.01-Education-and-Training-Act.pdf

Families and Children Act, Cap. 173, Revised Edition 2020. Available from https://www.agm.gov.bz/wp-content/uploads/2021/11/Cap-173-Families-and-Children-Act.pdf

Dominica

Education Act, 1997. Available from https://www.dominica.gov.dm/laws/1997/act11-1997.pdf

Education Regulations, 2011. Available from https://www.dominica.gov.dm/laws/2011/Education%20Regulations%20No.7.pdf

Grenada

Child (Protection and Adoption) Act, 2010, Cap 44A. Available from https://laws.gov.gd/index.php?option=com_content&view=article&id=9&Itemid=101

Education Act, 2002, Cap 86. Available from https://laws.gov.gd/index.php?option=com_content&view=article&id=9&Itemid=101

Guyana

Adoption of Children Act, Cap. 46:04. Available from https://mola.gov.gy/sites/default/files/Cap.%204604%20Adoption%20of%20Children.pdf

Education Act, Cap. 39:01. Available from https://mola.gov.gy/sites/default/files/Cap.%203901%20Education.pdf

Equal Rights Act, Cap. 38:01. Available from https://mola.gov.gy/sites/default/files/Cap.%203801.pdf

Persons with Disabilities Act, Cap. 36:05. Available from https://mola.gov.gy/sites/default/files/Cap.%203605%20Person%20with%20Disabilities.pdf

Prevention of Discrimination Act, Cap. 99:08. Available from https://mola.gov.gy/sites/default/files/Cap.%209908.pdf

Protection of Children Act, Cap. 46:06. Available from https://mola.gov.gy/sites/default/files/Cap.%204606%20Protection%20of%20Children.pdf

Jamaica

The Child Care and Protection Act, 2004. Available from https://laws.moj.gov.jm/library/statute/the-child-care-and-protection-act

The Disabilities Act, 2014. Available from https://japarliament.gov.jm/attachments/341_The%20Disabilities%20bill%202014%20No.13.pdf

The Education Act, 1965. Available from https://laws.moj.gov.jm/library/statute/the-education-act

St Kitts and Nevis

The Child (Care and Adoption) Act, Cap. 12.01. Available from https://aglcskn.info/wp-content/documents/Act17TOC/Ch-12_01-Children-Care-and-Adoption-Act.pdf

The Education Act, Cap 13:01. Available from https://aglcskn.info/wp-content/documents/Act02and09TOC/Ch-13_01-Education-Act.pdf

St Lucia

Child Justice Act, 2018. Available from http://slugovprintery.com/template/files/document_for_sale/laws/4258/Act%209%20of%202018.pdf

Education Act, Cap. 18:01. Available from https://www.govt.lc/media.govt.lc/www/resources/legislation/EducationAct.pdf

St Vincent and the Grenadines

Child (Care and Adoption) Act, Cap. 25. Available from https://www.warnathgroup.com/wp-content/uploads/2018/02/Children-Care-and-Adoption-Act.pdf

Education Act, Cap 202. Available from http://education.gov.vc/education/images/PDF/education_act_2006.pdf

The Bahamas

Child Protection Act, 2010. Available from http://laws.bahamas.gov.bs/cms/images/LEGISLATION/PRINCIPAL/2007/2007-0001/ChildProtectionAct_1.pdf

Education Act, 2001. Available from http://laws.bahamas.gov.bs/cms/images/LEGISLATION/PRINCIPAL/1962/1962-0015/EducationAct_1.pdf

Persons with Disabilities (Equal Opportunities) Act, 2014. Available from http://laws.bahamas.gov.bs/cms/images/LEGISLATION/PRINCIPAL/2014/2014-0031/PersonswithDisabilitiesEqualOpportunitiesAct2014_1.pdf

Trinidad and Tobago

Education Act, Ch. 39:01 (Revised Laws of Trinidad and Tobago, 2016). Available from https://agla.gov.tt/downloads/laws/39.01.pdf

Equal Opportunities Act, Ch. 22:03. (Revised Laws of Trinidad and Tobago, 2016). Available from https://agla.gov.tt/downloads/laws/22.03.pdf

CHAPTER 4

Disability, Information Technology, Assistive Devices and Employment in the Caribbean

Introduction

This chapter analyses workplace provisions, such as information technology and assistive devices and whether and the extent to which, they are likely to provide the support required by persons with disabilities, such that their duties towards the organisation's goals are achieved and any obstacles to productivity and job satisfaction are mediated (Vornholt et al., 2018). Extant Caribbean laws which prohibit discrimination against persons with disabilities, require employers to make accommodations for persons with disabilities, where needed. These accommodations may vary from simply allowing an employee additional time to complete an assignment, to making physical changes to their work area to accommodate an employee. Whether or not organisations are willing to make accommodations, may be one of the most fundamental considerations for persons with disabilities, with respect to obtaining and retaining employment. It is important to note that organisations are not mandated by law to make any changes that will be unduly financially burdensome. Indeed, some organisations may not need to make changes, where modifications have already been made to make the organisation accessible to relevant stakeholders (e.g. customers). Continued innovations in technology have facilitated the ongoing development of software applications (*apps*) and

J. H. Stephenson and N. Persadie, *Disability in the Workplace*, Palgrave Explorations in Workplace Stigma,
https://doi.org/10.1007/978-3-031-19340-8_4

devices that adapt to the physical environment such that the limitations which were previously faced by persons with disabilities can be overcome (Blanck et al., 2007; Morris et al., 2018; Wehmeyer et al., 2006).

Living with Disabilities

According to the World Health Organisation (WHO), there are approximately 1 billion people in the world that currently live with a disability of some type, and within the Caribbean developing states, there are 1 million persons with disabilities, notwithstanding this, resources available to treat and reintegrate persons so diagnosed are limited, relative to those available to persons with disabilities (PWD) in developed nations (WHO, 2022a, 2022b). Notwithstanding this, for the islands of the Anglophone Caribbean which have committed to equality and inclusion of PWD through becoming a signatory to the Convention on the Rights of Persons with Disabilities (CRPD) and/or by implementing legislation prohibiting discrimination based on disabilities, one approach which may be used to bridge the gap in information and communication technologies or assistive technologies.

Access to and use of accessible technologies are largely determined by the prevailing national and organisational policies and practices (education employment and the provision of goods and services) (Samant et al., 2013). In practice, PWD encounter multiple challenges when seeking employment and in an effort to mitigate the effects of these socially constructed (*or otherwise imposed*) barriers, information and communication technology (ICT) and assistive technology (AT) may be relied on, to enhance their economic and societal participation (Samant et al., 2013).

Article 9 of the CRPD mandates signatories to "*enable persons with disabilities to live independently and participate fully in all aspects of life, take appropriate measured to ensure to PWD, access on an equal basis with others to the physical environment, transportation and to information and communication inter alia, to include the identification and elimination of obstacles and barriers to accessibility*". In defining discrimination on the basis of disabilities, the CRPD states that in addition to disparate treatment for PWD, discrimination may need to be addressed, and this may include the possible denial of reasonable accommodation.

The CRPD defines reasonable accommodation[1] as "*necessary and appropriate modification and adjustments, (not imposing a disproportionate or undue burden), where needed, to PWD enjoy on an equal basis with others, all human rights and fundamental freedoms*".

The social model of disability suggests that PWD are adversely affected, not primarily by their impairment, but by societal barriers (prejudicial attitudes, social exclusion *inter alia*) and physical structures (e.g. the absence of ramps for persons with mobility impairments) which impose disabling restrictions on this marginalised group, which results in PWD who are unable to navigate and access all aspects of life as others without known disabilities (Oliver, 2013; Riddle, 2020; Samaha, 2007). Further, Berghs et al. (2016) emphasises the importance of accessibility for organisations when developing and implementing employment policies and practices for persons with disabilities (PWD). It is useful to note here that among the antecedents for the use of an ICT or AT are the political, social, and economic support needed, in order to realise the desired outcomes when seeking employment (Samant et al., 2013). The relationship between poverty and disabilities in the Anglophone Caribbean, could be addressed by ensuring, employment barriers (where they exist) may be mitigated by AT or ICT, every effort is made to support PWD and to improve their quality of life and contribution to society (Borg et al., 2009).

The International Classification of Functioning, Disability and Health (ICF) categorised three broad dimensions of disability: (i) Body structure and function (and impairment); (ii) activity (and activity restrictions); and (iii) participation (and participation restrictions). These can be further sub-categorised as follows: (i) mobility/physical (amputated limb); (ii) spinal cord; (iii) head injuries (e.g., traumatic brain injury); (iv) vision (e.g. blindness); (v) hearing; (vi) cognitive/learning; (vii) psychological (e.g. schizophrenia) and (viii) invisible (e.g. Crohn's disease) (Fig. 4.1).

[1] In addition, the Bahamas Persons with disabilities (Equal Opportunities Bill) 2014, defines reasonable accommodation as necessary and appropriate modification and adjustments not imposing a disproportionate or undue burden where needed in a particular case to ensure persons with disabilities the enjoyment or exercise on an equal basis with others of all human rights and fundamental freedoms.

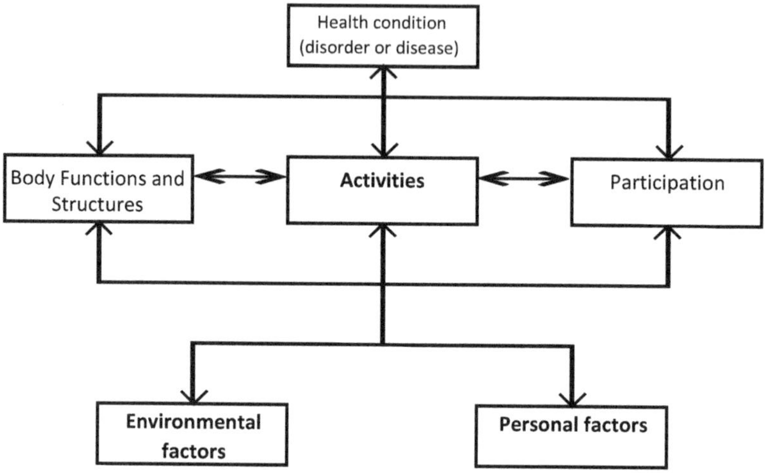

Fig. 4.1 Interactions between the components of ICF. (*Source* World Health Organisation [WHO]. The ICF: An overview. International Classification of Functioning, Disability and Health [ICF])

Understanding the Role of Assistive Technology

The Bahamas Persons with disabilities (Equal Opportunities Bill) 2014[2] defines assistive or adaptive devices and services as implements, tools and specialised services (including the services of qualified technicians and tutors for persons with learning disabilities, interpreters for the deaf and qualified teachers for the blind) provided to persons with disabilities to assists them in education, employment or activities of daily living. Assistive devices may be categorised as low and high tech. Low tech AT does not have complex or mechanical features, e.g. wheelchair ramps, pen grips. High Tech AT has digital or electronic components, will require training to be used effectively and will cost relatively more than low-tech AT.

[2] Bahamas Persons with disabilities (Equal Opportunities Bill) 2014, Sect. Living with Disabilities defines discrimination on the basis of disability means the distinction, exclusion or restriction on the basis of disability which has the purpose or effect of impairing or eliminating the recognition, enjoyment or exercise on an equal basis with others, of all human rights and fundamental freedoms in the political economic social, cultural civil or any other field inclusion all forms of discrimination such as the denial of reasonable accommodation.

Riddell and Song (2017) have argued that highly educated workers tend to adopt new technologies faster than those with less education.

Information and communication technology (ICT) and assistive technology (AT) allows PWD access to information and resources which they would not otherwise have. However, when thinking about accessibility issues, it is not enough to consider the availability of resources, but as the social model of disability suggests, there are other environmental and societal factors that may determine whether and the extent to which PWD are able to enjoy such accessibility (Leonardi & Hollenweger, 2015; Samant et al., 2013). For the avoidance of doubt, it is necessary to adopt a multidimensional approach, in an effort to address the issues of accessibility facing PWD. To this end, determining /influential factors include: *(i)* ***personal*** *(gender, race, age, other health conditions, fitness, lifestyle, habits, upbringing, coping styles, social background, education, profession, experience, behaviour pattern, character*), *(ii)* ***environmental*** *(products and technology, the natural and built environment, support and relationships, attitudes, services, systems*); social, financial, *(iii)* ***governmental*** (political support, *policies and laws*), *(v)* ***infrastructure and financing***, which constitute a holistic ICT ecosystem as proposed by Smith and Elder (2010—see also Carlson & Ehrlich, 2005; Leonardi & Hollenweger, 2015; Samant et al., 2013; Wilson, 2004). The challenge for developing nations (where 80% of PWD live) such as those represented in the English-speaking Caribbean, co-ordinating such an ecosystem to improve accessibility for PWD, requires knowledge and resources which may not be readily available in the regions where the need is greatest and the ability to outsource is hampered by limited national resources (Samant et al., 2013). Integration of assistive technology (across all aspects of society) is really contingent on the existing political climate, extant legislation and prevailing support (Tables 4.1 and 4.2).

As it relates to improving participation in the context of work for PWD, ICT can be operationalised for persons with visual impairments, in a text to speech technology (e.g. screen readers) and the inclusion of braille on currency, access doors, ATM machines and calculators *inter alia* and for persons with hearing impairments, email, closed captioning and text communication and for persons with mobility and/or dexterity challenges, ramps, motion controlled doors, voice recognition devices *inter alia* (Davison et al., 2009; Hartnett et al., 2011; Samant et al., 2013). These measures can facilitate teleworking and e-commerce engagement at work for persons with disabilities and will also make their daily lives

Table 4.1 Accommodating employees—Questions to Consider

1.	What limitations is the EWD experiencing?
2.	How do these limitations affect the employee and the employee's job performance?
3.	What specific job tasks are problematic as a result of these limitations?
4.	What accommodations are available to reduce or eliminate these problems?
5.	Are all possible resources being used to determine possible accommodations?
6.	Has the employee with the impairment been consulted regarding possible accommodations?
7.	Once accommodations are in place, would it be useful to meet with the employee with the impairment to evaluate the effectiveness of the accommodations and to determine whether additional accommodations are needed?
8.	Do supervisory personnel and employees need training regarding the impairment(s) under consideration?

Source Office of Disability Employment Policy—U.S.A. (ODEP) (2009)

much less burdensome. Of course, in a broader societal sense, such ICT initiatives can also be beneficial for PWD in the areas of civic responsibility (voting in elections); access to health care information and services, access to education and related resources, access to emergency/disaster information and the ability to request assistance; entrepreneurial opportunities (MacDonald-Wilson et al., 2002; Samant et al., 2013; Schartz et al., 2006).

To this end, continued communication with PWD is very important, again the motto of PWD "nothing about us, without us" must be observed such that when deciding whether accessibility would be required by an employee with disabilities (EWD), they must be consulted and the options discussed with them to ensure that the organisation's limited resources are used in such a way that these employees derive the greatest benefit from the product or service, and the organisation benefits from their increased efficiency (Solovieva et al., 2011; Sunstein, 2007). When considering such a comprehensive approach, it is imperative for companies to consider whether the adoption of ICT and AT would be appropriate for employees with disabilities (EWD) and whether and the extent to which the organisational culture and prevailing policies and practices will allow for the seamless integration of PWD using the accessible devices, without being further singled out and meted with disparate outcomes or effects in their search for work or their tenure with the organisation (Bruyere et al., 2005; Samant et al., 2013).

Table 4.2 Assistive technology products classification according to ISO 9999:2016

ISO 9999:2016 Product class	*Product examples (Not comprehensive but intended to illustrate the vast range, one product may belong to more than one class)*
For measuring, supporting, training or replacing body functions	Pressure relief wheelchair cushion (for tissue integrity)
For education and for training in skills	*Mobile application to train in everyday activities *Paint brush with thick handle to train in painting skills
Attached to the body for supporting neuromusculoskeletal or movement related functions and replacing anatomical structures	*Below-knee prosthesis *Spine orthosis
For self-care activities and participation in self care	*Kids protective cap *One-handed buttoning devices and fasteners
For activities and participation relating to personal mobility and transportation	*Van that can be driven from a power wheelchair *Elbow crutches *White cane
For domestic activities and participation in domestic life	*Easy grip garden fork *Fixed food cutting board
Furnishings, fixtures and other assistive products for supporting activities in indoor and outdoor human-made environments	*Chair with special mechanism to assist the person to stand *Kids floor seats
For communication and information management	*Magnifier lens *Face-to-face communication software *Computer joystick
For controlling, carrying, moving and handling objects and devices	*Reacher *Small table on wheels
For controlling, adapting or measuring elements of physical environments	*Noise reduction board *Barometer
For work activities and participation in employment	*Workplace mat for reducing vibration *Height adjustable work bench
For recreation and leisure	*Switch-activated toys *Blind-soccer ball

Source Toro-Hernández et al. (2019). Assistive Technology products classification according to ISO 9999:2016—The International Organization for Standardization—[Adapted from the European Search Engine on Assistive Technology]

Universal Design

The CRPD describes universal design as "*the design of products, environments, programmes and services to be usable by all people, without the need for adaptation or specialized design, but not to exclude assistive devices for particular groups of persons with disabilities where this is needed*". To this end, the concept of "universal design" or "design for all" emerged, where instead of relying on the creation and development of specialised accessible products or services, all products when developed should cater to the needs of the entire populous without having to be adapted for PWD (Björk, 2009; Newell, 2003; Story & Mueller, 2001; Williams & Moore, 2011). The notion of developing multiple products to achieve the same goal but with some products being deliberately modified for the needs of PWD, which may be referred to as the medical model of AT and this furthers the ideas of different groups of individuals and as such and us/them, in group/out group; social integrated and socially isolated individuals (Gudykunst, 2003; Mannix & Neale, 2005; Newell, 2003). Such disparities, further signals and amplify differences between groups, while the universal design takes a social model approach by eroding the barriers caused by factions within society, and as such products and services are accessible by a wider range of customers and markets, which boosts the providing company's reach and profitability (Crocker & Major, 1989; Mazur, 2010; Newell, 2003).

It may be argued that products/services which are designed and marketed as useful for multiple markets, will be beneficial for PWD who find them useful, insofar as they are not forced to use customised products to support them at work. Borg et al. (2009), suggest affordability for end users is important in terms of the assistive devices, demand and supply affect costs, hence universal design would be more appealing, and higher costs which makes accessing the product prohibitive for most people and organisations (*see also*, Delisio & Bukaty, 2019). Demographics are changing and PWD may have multiple disabilities (intersectionality), which product designers must take into account. In developing countries, such as the islands of the Anglophone Caribbean, not all PWD whose lives would benefit from the use of assistive technology may not be able to easily access them due to cost or ignorance of their existence (Boot et al., 2017; Mansour & Elsayed, 2017; Nisbet, 2020). With a view to ensuring that the regulations/mandates of the CRPD are actioned, the WHO created the Global Cooperation on Assistive Technology (GATE)

Table 4.3 WHO—Priority assistive products list © World Health Organization (2016a, 2016b)

1. Alarm signallers with light/sound/vibration	21. Magnifiers, digital hand-held	41. Travel aids, portable
2. Audio players with DAISY capability	22. Magnifiers, optical	42. Tricycles
3. Braille displays (note takers)	23. Orthoses, lower limb	43. Video communication devices
4. Braille writing equipment/braillers	24. Orthoses, spinal	44. Walking frames/walkers
5. Canes/sticks	25. Orthoses, upper limb	45 Watches, talking/ touching
6. Chairs for shower/ bath/toilet	26. Personal digital assistant (PDA)	46. Wheelchairs, manual for active use
7. Closed captioning displays	27. Personal emergency alarm systems	47. Wheelchairs, manual assistant-controlled
8. Club foot braces	28. Pill organizers	48. Wheelchairs, manual with postural support
9. Communication boards/books/cards	29. Pressure relief cushions	49. Wheelchairs, electrically powered
10. Communication software	30. Pressure relief mattresses	50. White canes
11. Crutches, axillary/elbow	31. Prostheses, lower limb	
12. Deafblind communicators	32. Ramps, portable	
13. Fall detectors	33. Recorders	
14. Gesture to voice technology	34. Rollators	
15. Global positioning system (GPS) locators	35. Screen readers	
16. Handrails/grab bars	36. Simplified mobile	
17. Hearing aids (digital) and batteries	37. Spectacles; low vision, short distance, long distance, filters and protection	
18. Hearing loops/FM systems	38. Standing frames, adjustable	
19. Incontinence products, absorbent	39. Therapeutic footwear; diabetic, neuropathic, orthopaedic	
20. Keyboard and mouse emulation software	40. Time management products	

Source Priority assistive products list © World Health Organization (2016a, 2016b)

programme, specifically to ensure access and availability of assistive products (AP). One aspect of the GATE programme is the development of an assistive product list (APL) (see Table 4.3), which comprises 50 assistive products chosen because of the greatest need and likely impact on the lives of users. One of the objectives of the development of this list by the WHO is for it to be used as a template, which will be further modified by taking into consideration the needs of PWD in each country and the available resources (Boot et al., 2017, WHO, 2016a, 2016b). These assistive products vary with respect to the nature and severity of the impairment and are useful in compensating for an impairment, offering PWD more independence and facilitating greater inclusion within work and society for PWD (WHO, 2016a, 2016b).

The World Wide Web Consortium (W3C) is an organisation that develops standards for the internet. In so doing this organisation influences web accessibility and the extent that it can be universally available to all people including but not limited to PWD. This organisation has developed web content accessibility guidelines to this end, these include success criteria and technique. To wit, in order to be universally accessible, web content should be *(i) perceivable* (e.g. closed captioning for persons with hearing impairments); *(ii) operable* (websites should be accessible through a keyboard to help users navigate and find required content); *(iii) understandable* (making text readable and understandable); and *(iv) robust* (maximise compatibility with current and future user tools) (W3C website).

Costs of Assistive Technology (AT) and Assistive Devices (AD)

One of the primary challenges with respect to the provision of AT or ICT is the associated costs. According to Kelly et al. (2010), where costs are prohibitive, reasonable steps may be taken to obviate challenges to accessible service, to include continued engagement PWD (Kelly et al., 2010; Nisbet, 2020; Tripathi & Shukla, 2014). The use of assistive technology is quite commonplace and with the development of universal design products will have features that facilitate their use by PWD without having to use specially designed products thus perhaps unintentionally identifying themselves as PWD (Lewis & Lewis, 1998; Vanderheiden, 2008). Technology may be categorised as high (e.g. computers with specialised software, closed captions) or low (e.g. pencil grips, handheld magnifiers).

One of the major concerns in relation to the provision of accommodations is associated costs, indeed, anti-discrimination laws in the Caribbean region acknowledge this and mandate that the provision of accommodations by organisations should not be so financially onerous that it results in the businesses winding up, due to the weight of the associated cost. Borg et al. (2009: 1864) argue that the AT supported by the company should "meet *users needs, conditions, be safe, durable, available in the country, obtained and maintained, with service sustained*". This suggests that after the service or product has been acquired, it is important that a systematic process is in place to ensure "efficient use" is maintained, and any further modifications that may be made are facilitated, and the product or service continues to be "equitable" and removes the previously recognised barriers to PWD with respect to contributions to the organisation (Borg et al., 2009; Kendall & Karns, 2018).

Kaye et al. (2011) suggest that employers are hesitant to hire PWD due to the expected astronomical costs of accommodations that may be required for them to compete within their places of work. There seems to be a prevailing acceptance, that any accommodations made for PWD will be associated with high prohibitive costs, such that these costs outweigh any potential benefits to accrue to the organisation. Further, organisations appear also to want to avoid potential litigation by PWD, should their employment policies and practices constitute a violation of the enacted anti-discrimination legislation, or where their standards fall below what has been agreed by the jurisdiction as a signatory to the CRPD. On the contrary, research has found that individual accommodations are inexpensive and are quite feasible for organisations to hire and develop PWD who excel within their field of endeavour (Carlson & Ehrlich, 2006; Chirikos, 1999; Sunstein, 2007).

In reality, what appears to be typical, is that where a PWD requires an assistive device, this has typically been acquired prior to joining the organisation and as such major devices or products will not present a financial burden for the company. Within the jurisdiction, there may exist government programs that pay for accommodation requests (via subsidies), where covered by insurance policies, the AT will undertake the costs of assistive devices, hence PWD are not seeking to impose financial burdens on their employers. In fact, PWD simply want to be productive, contribute to society and derive the other social benefits from employment as their counterparts. In fact, there would be a greater adverse impact on governments and societies, where PWD are compelled (because of their inability to secure employment) to rely on state social payments for subsistence.

Lewis and Lewis (1998) suggest that in order to ensure the continued efficacy of assistive technology, equity of access, ease of use and continuous development (developing new and improved AT). Hence, the fear oft articulated by employers, is not really based on empirical evidence. In fact, if the standard were to be lowered, such hesitant employers, managers, are unable to point to businesses that have folded or been bankrupted because of this imposition by a PWD they hire.

In light of this, is the cost of assistive equipment or technology really a moot point? This is because research indicates that for a large percentage of the assistive devices in the possession of persons with disabilities most of the cost is undertaken by the disabled person by insurance by government agencies. Less than 1% is actually undertaken by the employer so why are employers so adamant that the cost of the hiring process with disabilities will be prohibitive according to research they don't even undertake the cost themselves in most cases. When an individual has a career objective in mind, for example, the desire to become an attorney at law, one would not go to the offices of "*Caribe-Indies and Associates*",[3] after leaving secondary education and expect to be hired to practise law with immediate effect. Instead, one would read for a law degree at a reputable university, after which one would proceed and complete law school, pass the bar and become a qualified attorney-at-law. One would simply not go to a law office and ask the human resources manager to send you to law school. In the same way, PWD apply for jobs for which they are typically overqualified and as such arrive to work with the requisite skills, knowledge, abilities, experience and training required to fulfil the role of the job being sought. Thus, the logical question which must emerge, is whether and the extent to which such hesitation by organisations, is a proxy for something unspoken such as underlying prejudice. Consider whether as an employer, you would expect an employee to retire or resign if a limb was amputated whilst performing their job in a manufacturing firm? No, accommodations would likely be made for the employee (Table 4.4).

[3] A fictitious company, used only for illustrative purposes.

Table 4.4 Assistive technology which may facilitate efficient participation in the labour force by PWD (*Not an exhaustive list*)

No	*Categories of disabilities (ICF) Categories here are as prescribed by the International Classification of Functioning, Disability and Health (ICF)*	*Assistive technology (Low technology and High technology)*
1.	Mobility/Physical (amputated limb)	Prosthetics, Wheelchairs, wheelchair friendly Ramps, Canes, Crutches, automated doors and/or door openers, dictation software, accessible websites, Voice activated devices, adjustable office desk, workstation redesign
2.	Spinal cord	Assistive computer technology, prosthetics, orthotics, assistive listening, wheelchair/ambulatory support, adjustable office equipment (chairs/desks/conference table),
3.	Head injuries (e.g. traumatic brain injury)	Speech to text (e.g. Dragon Naturally speaking software); speech generating devices, voice recorder, canes, lever doorknobs, scooters, walkers, automatic page turners, document holders, reading software (e.g. Kurzweil)
4.	Vision impairment	Screen magnifiers, Large print text, Screen readers, Voice recognition software, Braille on buildings and equipment. Voice activated devices, accessible websites, dictation software
5.	Hearing impairments	Captioning, Hearing aids, Sign language, visual alerting devices, real time transcription, voice amplification systems, audio induction loop systems, natural synthesized speech—*text to speech*, accessible websites
6.	Cognitive/Learning	Text to speech; Speech to text (e.g. Dragon Naturally speaking software); word prediction software, Electronic graphic organisers, audio recorders, colour coded notes, cue cards, touch screens, alternative keyboards, Focus Assist, accessible websites, dictation software, voice recognition software
7.	Psychological (e.g. schizophrenia)	Recording devices, reminders/schedulers, symptom trackers, calming/comforting aids

(continued)

Table 4.4 (continued)

No	*Categories of disabilities (ICF) Categories here are as prescribed by the International Classification of Functioning, Disability and Health (ICF)*	*Assistive technology (Low technology and High technology)*
8.	Invisible (e.g. Crohn's disease)	***These are specifically in relation to Crohn's disease as there are a wide-ranging variety of invisible conditions*** Accessible toilets and toilet seats; flexible schedules, grab bars, modified break schedule, scooters, walkers, modified workspace, anti-fatigue mats, sound machines, mobile apps to track symptoms

Categories here are as prescribed by the International Classification of Functioning, Disability and Health (ICF)

Sources Asghar et al. (2018), Borg et al. (2009), Brown (1992), Carlson and Ehrlich (2006), Houtenville and Kalargyrou (2015), Kaye et al. (2011), Kbar et al. (2015), Lewis and Lewis (1998), ODEP (2009), Pal and Lakshmanan (2012), Riddell and Song (2017)

Heterogeneity and Multiple Impairments

The aforementioned categories and types of disabilities are not mutually exclusive, and employees may have been diagnosed with multiple impairments for which they may need support to ensure their ability to participate in the workforce. Consequent to the nature and severity of impairment, PWD may include face print barriers (where needed information is only available in print form and they need to access information in another format), communication barriers (in respect of speech and language impairments), learning barriers (e.g. ADHD). As previously indicated the incorporation of assistive technology will be beneficial for employees where the technology is used to restore any competence imbalance which might result from an impairment, with which they have been diagnosed (Lewis, 1993). Otherwise stated, AT can be used as a "*cognitive prosthesis*", which fills the gap of the missing or impaired ability, and/or "*cognitive scaffold*" which supports PWD in undertaking their daily work tasks (Cavalier et al., 1994).

Simply by virtue of its existence, assistive technology will not meet the needs of all persons diagnosed with the conditions for whom the technology was designed. This is because each person is an individual and impairments vary in severity and the manner in which each individual is affected. Thus, it is not enough for businesses to acquire technology designed for persons with hearing impairments, *for example*, to assist employees and believe that in so doing they have discharged their responsibilities to employees with hearing impairments. It is important for organisations to take a strategic structured approach in implementing solutions where PWD are disadvantaged, and where societal barriers prohibit them from achieving optimal performance in their organisational roles.

Employment Policies and Practices

To this end, the human resource development (HRD) cycle offers such an approach. This is a systematic process that may be utilised to assist employees to improve their skills, knowledge and abilities (KSAs) by first identifying needs, designing a solution to meet that identified need, implementing the solution and finally evaluating the solution to assess its efficacy (Spooner et al., 2007; Zhu et al., 2019). Assessing needs requires the organisation engage with the PWD to find out exactly what they need, the detailed specifications are needed to ensure that the product or service solution purchased and provided, is fit for purpose (Hergenrather et al., 2008; Martin & Honig, 2020). Where this requires customisation, this may mean that fittings and training are needed in order to ensure the solution is the right one for the PWD and will function effectively in the organisation's environment, without being disruptive to the flow of work.

Employers shouldn't be overly concerned about the cost of AD and disadvantages PWD might face at work. People with disabilities are aware of the negative stereotypes which exist regarding their capabilities, and as such they know that will face organisational challenges, due to prevailing negative perceptions, prejudices, discriminatory policies and practices. Consequently when PWD apply for vacancies, they want to be well qualified, with the requisite experience and as such to be favourably considered for the job (Pilgrim, 2014; Saben, 2017).

If you're a person with disabilities when you come to the organisation, you have to live on things that you require a work in terms of assistive technology or probably things that you use, that home so that you have them in your possession or tea you've purchased them or the insurance company, what are the government system of government programme in place that allows you to get them through the programme, right so you're not coming to the organisation then and you're not saying to them I'm here I'm ready to work, but in order for me to wear in order for me to be able to contribute to your organisation you have to provide me, with eczema and that you're not doing that you're coming to them with the equipment that you need with the, skills that you need with the experience that you need and with the education that you need you're not asking, them to be so burden that they will go out of business that's not realistic and fear isn't really grounded in evidence, or empirical research (Erickson et al., 2014; Islam & Patwary, 2013; Nevala et al., 2015). In fact, the legislation mandates that organisations should not be so burdened by providing accommodations which are not financially feasible.

With changing demographics, including PWD into the labour force could be profitable for organisations who are prepared to offer them any accommodations which may be required in order to them to support the organisation's strategic objectives. By including this group of employees in the workplace, and seeking their input on decision-making, the company's products and services offered could have a more comprehensive appeal to a wider cross-section of customers. The innovative ideas contributed by this group could also result enhanced competitive advantage for the company (Carlson, 2005; Riddell & Song, 2017). "*ICTs enable social change through their ability to facilitate information storage, processing, and communication*" (Smith & Elder, 2010: 68).

Where discrimination is rife in any of the labour market, for a specific industry or for a particular company, this suggests that nonrepresentation persists for this marginalised group. Kearney et al. (2019) suggest that this perpetuates the acceptance of ableist narratives, such that PWD who, *prima facie*, don't have any expected symptoms, behaviours or mannerisms associated with disabilities, appear to be more readily accepted in the workplace than other PWD whose impairment is visible, and which is not easily concealed (mobility impairments, wheelchair users). Productivity expectations for the latter group are low compared to the former group of individuals who are believed to be free from any disabling impairment (Hernandez et al., 2000; Kendall & Karns, 2018; Leber et al., 2018;

Miethlich & Oldenburg, 2019). Ableists assume that PWD are fundamentally different and are unable to function in a workplace and contribute successfully.

Within work, organisational members who have previously worked with PWD or are related to PWD have less discriminatory attitudes towards this group, relative to employees who have had minimal interactions and/or experience with PWD (McKinney & Swartz, 2021; McMahon et al., 2008; Snyder et al., 2010). Conversely, organisational members who have not worked with PWD in the past may have subscribed to stereotypes regarding this heterogenous group, in the absence of evidence-based accurate information, or experiences that dispel such negative perceptions. To encourage more inclusion of PWD in the labour force, one of the issues that may need to be broached is a change in attitudes of stakeholders, which may be achieved through training and re-education (Houtenville & Kalargyrou, 2015). Access and use of assistive technology can facilitate the independent participation of PWD in organisations and other elements within society, and result in members of this marginalised group feeling less vulnerable and less isolated (Delisio & Bukaty, 2019; Ender et al., 2007; Toro-Hernández et al., 2019).

PWD may require physical modifications in the workplace, but major structural modifications are not typically implemented, this is reportedly because "*employers did not see the cost–benefit of making any architectural modifications*" (Neal-Boylan & Guillett, 2008; Nevala et al., 2015; Purc-Stephenson et al., 2017; Sundar, 2017). This means that where such structural changes are required the EWD had to decide whether there was an alternative approach that they could adopt in order to continue working with the organisation. For example, taking a service entrance instead of using the main entrance where an employee has mobility challenges and a ramp is in place at the service entrance, but not the employee entrance. Employees who prefer not to declare their disability may be forced to declare the nature and severity of their disability if they need AT in order to assist them in the execution of their work functions (Ender et al., 2007; Mansour & Elsayed, 2017; Purc-Stephenson et al., 2017). It is relatively easy for organisations to espouse their commitment to inclusion and diversity but when PWD encounter seemingly impossible bureaucracy or other barriers in seeking accommodation, then it became clear that the policy is useful on paper but not in practice (Dong et al., 2021; Lindsay, 2011; Purc-Stephenson et al., 2017; Schur, 2003).

Further, employees with disabilities are sometimes hesitant to request accommodation and access to assistive devices, even if the organisation is willing to provide them, this is because in so doing PWD, make organisational members aware of their disability, and as such, make themselves more visible and potentially more vulnerable (Ali et al., 2011; Banks, 2014; Jans et al., 2012). Further complications associated with disclosure, might be negative responses from colleagues, who believe that the provision of accommodation (in any form), may provide an advantage to EWD an advantage, which might be perceived by colleagues as unjust (Dong et al., 2021; Schur, 2003). These perceptions these negative perceptions are referred to as anticipated image cost (Purc-Stephenson et al., 2017), this is misplaced, but may result from the absence of education, training, knowledge and understanding about the individual's needs. In reality, through the provision of accommodation or assistive devices, PWD are not, in fact, gaining an advantage, but the availability and use of assistive devices allows PWD to work as efficiently as their colleagues who have not been diagnosed with a disability. Willingness of organisations to remove social barriers for PWD, signals a desire by the organisation to be more inclusive by changing the extant organisational culture, practices and policies.

The global cooperation on assistive technology (GATE) exists to assist WHO member states in achieving the objectives of the CRPD, specifically as it relates to increasing access to assistive devices to PWD (Article 32—CRPD). The GATE initiative emphasises the importance of 5 factors, namely: People (end users), Policy (policies of the jurisdiction), Products (must be fit for purpose—see Tables 4.3 and 4.4), Provision (distribution of the AT/AD) and Personnel (must be appropriate to assess the needs of PWD, provide training and future modifications). It has been suggested that governments may have a department charged with the responsibility of acquiring items on the priority assistive products list (PPL) (Table 4.3) for distribution. This is with the understanding that for each jurisdiction, the most prevalent disabilities will vary, thus the products required will also vary, with the jurisdiction under consideration.

It has also been suggested that government subsidies may facilitate more widespread access and use of PPL, by PWD. It is also possible for organisations in the private sector and disability allies to fulfil this role (see Table 4.3). This is consistent with the assertions made by Kelly et al. (2010) about the fundamental areas within society is very important in order to facilitate further integration and inclusion of PWD primarily within organisations. Legislation is important to ensure that changes are enacted. Of course, legislation alone is unlikely to be effective without enforcement and associated penalties. Regarding this, the penalties for non-compliance should not be so onerous as to create unrealistic debt for the organisation, but they should be forceful enough to send a message to the company that is in breach of the law, as well as organisations who are not a party to the legal action being assessed. The development and enactment of toothless legislation is an exercise in futility. Effective legislation may be further supported by a re-education and training programme.

Allies[4] are important catalysts for change towards inclusive and equitable organisations, to wit, allies to marginalised employees, "drive systemic improvements to workplace policies, practices and culture (Jordan et al., 2021; Melaku et al., 2020). PWD particularly in the workplace want to have an ally or someone advocating on their behalf where there are lots of organisations intending to intended to assist the integration of persons with disabilities you also want to have an advocate for

[4] Within organisations, allies are dominant (*typically non-stigmatised*) group members, who support and advocate for persons in marginalized, oppressed and stigmatized groups (Brooks & Edwards, 2009; Cheng et al., 2019; Ragins, 2008; Webster et al., 2018), with a view of creating an inclusive and diverse organisational climate (Sabat et al., 2014). In order to be an effective ally, organisational members (including managers and executives) must actively and consistently engage in continuous education and critical self-reflection, to ensure that their beliefs and behaviours are not having a deleterious effect on marginalized group members; further, where possible, allies act as a mentor to support and encourage targets (of discrimination) and discourage the unchallenged maintenance of the status quo (particularly, where this has adverse effects on marginalized employee groups) (Cheng et al., 2019; Erskine & Bilimoria, 2019; Spanierman & Smith, 2017; Webster et al., 2018). In short, allies must promote and advocate for social justice, support targeted organisational groups (including but not limited to persons with disabilities), however, inauthentic, shallow efforts and transitional exchanges in the name of allyship are performative and inefficacious (Erskine & Bilimoria, 2019; Jones et al., 2017; Kalina, 2020; Spanierman & Smith, 2017). Allies who are associated with persons with disabilities must be actively engaged in support and advocacy behaviours, including but not limited to:- advocating for workplace accommodations; confronting instances of prejudice; providing social support; creating and/or supporting inclusive policies; acknowledging or giving credit to ideas or work; providing job- or task-related information (Cheng et al., 2019; Sabat et al., 2014). The expected outcomes of organisational allyship include (but are not limited to): improved work environment and organisational effectiveness, increased job satisfaction, organisational commitment and ethical behaviour, the promotion of an inclusive organisational culture, lower employee turnover, increased innovation and organisational citizenship behaviour and improved competitive advantages (Cheng et al., 2019; Erskine & Bilimoria, 2019; Spanierman & Smith, 2017).

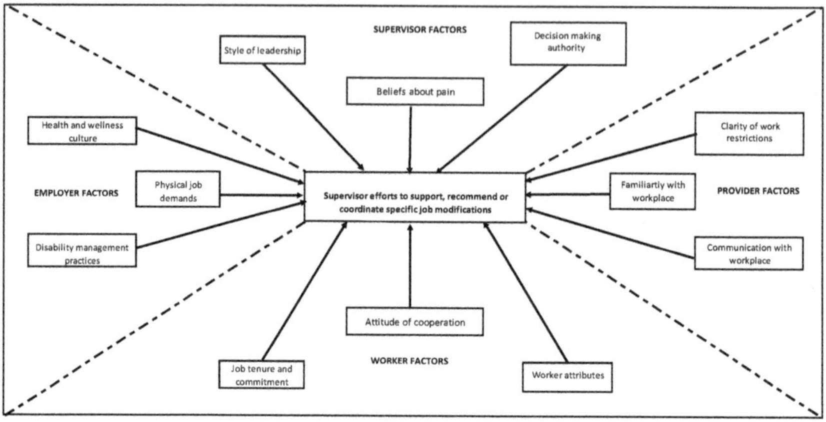

Fig. 4.2 Conceptual framework showing potential factors influencing supervisor support for job modification (*Source* Shaw, W. S., Kristman, V. L., Williams-Whitt, K., Soklaridis, S., Huang, Y. H., Côté, P., & Loisel, P. [2014]. The Job Accommodation Scale [JAS]: psychometric evaluation of a new measure of employer support for temporary job modifications. *Journal of occupational rehabilitation*, *24*(4), 755–765)

example within the organisation where policies are made at the executive level but also at the operational level so that you have consistency in terms of someone being available advocating for equality or integration of persons with disabilities at the level of policy and operations (Evans et al., 2005; Knapp & Midgley, 2010). According to Newell et al. (2003) the integration of the perspectives or the organisation should see the prospective thoughts the input from PWD, who are the end user persons of the products. Failure to integrate the input of PWD in the design process, increases the likelihood that the product/service is abandoned/discarded.

The disability equality index (DEI) report (*compiled by the American Association of Persons with disabilities*) evaluates the disability inclusion policies and practices of a range of organisations, the assessment tool is easily accessible for any organisation to complete and have their employment policies and practices evaluated. Using the DEI measure, organisations are assessed on culture and leadership (*30 points*); organisation-wide accessibility (*10 points*); employment practices which include a commitment by the organisation's benefits, recruitment, employment and accommodation practices which are inclusive of PWD (*40 points*); community engagement (*10 points*); supplier diversity (*10 points*). The large weight assigned to the accommodation category signals its importance of its role, in facilitating inclusive and diverse organisations. The top-ranking organisations in the DEI offer flexible work accommodations, and provide access to organisational funds to finance any needed accommodation.

Concluding Comments

Extant literature provides us with multiple accommodation models and each of these models suggests that the provision of accommodation is not done in silos, there are other influential factors which must be considered if the provision of accommodation is to be effective in meeting the needs of PWD. One such model was proposed by Shaw et al. (2014) (see Fig. 4.2), and suggests that several factors affect organisations decisions to provide accommodations including: supervisor's—style of leadership, beliefs about pain, decision-making authority; provider's—communication with the organisation, familiarity with the organisation and clarity of parameters of work; organisation's—disability management policies and practices, physical job demands, prevailing health and wellness culture; and EWD's—attributes, attitude of cooperation, job tenure and commitment. The comprehensive approach to decisions about the provision of accommodations is also reflected by Gould et al. (2018), who argue that the critical organisational factors regarding accommodation decisions include the employer's characteristics, communication and resources; the interventions available publicly and the EWD's characteristics, including tenure, work role, work performance and type of health condition. Gould et al. (2018) further suggests that provision of accommodation is not guaranteed after these factors are considered, and organisations may decide variously to ask the employee to take a leave of absence or offer no accommodation at all. Alternatively, modifications may be made to the workspace or equipment, the duties of the EWD may be modified, the hours of work reduced or flexibility introduced, such that the EWD may be permitted to work from their home. It is important to note that although the organisation may make decisions that are thought to be in its best interest, however, where such acts or omissions are in breach of the anti-discrimination legislation, the aggrieved party (i.e. the EWD), would be permitted to file a claim of discrimination against the employer. Communication, education and advocacy are some of the elements to be considered by organisations and EWD as it relates to seeking and granting accommodation of any type (Kelly et al., 2010). Their importance and impact cannot be underestimated.

References

Ali, M., Schur, L., & Blanck, P. (2011). What types of jobs do people with disabilities want? *Journal of Occupational Rehabilitation, 21*(2), 199–210.

Asghar, I., Cang, S., & Yu, H. (2018). Usability evaluation of assistive technologies through qualitative research focusing on people with mild dementia. *Computers in Human Behavior, 79*, 192–201.

Banks, J. (2014). Barriers and supports to postsecondary transition: Case studies of African American students with disabilities. *Remedial and Special Education, 35*(1), 28–39.

Berghs, M., Atkin, K., Graham, H., Hatton, C., & Thomas, C. (2016). Implications for public health research of models and theories of disability: A scoping study and evidence synthesis. *Public Health Research, 4*(8), 1–166.

Björk, E. (2009). Many become losers when the Universal Design perspective is neglected: Exploring the true cost of ignoring Universal Design principles. *Technology and Disability, 21*(4), 117–125.

Blanck, P., Adya, M., Myhill, W. N., & Samant, D. (2007). Employment of people with disabilities: Twenty-five years back and ahead. *Law & Inequality, 25*, 323.

Boot, F. H., Dinsmore, J., Khasnabis, C., & MacLachlan, M. (2017). Intellectual disability and assistive technology: Opening the GATE wider. *Frontiers in Public Health, 5*, 10.

Borg, J., Lindström, A., & Larsson, S. (2009). Assistive technology in developing countries: National and international responsibilities to implement the convention on the rights of persons with disabilities. *The Lancet, 374*(9704), 1863–1865.

Brooks, A. K., & Edwards, K. (2009). Allies in the workplace: Including LGBT in HRD. *Advances in Developing Human Resources, 11*(1), 136–149.

Brown, C. (1992). Assistive technology computers and persons with disabilities. *Communications of the ACM, 35*(5), 36–45.

Bruyere, O., Wuidart, M. A., Di Palma, E., Gourlay, M., Ethgen, O., Richy, F., & Reginster, J. Y. (2005). Controlled whole body vibration to decrease fall risk and improve health-related quality of life of nursing home residents. *Archives of Physical Medicine and Rehabilitation, 86*(2), 303–307.

Carlson D. & Ehrlich, N. (2005). Assistive technology and information use and need by persons with disabilities in the Unites States, 2001. http://www2.ed.gov/rschstat/research/pubs/at-use/index.html

Carlson, D., & Ehrlich, N. (2006). Sources of payment for assistive technology: Findings from a national survey of persons with disabilities. *Assistive Technology, 18*(1), 77–86.

Cheng, S. K., Ng, L. C., Traylor, A. M., & King, E. B. (2019). Helping or hurting?: Understanding women's perceptions of male allies. *Personnel Assessment and Decisions, 5*(2), 44–58.

Chirikos, T. N. (1999). Will the costs of accommodating workers with disabilities remain low? *Behavioral Sciences & the Law, 17*(1), 93–106.

Crocker, J., & Major, B. (1989). Social stigma and self-esteem: the self-protective properties of stigma. *Psychological Review, 96*, 608–630.

Davison, S. L., Bell, R. J., LaChina, M., Holden, S. L., & Davis, S. R. (2009). Psychology: The relationship between self-reported sexual satisfaction and general well-being in women. *The Journal of Sexual Medicine, 6*(10), 2690–2697.

Delisio, L. A., & Bukaty, C. A. (2019). UDL and Assistive Technology. *What Really Works With Universal Design for Learning*, 157.

Dong, S., Eto, O., & Spitz, C. (2021). Barriers and facilitators to requesting accommodation among individuals with psychiatric disabilities: A qualitative approach. *Journal of Vocational Rehabilitation*, (Preprint), 1–12.

Ender, K. E., Kinney, B. J., Penrod, W. M., Bauder, D. K., & Simmons, T. (2007). Achieving systemic change with universal design for learning and digital content. *Assistive Technology Outcomes and Benefits, 4*(1), 115–129.

Erickson, W. A., von Schrader, S., Bruyère, S. M., & VanLooy, S. A. (2014). The employment environment: Employer perspectives, policies, and practices regarding the employment of persons with disabilities. *Rehabilitation Counseling Bulletin, 57*(4), 195–208.

Erskine, S. E., & Bilimoria, D. (2019). White allyship of Afro-Diasporic women in the workplace: A transformative strategy for organizational change. *Journal of Leadership & Organizational Studies, 26*(3), 319–338.

Evans, N. J., Assadi, J. L., & Herriott, T. K. (2005). Encouraging the development of disability allies. *New Directions for Student Services, 2005*(110), 67–79.

Gudykunst, W. B. (2003). *Bridging differences: Effective intergroup communication*. Sage Publications.

Hartnett, H. P., Stuart, H., Thurman, H., Loy, B., & Batiste, L. C. (2011). Employers' perceptions of the benefits of workplace accommodations: Reasons to hire, retain and promote people with disabilities. *Journal of Vocational Rehabilitation, 34*(1), 17–23.

Hergenrather, K. C., Rhodes, S. D., Turner, A. P., & Barlow, J. (2008). Persons with disabilities and employment: Application of the self-efficacy of job-seeking skills scale. *Journal of Rehabilitation, 74*(3), 34.

Hernandez, B., Keys, C., & Balcazar, F. (2000). Employer attitudes toward workers with disabilities and their ADA employment rights: A literature review. *Journal of Rehabilitation-Washington-, 66*(4), 4–16.

Houtenville, A., & Kalargyrou, V. (2015). Employers' perspectives about employing people with disabilities: A comparative study across industries. *Cornell Hospitality Quarterly, 56*(2), 168–179.

Islam, R., & Patwary, A. K. (2013). Factors influencing to the policy and strategies used to disabled employment in hospitality industry. *Advances in Environmental Biology*, 2598–2606.

Jans, L. H., Kaye, H. S., & Jones, E. C. (2012). Getting hired: Successfully employed people with disabilities offer advice on disclosure, interviewing, and job search. *Journal of Occupational Rehabilitation, 22*(2), 155–165.

Jones, K. P., Arena, D. F., Nittrouer, C. L., Alonso, N. M., & Lindsey, A. P. (2017). Subtle discrimination in the workplace: A vicious cycle. *Industrial and Organizational Psychology, 10*(1), 51–76.

Jordan, S., Li, Y., Paik, M., Daniels, S. (2021). Understanding allyship at work. An investigation of the antecedents of allyship behaviour toward marginalized employees. *Dismantling Bias Conference Series, 3*(8), 4–12.

Kalina, P. (2020). Performative allyship. *Technium Social Science Journal, 11*, 478–481.

Kaye, H. S., Jans, L. H., & Jones, E. C. (2011). Why don't employers hire and retain workers with disabilities? *Journal of Occupational Rehabilitation, 21*(4), 526–536.

Kbar, G., Aly, S., Elsharawy, I., Bhatia, A., Alhasan, N., & Enriquez, R. (2015). Smart help at the workplace for persons with disabilities (SHW-PWD). *International Journal of Computer, Control, Quantum and Information Engineering, 9*(1), 84–90.

Kearney, S., Brittain, I., & Kipnis, E. (2019). 'Super disabilities' vs 'Disabilities'? Theorizing the role of ableism in (mis)representational mythology of disability in the marketplace. *Consumption, Markets and Culture, 22*(5–6), 545–567. ISSN 1025-3866.

Kelly, B., Lewthwaite, S., & Sloan, D. (2010, April). Developing countries; developing experiences: Approaches to accessibility for the real world. In *Proceedings of the 2010 international cross disciplinary conference on web accessibility (W4A)* (pp. 1–4).

Kendall, K. M., & Karns, G. L. (2018). The business case for hiring people with disabilities. *Social Business, 8*(3), 277–292.

Knapp, J., & Midgley, J. (2010). Developmental social work and people with disabilities. *Social Work and Social Development*, 87–104.

Leber, M., Bastič, M., Moody, L., & Krajnc, M. S. (2018). A study of the impact of ergonomically designed workplaces on employee productivity. *Advances in Production Engineering & Management, 13*(1), 107–117.

Leonardi, M., & Hollenweger, J. (2015). ICF Personal factors: Why and where. A challenge for WHO-FIC.

Lewis, R. B., & Lewis, R. B. (1998). Assistive technology and learning disabilities: Today's realities and tomorrow's promises. *Journal of Learning Disabilities, 31*(1), 16–26.

Lindsay, S. (2011). Discrimination and other barriers to employment for teens and young adults with disabilities. *Disability and Rehabilitation, 33*(15–16), 1340–1350.

MacDonald-Wilson, K. L., Rogers, E. S., Massaro, J. M., Lyass, A., & Crean, T. (2002). An investigation of reasonable workplace accommodations for people with psychiatric disabilities: Quantitative findings from a multi-site study. *Community Mental Health Journal, 38*(1), 35–50.

Mannix, E., & Neale, M. A. (2005). What differences make a difference? The promise and reality of diverse teams in organizations. *Psychological Science in the Public Interest, 6*(2), 31–55.

Mansour, S. O., & Elsayed, S. F. (2017). Assistive devices for hearing impaired hotels guests (Applying to Hurghada Resorts). *International Journal on Recent Trends in Business and Tourism (IJRTBT), 1*(1), 1–11.

Martin, B. C., & Honig, B. (2020). Inclusive management research: Persons with disabilities and self-employment activity as an exemplar. *Journal of Business Ethics, 166*(3), 553–575.

Mazur, B. (2010). Cultural diversity in organisational theory and practice. *Journal of Intercultural Management, 2*(2), 5–15.

McKinney, E. L., & Swartz, L. (2021). Employment integration barriers: Experiences of people with disabilities. *The International Journal of Human Resource Management, 32*(10), 2298–2320.

McMahon, B. T., Roessler, R., Rumrill, P. D., Hurley, J. E., West, S. L., Chan, F., & Carlson, L. (2008). Hiring discrimination against people with disabilities under the ADA: Characteristics of charging parties. *Journal of Occupational Rehabilitation, 18*(2), 122–132.

Melaku, T., Beeman, A., Smith, D., & Johnson, B. (2020). Be a better ally. *Harvard Business Review, 98*(6), 135–139.

Miethlich, B., & Oldenburg, A. G. (2019). Employment of persons with disabilities as competitive advantage: An analysis of the competitive implications. In *33nd International Business Information Management Association Conference (IBIMA), Education Excellence and Innovation Management through Vision 2020, Granada, Spain, 10–11.04. 2019* (pp. 7146–7158). IBIMA Publishing.

Morris, S. P., Fawcett, G., Brisebois, L., & Hughes, J. (2018). A demographic, employment and income profile of Canadians with disabilities aged 15 years and over, 2017. https://www150.statcan.gc.ca/n1/pub/89-654-x/89-654-x2018002-eng.htm

Neal-Boylan, L., & Guillett, S. E. (2008). Work experiences of RNs with physical disabilities. *Rehabilitation Nursing, 33*(2), 67–72.

Nevala, N., Pehkonen, I., Koskela, I., Ruusuvuori, J., & Anttila, H. (2015). Workplace accommodation among persons with disabilities: A systematic review of its effectiveness and barriers or facilitators. *Journal of Occupational Rehabilitation, 25*(2), 432–448.

Newell, A. (2003). Inclusive design or assistive technology. In *Inclusive design* (pp. 172–181). Springer.

Nisbet, P. D. (2020). Assistive technologies to access print resources for students with visual impairment: Implications for accommodations in high stakes assessments. *British Journal of Visual Impairment, 38*(2), 222–247.

Office of Disability Employment Policy (ODEP). (2009). Employees with mental health impairments. Accommodation and compliance series. Job Accommodation Network. Office of Disability Employment Policy. US Department of Labour. West Virginia. USA.

Oliver, M. (2013). The social model of disability. Thirty Years on. *Disability and Society, 28*(7), 1024–1026.

Pal, J., & Lakshmanan, M. (2012, March). Assistive technology and the employment of people with vision impairments in India. In Proceedings of the Fifth International Conference on Information and Communication Technologies and Development (pp. 307–317).

Purc-Stephenson, R. J., Jones, S. K., & Ferguson, C. L. (2017). "Forget about the glass ceiling, I'm stuck in a glass box": A meta-ethnography of work participation for persons with physical disabilities. *Journal of Vocational Rehabilitation, 46*(1), 49–65.

Ragins, B. R. (2008). Disclosure disconnects: Antecedents and consequences of disclosing invisible stigmas across life domains. *Academy of Management Review, 33*(1), 194–215.

Riddell, W. C., & Song, X. (2017). The role of education in technology use and adoption: Evidence from the Canadian workplace and employee survey. *ILR Review, 70*(5), 1219–1253.

Riddle, C. A. (2020). Why we do not need a stronger social model of disability. *Disability & Society, 35*(9), 1509–1513.

Sabat, I. E., Lindsey, A. P., Membere, A., Anderson, A., Ahmad, A., King, E., & Bolunmez, B. (2014). Invisible disabilities: Unique strategies for workplace allies. *Industrial and Organizational Psychology, 7*(2), 259–265.

Samaha, A. M. (2007). What good is the social model of disability? *The University of Chicago Law Review, 74*(4), 1251–1308.

Samant, D., Matter, R., & Harniss, M. (2013). Realizing the potential of accessible ICTs in developing countries. *Disability and Rehabilitation: Assistive Technology, 8*(1), 11–20.

Schartz, H. A., Hendricks, D. J., & Blanck, P. (2006). Workplace accommodations: Evidence based outcomes. *Work, 27*(4), 345–354.

Schur, L. A. (2003). Barriers or opportunities? The causes of contingent and part-time work among people with disabilities. *Industrial Relations: A Journal of Economy and Society, 42*(4), 589–622.

Smith, M., & Elder, L. (2010). Open ICT ecosystems transforming the developing world. *Information Technology and International Development, 6*(1), 65–71.

Snyder, L. A., Carmichael, J. S., Blackwell, L. V., Cleveland, J. N., & Thornton, G. C. (2010). Perceptions of discrimination and justice among employees with disabilities. *Employee Responsibilities and Rights Journal, 22*(1), 5–19.

Solovieva, T. I., Dowler, D. L., & Walls, R. T. (2011). Employer benefits from making workplace accommodations. *Disability and Health Journal, 4*(1), 39–45.

Spanierman, L. B., & Smith, L. (2017). Roles and responsibilities of White allies: Implications for research, teaching, and practice. *The Counseling Psychologist, 45*(5), 606–617.

Spooner, F., Baker, J. N., Harris, A. A., Ahlgrim-Delzell, L., & Browder, D. M. (2007). Effects of training in universal design for learning on lesson plan development. *Remedial and Special Education, 28*(2), 108–116.

Story, M. F., & Mueller, J. L. (2001). Universal design of products. *Universal Design Handbook*. McGraw-Hill.

Sundar, V. (2017). Operationalizing workplace accommodations for individuals with disabilities: A scoping review. *Work, 56*(1), 135–155.

Sunstein, C. R. (2007). Cost-benefit analysis without analyzing costs or benefits: Reasonable accommodation, balancing, and stigmatic harms. *The University of Chicago Law Review, 74*, 1895–1909.

Toro-Hernández, M. L., Kankipati, P., Goldberg, M., Contepomi, S., Tsukimoto, D. R., & Bray, N. (2019). Appropriate assistive technology for developing countries. *Physical Medicine and Rehabilitation Clinics, 30*(4), 847–865.

Tripathi, M., & Shukla, A. (2014). Use of assistive technologies in academic libraries: A survey. *Assistive Technology, 26*(2), 105–118.

Vanderheiden, G. C. (2008). Ubiquitous accessibility, common technology core, and micro assistive technology: Commentary on "computers and people with disabilities". *ACM Transactions on Accessible Computing (TACCESS), 1*(2), 1–7.

Vornholt, K., Villotti, P., Muschalla, B., Bauer, J., Colella, A., Zijlstra, F., ... & Corbière, M. (2018). Disability and employment–overview and highlights. *European Journal of Work and Organizational Psychology, 27*(1), 40–55.

Webster, J. R., Adams, G. A., Maranto, C. L., Sawyer, K., & Thoroughgood, C. (2018). Workplace contextual supports for LGBT employees: A review, meta-analysis, and agenda for future research. *Human Resource Management, 57*(1), 193–210.

Wehmeyer, M. L., Palmer, S. B., Smith, S. J., Parent, W., Davies, D. K., & Stock, S. (2006). Technology use by people with intellectual and developmental disabilities to support employment activities: A single-subject design meta analysis. *Journal of Vocational Rehabilitation, 24*(2), 81–86.

Wilson, E. J., III. (2004). *The information revolution and developing countries.* MIT Press.

Williams, A. S., & Moore, S. M. (2011). Universal design of research: Inclusion of persons with disabilities in mainstream biomedical studies. *Science Translational Medicine, 3*(82), 1–10.

World Health Organization (WHO). (2016a). Priority Assistive Products List. Geneva. World Health Organization.

World Health Organisation (WHO). (2016b). The ICF: An overview. International Classification of Functioning, Disability and Health (ICF). https://www.who.int/standards/classifications/international-classification-of-functioning-disability-and-health

World Health Organization (WHO). (2022a). Global Cooperation on Assistive Technology. Geneva. World Health Organization. https://www.who.int/news-room/feature-stories/detail/global-cooperation-on-assistive-technology-(gate)

World Health Organisation (WHO). (2022b). World Health Statistics. Monitoring health for the sustainable development goals (SDGs). Geneva. World Health Organization.

Zhu, X., Law, K. S., Sun, C., & Yang, D. (2019). Thriving of employees with disabilities: The roles of job self-efficacy, inclusion, and team-learning climate. *Human Resource Management, 58*(1), 21–34.

CHAPTER 5

Mental Health Disabilities and Work in the Caribbean Region

Introduction

Of the types of disabilities which exist, mental health disabilities are perhaps the most stigmatised. Some of the prevailing stereotypes associated with mental illnesses include, (but are not limited to), beliefs that they may be unpredictable, unproductive, difficult with whom to work, their condition likely to deteriorate at any point in time, and they will either harm others or become disruptive in a workplace setting, and as such, they are regarded as less desirable employees, than persons with physical disabilities (Ali et al., 2013; Ren et al., 2008). Hence, employers appear less likely to hire someone with a history of mental illness, preferring to hire someone with a physical disability (Krupa et al., 2009). As a consequence, it is more likely that an employee will reveal physical limitations rather than mental health challenges. Once diagnosed, most mental illnesses can be treated, indeed, some organisations offer wellness programmes through which mental health services are accessible, however, due to the stigma associated with having a diagnosed mental illness, some employees are reluctant to access these potentially beneficial services. This chapter will examine the engagement of persons with mental illnesses, in contemporary Caribbean organisations. Concerns about their potential level of performance, particularly, in the face of organisational, economic and other environmental pressures to maintain

J. H. Stephenson and N. Persadie, *Disability in the Workplace*, Palgrave Explorations in Workplace Stigma,
https://doi.org/10.1007/978-3-031-19340-8_5

high levels of productivity and profitability are noted by employers, as further reasons for their reluctance to employ individuals with mental illnesses (Keyes, 2007; Krupa et al., 2009). Regrettably, in the Caribbean, pejorative terms such as "*mad*" or "*crazy*" continue to be liberally used to describe individuals with mental illnesses, which has a deleterious effect on the way they are perceived in every aspect of society (i.e. economic, cultural, societal, education, government, *inter alia*) (Arthur & Whitley, 2015; Arthur et al., 2010). Moreover, this contributes to further declines in their mental health and wellness and consequently, has an adverse impact on their ability to contribute to their societies and economies in a productive manner.

Understanding Mental Disorders

Ubiquitous in the islands of the Anglophone Caribbean is the use of the words "mad" or "crazy" to describe any type of erratic behaviour (Arthur & Whitley, 2015; Arthur et al., 2010; Devonish, 2017; Robinson et al., 2021). The fact that these words have no medical meaning does not factor into the thought process of the users. Depending on the severity of the behaviour, some people may even speculate that the person should be hospitalised without delay, either to seek medical help or to protect other societal members. So frequent is the use of these disparaging terms, their use no longer causes alarm and they have become accepted terms in the regional lexicon. The result is that persons who ordinarily engage in behaviours which are thought to be atypical or at variance with societal expectations, are frequently dismissed as abnormal or pitied. One of the anomalous occurrences with respect to mental health, which is at variance with physical health is in regular discourse the terms "mental health" and "mental illnesses" are used synonymously. It is clearly understood that one is unlikely to be mentally healthy and ill at the same time, in fact, Keyes (2005: 542) asserts that "the de facto conception of mental health is psychiatric: Individuals are either mentally ill or presumed mentally healthy".

The American Psychiatric Association's (APA), Diagnostic and Statistical Manual of Mental Disorders (DSM) defines a mental disorder as "*a clinically significant disturbance in an individual's cognition, emotion regulation or behaviour, which reflects a dysfunction in the psychological, biological or developmental processes underlying mental functioning*" (DSM-5, 2013; Stein et al., 2021). According to the manual, "*mental disorders are usually associated with significant distress or disability in social, occupational or other important activities*" (DSM-5, 2013; Stein et al., 2021). The manual further clarifies this by noting that expected responses to job losses or life events like a divorce, do not constitute mental disorders. Some diagnosable mental disorders include, (but are not limited to), the following: Schizophrenia Spectrum, Bipolar Disorders, Depressive and Anxiety Disorders; Obsessive–Compulsive Disorders; Trauma-Related Disorders, Dissociative Disorders, Disruptive, Impulse-Control and Conduct Disorders; Substance-Related and Addictive Disorders; Personality Disorders; Paraphilic Disorders *inter alia*.

The main categories of disorders in the DSM are developmental disorders, cognitive disorders, mental disorders due to a general medical condition, substance-related disorders, schizophrenia and other psychotic disorders, mood disorders, anxiety disorders, somatoform disorders, factitious disorders, dissociative disorders, sexual and gender dysphoria, eating disorders, sleep disorders, impulse control disorders, adjustment disorders, personality disorders. These are consistent with the classification of mental and behavioural disorders categorised by the International Classification of Diseases,[1] namely: (F0) Organic, including symptomatic mental disorders; (F1) Mental and behavioural disorders due to the use of psychoactive substances; (F2) Schizophrenia, schizotypal and delusional disorders, mood (affective) disorders; (F3) Mood disorders; (F4) Neurotic, stress-related and somatoform disorders; (F5) Behavioural syndromes associated with physiological disturbances and physical factors; (F6) Disorders of personality and behaviour in adult persons; (F7) Mental retardation; (F8) Disorders of psychological development; (F9) Behavioural and emotional disorders with onset usually occurring in childhood and adolescence; and unspecified mental disorders.

[1] International Classification of Diseases (ICD) is an international standard diagnostic classification for a wide variety of health conditions, ICD-10 focuses on mental and behavioural disorders.

Mental Disorders and Employment

The Pan American Health Organisation (PAHO) reports depression as the leading mental health disorder in the Caribbean region (see Fig. 5.1) and affects women twice as frequently as it does men (see Fig. 5.2). Women, as is the case in developing regions like the Caribbean, are frequently diagnosed with disorders like depression and postpartum depression, during or after pregnancy. Further, mental disorders including dementia, Alzheimer's and depression disproportionately affect the elderly are the rate is expected to increase in the future as the number of elderly persons in the region increases. The treatment for persons diagnosed with mental disorders in the Caribbean region is said to be limited, and this may be attributed to the limited resources expended on this by the regional governments. In fact, PAHO reported that approximately 2% of the allocated public health care budget is spent on mental health across the region, and this, primarily on psychiatric hospitals (PAHO, 2021). PAHO reports a 78% treatment gap[2] for persons in Latin America and the Caribbean for persons diagnosed with moderate and severe affective, anxiety and substance use disorders. Treatment received for the mental disorders is reported as poor, but may also be limited, this may be due to the restricted level of resources available in developing countries, as well as their "inequitable distribution and inefficient use" (WHO, 2021). Treatment may also be limited because of the hesitation, by affected individuals, in seeking help when a mental disorder is suspected. Indeed, even when a diagnosis has made and a treatment regime recommended, there may still be reticence by patients to follow the regime, for fear that it might make them worst or that upon disclosing their mental illness to others, this would result in discrimination, avoidance and isolation, as the stigma associated with mental disorders are erroneously believed to be accurate, in relation to all persons diagnosed with mental disorders (WHO, 2021).

We have noted the importance of gainful employment for individuals as it provides an outlet for employees to efficiently use their knowledge, skills and abilities, to promote social interaction with other organisational members and to realise the financial benefits from their labour (Brouwers, 2020; Lu et al., 2019; Seeman, 2009; Saavedra et al., 2016). It must

[2] The treatment gap for mental disorders "refers to the difference that exists between the number of people who need care and those who receive care" (Jansen et al., 2015).

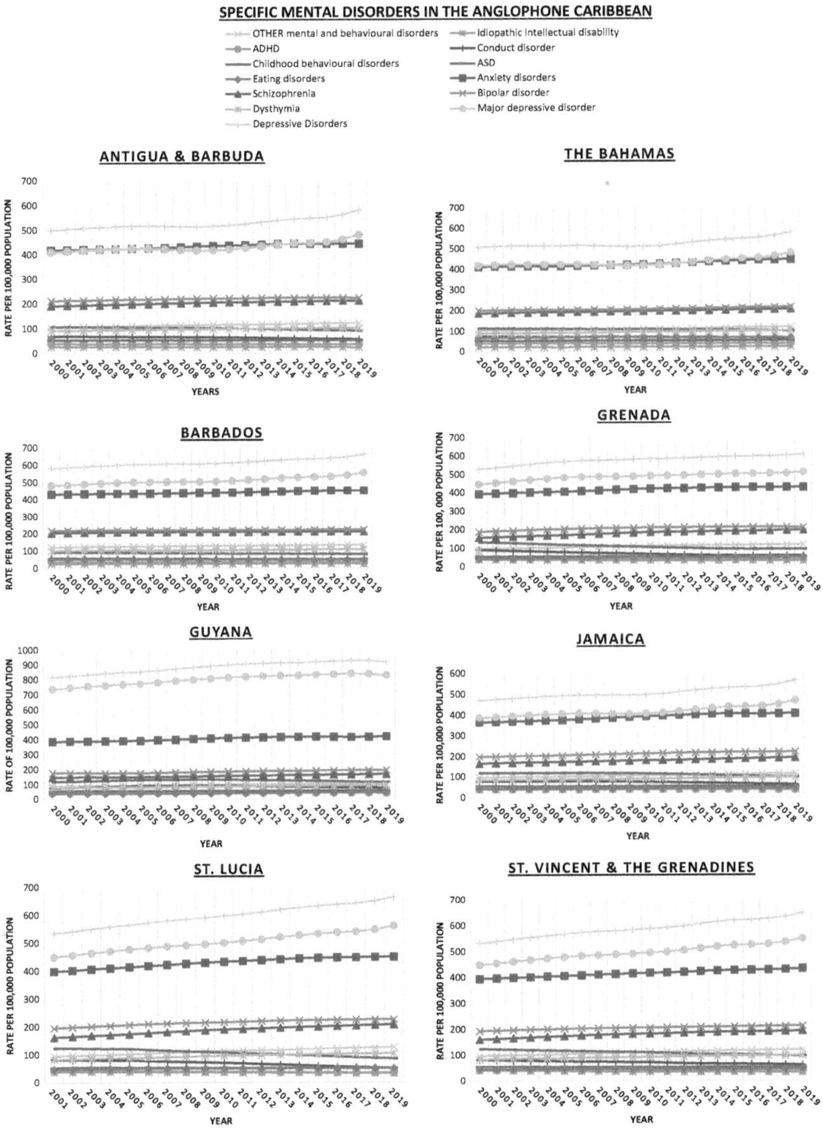

Fig. 5.1 Burden of specific mental disorders—trends over time (*Source* PAHO. The burden of mental disorders in the Region of the Americas, 2000–2019. Pan American Health Organization, 2021, https://www.paho.org/en/noncommunicable-diseases-and-mental-health/enlace-data-portal-noncommunicable-diseases-mental-2)

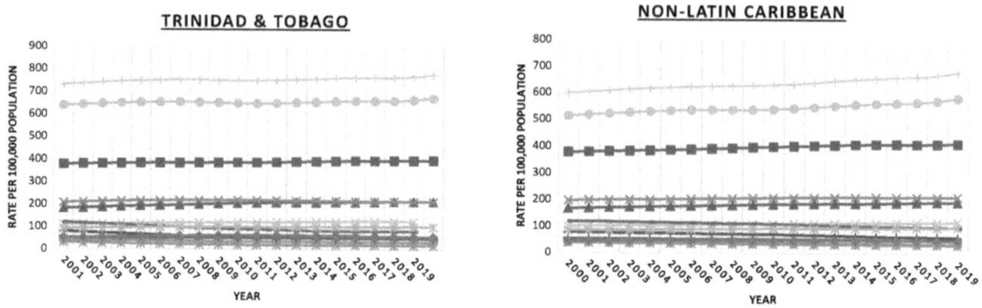

Fig. 5.1 (continued)

also be accepted that persons diagnosed with mental disorders are not homogeneous (Cimera & Cowan, 2009), which is consistent with the heterogeneous nature and severity of mental disorders. Prejudicial attitudes may result in the failure of persons with mental disorders to access gainful employment, and where this occurs, the result can be economic impoverishment, homelessness and incarceration, due to the resulting marginalisation and vulnerability of this group (Brouwers, 2020; WHO, 2021). This has a multiplier effect on the island's economy, as should this occur, relevant government ministries would be compelled to take financial responsibility for this group of potentially productive individuals, either through social security payments, or the use of public resources to ensure their care when hospitalised or imprisoned at public institutions[3] (WHO, 2021).

Notwithstanding this, the employment rate for persons with mental illnesses remains low (Wheat et al., 2010) and it is imperative that employers, managers and other organisational members recognise and accept that (in addition to the advantages aforementioned), employment is "an essential milestone, in the recovery process of people with mental illnesses" (Saavedra et al., 2016: 512; see also Devine et al., 2020; Stuart, 2006). This can be accommodated for persons with mental illnesses in the same way that persons with physical impairments are offered access to assistive devices and technology. Though the requisite

[3] Though it has been noted in previous chapters, it bears repeating here that the Convention on the Rights of Persons with Disabilities (CRPD), which is binding on signatory islands that have ratified or acceded to it, mandates these jurisdictions to protect and promote the rights of all persons with disabilities, and to promote their inclusion (WHO, 2021).

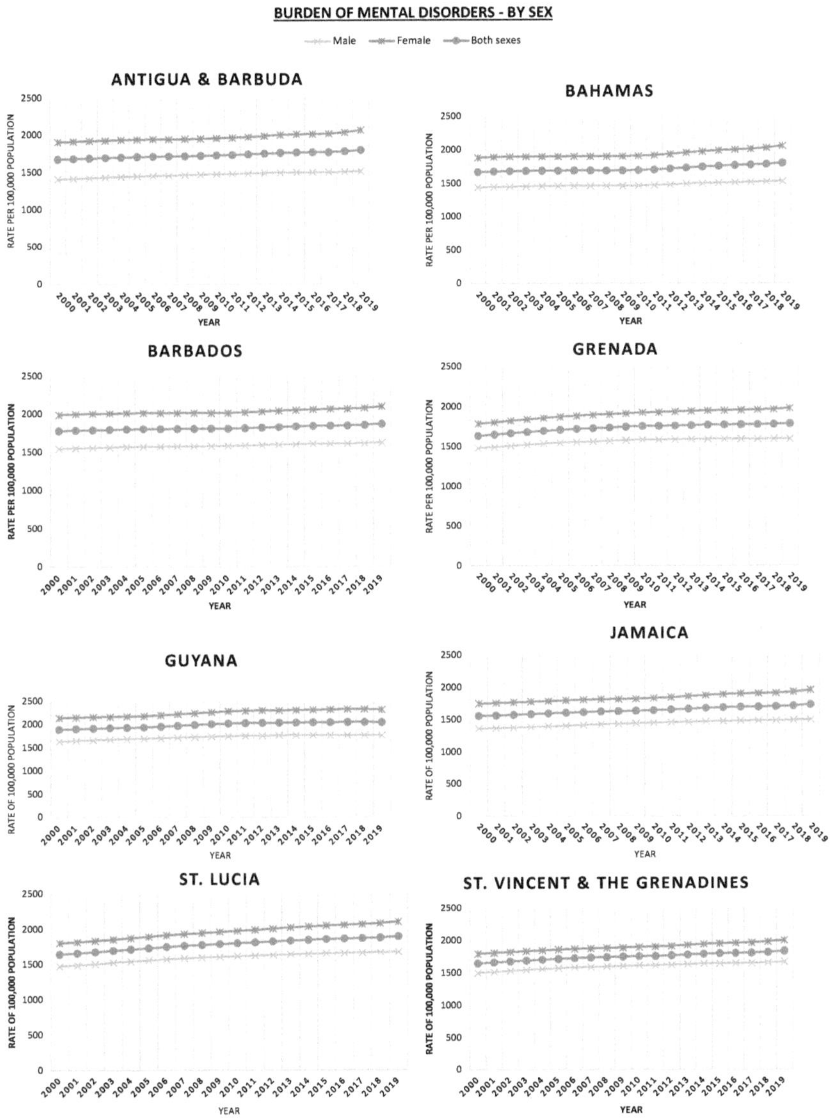

Fig. 5.2 Burden of mental disorders—Trends over time (*Source* PAHO. The burden of mental disorders in the Region of the Americas, 2000–2019. Pan American Health Organization, 2021, https://www.paho.org/en/noncommunicable-diseases-and-mental-health/enlace-data-portal-noncommunicable-diseases-mental-2)

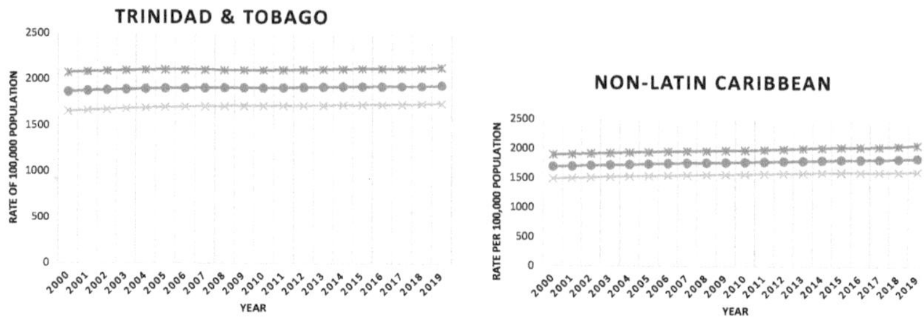

Fig. 5.2 (continued)

support may differ for persons with mental disorders, the principle of providing organisational support and assistance would be equally valuable and instrumental in enabling these applicants or employees to be productive, engaged and efficient. Some of the accommodations suitable for persons with disabilities, mental illnesses specifically, include flexible scheduling, psycho education of supervisors, job modification and a change in the way peers interact with disabled employees (Seeman, 2009). Where challenges persist, organisations determined to pursue diversity and inclusion in their employment policies and practice may assist organisational members to migrate towards inclusion by providing employees with training and offering access (for employees with mental disorders) to stress reduction and stress management training, an appropriately trained mentor, a manageable workload, frequent breaks, modification of supervision, conflict resolution mechanisms, flexibility to work remotely Markel and Barclay (2009); Elraz, 2018; Seeman, 2009). The costs associated with these accommodations are reasonable and are unlikely to create an onerous financial responsibility on the organisation which will affect its sustainability (Elraz, 2018).

The Role of Stigma

Research has identified social stigma as one of the key reasons for the unemployment of persons with diagnosed mental illnesses (Brouwers, 2020; Goldberg et al., 2005; Griffith et al., 2006; Krupa et al., 2009; Hampson et al., 2020; Seeman, 2009; Sniatecki et al., 2018). Some of the assumptions about this marginalised group include their perceived volatility, make colleagues uncomfortable; pose a danger, behaviour is erratic, potential for relapse, vulnerability to stress, disorganisation, easily fatigued, unreliability, lateness and absenteeism, attitude problems, social awkwardness, social withdrawal (Elraz, 2018; Kaye et al., 2011; Seeman, 2009). These are largely based on extant, cultural beliefs, a lack of understanding human differences, categorising people and labelling them; prevailing power imbalances within organisations (Blanck et al., 2020; Brouwers, 2020; Lyubykh et al., 2020). These can collectively lead to poor outcomes where persons with diagnosed mental disorders are considered different, less desirable, less employable by virtue of their diagnosis (Kirsh et al., 2012). Stigmatisation "results from inadequate or insufficient knowledge" (Brouwers, 2020; Earnshaw et al., 2013), and assumes attributes which have the effect of devaluing and discrediting employees with mental disorders (Earnshaw et al., 2013). This is concerning, as organisations typically make evidence-based decisions regarding their strategy, thus the apparent adoption of prevailing societal wisdom in respect of the abilities of this group is incongruent with the approach taken when making other organisational decisions. Indeed, each applicant or employee is assessed on their individual merit in relation to the job role that they are expected to fill, instead of having to face barriers erected by the organisation, to (either directly or indirectly) prohibit their participation in the labour force (Bonaccio et al., 2020).

Regarding the hierarchy of impairment, mental disorders are highly stigmatised (Baldwin & Marcus, 2006; Goldberg et al., 2005; Griffiths et al., 2006). Indeed, acceptance of stereotypes is likely to result in actions by managers, such as limiting their access to training and developmental opportunities, micromanaging, initiating and participating in malicious gossip and other insensitive counterproductive behaviours, engaging in social exclusion (Wheat et al., 2010). People diagnosed with schizophrenia are at least likely to be employed, in part because of social rejection of persons with this illness being perceived as perpetually disruptive, dangerous and angry (Arday, 2021; Markel and Barclay (2009) ; Corrigan et al., 2002; Manning & White, 1995; Tsang et al., 2007).

The likelihood of having to facing stigma hurdles (and other atypical challenges) in seeking employment, may result in employees with mental illnesses deciding not to disclose their invisible disability (Markel and Barclay (2009). As a result of non-disclosure, these employees are not exposed to positive role models within the organisation, and as a result experience stress of protecting their identity they may encounter social isolation, lack of job support, job failure and are labelled as an inefficient employee (Hampson et al., 2020; Rüsch et al., 2014; Wheat et al., 2010). Conversely, disclosure may promote sustainable work-through enabling employer education as well as contact and communication (Hampson et al., 2020). This includes with reference to improvements in financial positions of the company, loyalty of disabled customers who increased their custom because of the number the increased number of persons with disabilities who are now employed at the company, whether or not the organisation decides to include persons with disabilities when making decisions about them, what would serve their interests as a community, which is the same products or services offered, whether or not potential customers believe that they are represented within the company. It should be noted that persons with disabilities do not necessarily want to stand out for humiliation and to be marginalised so the idea of the universality is really quite important when designing or creating products and offering for offering them for consumption by the public (Migliaccio, 2019).

Advocates and Allies of Persons with Mental Illness

Persons who either have been diagnosed with mental illnesses; those who advocate for persons with mental illnesses, or persons who are allies of persons with mental illnesses, may face challenges within organisations, as they object to disparate treatment and negative prevailing assumptions made about the abilities of persons with mental illnesses within organisations. These challenges include inquiries as to their own mental health status, retaliatory treatment by organisational members who are desirous of removing (*perceived*) problematic employees from the organisation (e.g. via unfair dismissal), *inter alia*. In effect, these psychological stressors may disincentivize persons with mental illnesses from joining the labour force. In turn, this may be further compounded by unattractive compensation packages offered by organisations, relative to the state disability benefits to which PWD may be entitled, resulting in a *benefits trap* (Stuart, 2006). Thus, it is unsurprising that these antecedents may undermine the anticipated positive organisational outcomes of persons with mental illness. This is particularly notable (Devine et al., 2020; Krupa et al., 2009) when persons with disabilities are pressured into jobs or training that are incongruent with their own preferences, aptitudes, skills, and/or knowledge.

Globally, Suriname and Guyana are the two countries with the highest rates of suicide in the world (WHO, 2021). Suicide and mental health are indirectly linked through disorders such as depression, schizophrenia and bipolar disorder as suicide can become the reactionary response to these issues (WHO, 2021). Mental illnesses may be episodic, however, even if the symptoms of the disorder are not currently manifesting, one cannot stop the treatments for the disorder as the symptoms "can recur throughout one's life and can cause premature mortality when untreated" Keyes (2005: 543). Moreover, Corrigan et al. (2014) suggest that mental illness can have an adverse effect on an individual's quality of life (independence, education, employment and health). The DSM-III infers that an individual may either be languishing, moderately mentally healthy or flourishing (complete mental health). Table 5.1 offers 13 dimensions and characteristics associated with flourishing mental health. Further, Keyes (2005: 544) found that "mental health and mental illness are extremes of a continuum; they are different but related, such that the absence of mental illnesses in an individual, does not equate to complete mental health". The implication here is that employees who have been diagnosed with mental disorders may have periods where they are neither actively seeking employment or gainfully employed as they may need to exist in the labour force in order to undertake treatment in the event that the symptoms of the disorder require medical intervention, such that the employee would be ill-advised to return to work, during the treatment (Goldberg et al., 2005).

Sharpe and Sharpe (2016) argue that mental health appears to be a low priority for Caribbean governments and is only likely to be ascribed increased importance, when political leaders are seen to support the issue in word and deed, to wit, policies are enacted, resources are allocated to address the challenges associated with mental illness and new practices are actioned. Notwithstanding the anti-discrimination legislation, Caribbean jurisdictions have also enacted Mental Health laws, with the express purpose of "providing for the care and treatment of persons of unsound mind and related matters" Mental Health Act, 1998

Table 5.1 Factors and dimensions reflecting mental health as flourishing

Dimension	*Definition*
Positive emotions (i.e. emotional well-being)	
Positive affect	Regularly cheerful, interested in life, in good spirits, happy, calm and peaceful, full of life
Avowed quality of life	Mostly or highly satisfied with life overall or in domains of life
Positive psychological functioning (i.e. psychological well-being)	
Self-acceptance	Holds positive attitudes toward self, acknowledges, likes most parts of self, personality
Personal growth	Seeks challenge, has insight into own potential, feels a sense of continued development
Purpose in life	Finds own life has a direction and meaning
Environmental mastery	Exercises ability to select, manage, and mould personal environment to suit needs
Autonomy	Is guided by own, socially accepted, internal standards and values
Positive relations with others	Has, or can form, warm, trusting personal relationships
Positive social functioning (i.e. social well-being)	
Social acceptance	Holds positive attitudes toward, acknowledges, and is accepting of human differences
Social actualization	Believes people, groups, and society have potential and can evolve or grow positively
Social contribution	Sees own daily activities as useful to and valued by society and others
Social coherence	Interested in society and social life and finds them meaningful and somewhat intelligible
Social integration	A sense of belonging to, and comfort and support from, a community

Source Keyes, C. L. (2005). Mental illness and/or mental health? Investigating axioms of the complete state model of health. *Journal of Consulting and Clinical Psychology*, *73*(3), 539 (p. 541)

(Barbados[4]). With the high rates of suicide in Guyana, government leaders have recently (March, 2022) articulated their commitment to

[4] Additional mental health laws in the Caribbean include:—Mental Health Act of Jamaica, 2009; Mental Health Act, 1975 (Trinidad and Tobago); Mental Treatment Act, 1957 (Antigua & Barbuda); Mental Health Act, 2006 (Anguilla); Mental Health Act, 2008 (Grenada); Mental Health Act, 1969 (Bahamas); Mental Health Act, 1987 (Dominica); Mental Health Act, 1930 (Guyana); Mental Health Act, 1956 (St. Kitts and Nevis).

Table 5.2 Guide for changes in language in referring to mental health

Common/outdated terms	*Person-first language*
Mental health disorders	Mental health issues, conditions or illnesses
Individuals "struggling" or "suffering from" or having a mental illness, mental health condition or issue	Individuals living with mental illnesses, mental health condition or issue
Committed Suicide, "suicided", or successful/unsuccessful suicide	Died by suicide Attempted suicide
Mental illnesses	A mental illness (or specify specific disorder, rather than generalize by using the term "mental illness" to capture all mental illnesses.)
Mentally ill person	Someone who has a mental illness
Someone who is bipolar	Someone who is living with bipolar disorder
Patient/Client	People with lived experience or individuals we serve
Addict/Substance abuser	He/she has a substance use condition He/she has lived experience of substance use

Source The Canadian Mental Health Association (CMHA), https://ontario.cmha.ca/documents/stigma-and-discrimination/

revising the Mental Health Act 1930 (to include a new Suicide Bill), with a view of eliminating stigma around mental illnesses (and seeking help) making treatments more easily accessible. International jurisdictions can provide us with benchmarks regarding language, behaviour, policies, laws and practice which can effectively address problems associated with mental disorders, to wit the Canadian Mental Health Association (CMHA) offers some practical guidance regarding language and suggests replacing "committed suicide" with "died by suicide", replacing "mentally ill person" with "someone who has a mental illness" and replacing "addict" with "he/she has a substance use condition" (see Table 5.2).

Conclusion

A comprehensive approach is required by the islands of the Caribbean and by the region collectively, to advance a society, inclusive of workplaces which are more inclusive of persons with mental health conditions. Efforts to achieve this inclusion may follow the model outlined by the sextuple helix framework (Gouvea & Li, 2021; Logue & Blanck, 2020), and include (i) promoting inclusion and equity in the region's social economic environment; (ii) An economic environment, with efficient organisational practices, that result in the creation of jobs for persons with disabilities (PWD); (iii) advancing an equitable educational system that fosters research and education related to people with disabilities, including ICT; (iv) An inclusive and equitable infrastructure that illuminates or ameliorates physical barriers for persons with disabilities; and (v) An inclusive healthcare system that addresses the needs of PWD patient with disabilities. Investing in interventions designed to improve health can help reduce the burden of these illnesses, through cost-effective means.

In charting a way forward, research (Sharpe & Sharpe, 2016) suggests the pursuit of innovative approaches based on action proven to be successful in the Caribbean, which are aimed primarily at re-education and training in respect of the multiple erroneous stereotypes about persons who have been diagnosed with a mental illness. It is imperative that treatments are easily accessible and available for the entire populous, and in so doing, the island's human capital will be available and able to contribute to the economy, and to step the social and economic costs associated with mental illness. Practical guidance proffered by the CMHA suggests using S.T.O.P. as an acronym to question ourselves and others, in order to ensure that we are cognizant of the language being used to communicate about mental health conditions, as follows:

S—Stereotypes people with mental health conditions (that is, assumes they are all alike rather than individuals)?
T—Trivialises or belittles people with mental health conditions and/or the condition itself?
O—Offends people with mental health conditions by insulting them?
P—Patronises people with mental health conditions by treating them as if they were not as good as other people?

References

Aitken, Z., Simpson, J. A., Bentley, R., Milner, A., LaMontagne, A. D., & Kavanagh, A. M. (2020). Does the effect of disability World acquisition on mental health differ by employment characteristics? A longitudinal fixed-effects analysis. *Social Psychiatry and Psychiatric Epidemiology, 55*(8), 1031–1039.

Ali, L., Ahlström, B. H., Krevers, B., Sjöström, N., & Skärsäter, I. (2013). Support for young informal carers of persons with mental illness: A mixed-method study. *Issues in mental health nursing, 34*(8), 611–618.

Almond, S., & Healey, A. (2003). Mental health and absence from work: New evidence from the UK Quarterly Labour Force Survey. *Work, Employment and Society, 17*(4), 731–742.

Alvarez-Galvez, J., & Rojas-Garcia, A. (2019). Measuring the impact of multiple discrimination on depression in Europe. *BMC Public Health, 19*(1), 1–11.

Arday, J. (2021). No one can see me cry: Understanding mental health issues for Black and minority ethnic staff in higher education. *Higher Education, 83*, 79–102.

Arthur, C. M., & Whitley, R. (2015). "Head take you": Causal attributions of mental illness in Jamaica. *Transcultural Psychiatry, 52*(1), 115–132.

Arthur, C. M., Hickling, F. W., Robertson-Hickling, H., Haynes-Robinson, T., Abel, W., & Whitley, R. (2010). "Mad, sick, head nuh good": Mental illness stigma in Jamaican communities. *Transcultural Psychiatry, 47*(2), 252–275.

Baldwin, M. L., & Marcus, S. C. (2006). Perceived and measured stigma among workers with serious mental illness. *Psychiatric Services, 57*(3), 388–392.

Berrigan, P., Scott, C. W., & Zwicker, J. D. (2020). Employment, Education, and Income for Canadians with Developmental Disability (DD): Analysis from the 2017 Canadian Survey on Disability. *Journal of Autism and Developmental Disorders, 2020*, 1–13.

Blanck, P., Hyseni, F., & Wise, F. A. (2020). Diversity and inclusion in the American legal profession: Workplace accommodations for lawyers with disabilities and lawyers who identify as LGBTQ+. *Journal of Occupational Rehabilitation, 30*(4), 537–564.

Bonaccio, S., Connelly, C. E., Gellatly, I. R., Jetha, A., & Ginis, K. A. M. (2020). The participation of people with disabilities in the workplace across the employment cycle: Employer concerns and research evidence. *Journal of Business and Psychology, 35*(2), 135–158.

Bosma, A. R., Boot, C. R. L., Snippen, N. C., Schaafsma, F. G., & Anema, J. R. (2021). Supporting employees with chronic conditions to stay at work: Perspectives of occupational health professionals and organizational representatives. *BMC Public Health, 21*(1), 1–13.

Brijnath, B., Mazza, D., Singh, N., Kosny, A., Ruseckaite, R., & Collie, A. (2014). Mental health claims management and return to work: Qualitative insights from Melbourne. *Australia. Journal of Occupational Rehabilitation, 24*(4), 766–776.

Brouwers, E. P. (2020). Social stigma is an underestimated contributing factor to unemployment in people with mental illness or mental health issues: Position paper and future directions. *BMC Psychology, 8*(1), 1–7.

Brucker, D. L., & Sundar, V. (2020). Job Crafting among American workers with disabilities. *Journal of Occupational Rehabilitation, 30*(4), 575–587.

Cimera, R. E., & Cowan, R. J. (2009). The costs of services and employment outcomes achieved by adults with autism in the US. *Autism*, 13(3), 285–302.

Colella, A. (2001). Coworker distributive fairness judgments of the workplace accommodation of employees with disabilities. *Academy of Management Review, 26*(1), 100–116.

Corrigan, P. W., Druss, B. G., & Perlick, D. A. (2014). The impact of mental illness stigma on seeking and participating in mental health care. *Psychological Science in the Public Interest, 15*(2), 37–70.

Corrigan, P. W., Rowan, D., Green, A., Lundin, R., River, P., Uphoff-Wasowski, K., White, K., & Kubiak, M. A. (2002). Challenging two mental illness stigmas: Personal responsibility and dangerousness. *Schizophrenia Bulletin, 28*(2), 293–309.

Devine, A., Vaughan, C., Kavanagh, A., Dickinson, H., Byars, S., Dimov, S., Gye, B. & Brophy, L. (2020). 'I'm proud of how far I've come. I'm just ready to work': Mental health recovery narratives within the context of Australia's Disability Employment Services (DES). *BMC Public Health*, *20*(1), 1–18

Devonish, D. (2017). Managers' perceptions of mental illness in Barbadian workplaces: An exploratory study. *The Journal of Mental Health Training, Education and Practice, 12*(3), 161–172.

Earnshaw, V. A., Quinn, D. M., Kalichman, S. C., & Park, C. L. (2013). Development and psychometric evaluation of the chronic illness anticipated stigma scale. *Journal of Behavioral Medicine, 36*(3), 270–282.

Elraz, H. (2018). Identity, mental health and work: How employees with mental health conditions recount stigma and the pejorative discourse of mental illness. *Human Relations, 71*(5), 722–741.

Fuhrmann, F., Scholl, M., & Bruggemann, R. (2018). How Can the Empowerment of Employees with Intellectual Disabilities Be Supported? *Social Indicators Research, 136*(3), 1269–1285.

Gibbons, B. J., & Salkever, D. S. (2019). Working with a severe mental illness: Estimating the causal effects of employment on mental health status and total mental health costs. *Administration and Policy in Mental Health and Mental Health Services Research, 46*(4), 474–487.

Gignac, M. A., Bowring, J., Jetha, A., Beaton, D. E., Breslin, F. C., Franche, R. L., Irvin, E., Macdermid, J. C., Shaw, W. S., Smith, P. M., Thompson, A., Tompa, E., Van Eerd, D., & Saunders, R. (2021). Disclosure, privacy and workplace accommodation of episodic disabilities: Organizational perspectives on disability communication-support processes to sustain employment. *Journal of Occupational Rehabilitation, 31*(1), 153–165.

Goldberg, S. G., Killeen, M. B., & O'Day, B. (2005). The disclosure conundrum: How people with psychiatric disabilities navigate employment. *Psychology, Public Policy, and Law, 11*(3), 463.

Gouvea, R., & Li, S. (2021). Smart nations for all, disability and jobs: A global perspective. *Journal of the Knowledge Economy*, 1–16. https://doi.org/10.1007/s13132-021-00796-9

Griffiths, K. M., Nakane, Y., Christensen, H., Yoshioka, K., Jorm, A. F., & Nakane, H. (2006). Stigma in response to mental disorders: A comparison of Australia and Japan. *BMC Psychiatry, 6*(1), 1–12.

Hampson, M. E., Watt, B. D., & Hicks, R. E. (2020). Impacts of stigma and discrimination in the workplace on people living with psychosis. *BMC Psychiatry, 20*, 1–11.

Harpur, P. (2019). *Ableism at work: Disablement and hierarchies of impairment*. Cambridge University Press.

Harpur, P., & Blanck, P. (2020). Gig workers with disabilities: Opportunities, challenges, and regulatory response. *Journal of Occupational Rehabilitation, 30*(4), 511–520.

Henderson, C., Williams, P., Little, K., & Thornicroft, G. (2013). Mental health problems in the workplace: Changes in employers' knowledge, attitudes and practices in England 2006–2010. *The British Journal of Psychiatry, 202*(s55), s70–s76.

Hocking, B. (2003). Reducing mental illness stigma and discrimination-everybody's business. *Medical Journal of Australia, 178*(9), S47.

Jansen, S., White, R., Hogwood, J., Jansen, A., Gishoma, D., Mukamana, D., & Richters, A. (2015). The treatment gap in global mental health reconsidered: Sociotherapy for collective trauma in Rwanda. *European Journal of Psychotraumatology, 6*(10), 1–6.

Jetha, A., Ginis, K. A. M., Ibrahim, S., & Gignac, M. A. (2020). The working disadvantaged: The role of age, job tenure and disability in precarious work. *BMC Public Health, 20*(1), 1–12.

Juurlink, T. T., Ten Have, M., Lamers, F., van Marle, H. J., Anema, J. R., de Graaf, R., & Beekman, A. T. (2018). Borderline personality symptoms and work performance: A population-based survey. *BMC Psychiatry, 18*(1), 1–9.

Kaye, H. S., Jans, L. H., & Jones, E. C. (2011). Why don't employers hire and retain workers with disabilities? *Journal of Occupational Rehabilitation, 21*(4), 526–536.

Keyes, C. (2007). Towards a mentally flourishing society: Mental health promotion, not cure. *Journal of Public Mental Health, 6*(2), 4–7.

Keyes, C. L. (2005). Mental Illness and/or Mental Health? Investigating Axioms of the Complete State Model of Health. *Journal of Consulting and Clinical Psychology, 73*(3), 539–548.

Kirsh, B., Slack, T., & King, C. A. (2012). The nature and impact of stigma towards injured workers. *Journal of Occupational Rehabilitation, 22*(2), 143–154.

Krisi, M., Eckhaus, E., & Nagar, R. (2021). Developing a Multilevel Scale to Assess Retention of Workers with Disabilities. *Journal of Occupational Rehabilitation*, 1–9

Krupa, T., Kirsh, B., Cockburn, L., & Gewurtz, R. (2009). Understanding the stigma of mental illness in employment. *Work, 33*(4), 413–425.

Kulkarni, M., & Kote, J. (2014). Increasing employment of people with disabilities: The role and views of disability training and placement agencies. *Employee Responsibilities and Rights Journal, 26*(3), 177–193.

Kulkarni, M., & Scullion, H. (2015). Talent management activities of disability training and placement agencies in India. *The International Journal of Human Resource Management, 26*(9), 1169–1181.

Logue, L. M., & Blanck, P. (2020). Before the accommodation principle: Disability and employment among Union army veterans. *Journal of Occupational Rehabilitation, 30*(4), 565–574.

Lu, S. J., Liou, T. H., Yen, C. F., Chang, F. H., Chen, Y. L., Escorpizo, R., . Strauser, D.R. & Pan, A. W. (2019). Determinants of employment outcome for the people with schizophrenia using the WHODAS 2.0. *Journal of Occupational Rehabilitation, 29*(2), 375–383

Lyubykh, Z., Ansari, M. A., Williams-Whitt, K., & Kristman, V. L. (2020). Disability Severity, Leader-Member Exchange, and Attitudinal Outcomes: Considering the Employee and Supervisor Perspectives. *Journal of Occupational Rehabilitation, 30*(4), 613–623.

Manning, C., & White, P. D. (1995). Attitudes of employers to the mentally ill. *Psychiatric Bulletin, 19*(9), 541–543.

Markel, K. S., & Barclay, L. A. (2009). Addressing the underemployment of persons with disabilities: Recommendations for expanding organizational social responsibility. *Employee Responsibilities and Rights Journal*, *21*(4), 305–318.

McMahon, B. T., Rumrill, P. D., Roessler, R., Hurley, J. E., West, S. L., Chan, F., & Carlson, L. (2008). Hiring discrimination against people with disabilities under the ADA: Characteristics of employers. *Journal of Occupational Rehabilitation, 18*(2), 112.

Meacham, H., Cavanagh, J., Bartram, T., & Laing, J. (2019). Ethical management in the hotel sector: Creating an authentic work experience for workers with intellectual disabilities. *Journal of Business Ethics, 155*(3), 823–835.

Migliaccio, G. (2019). Disabled people in the stakeholder theory: A literature analysis. *Journal of the Knowledge Economy, 10*(4), 1657–1678.

Mueser, K. T., & McGurk, S. R. (2014). Supported employment for persons with serious mental illness: Current status and future directions. *l'Encéphale, 40*, S45–S56

Pan American Health Organization (PAHO). (2021). *The burden of mental disorders in the Region of the Americas, 2000–2019*. PAHO.

Parey, B. (2020). Using Sen's capability approach to assess wellbeing among working-age persons with disabilities in Trinidad. *Social Indicators Research, 151*(3), 1129–1148.

Ren, L. R., Paetzold, R. L., & Colella, A. (2008). A meta-analysis of experimental studies on the effects of disability on human resource judgments. *Human Resource Management Review, 18*(3), 191–203.

Robinson, J. N., Lambert, M. A., & Allwood, M. A. (2021). Barriers to Addressing Mental Health Challenges across Caribbean Nations. *Caribbean Journal of Psychology, 13*(1), 7–31.

Robinson, P., Oades, L., & Caputi, P. (2015). Conceptualising and measuring mental fitness: A Delphi study. *International Journal of Wellbeing*, *5*(1)

Rodríguez, R. P., Sánchez, C. R., de Haro, C. O., & Maldonado, J. S. (2014). Older workers with disabilities: Job satisfaction differences in the public and private sectors in Europe. *Applied Research in Quality of Life, 9*(3), 711–731.

Rüsch, N., Nordt, C., Kawohl, W., Brantschen, E., Bärtsch, B., Müller, M., & Rössler, W. (2014). Work-related discrimination and change in self-stigma among people with mental illness during supported employment. *Psychiatric Services, 65*(12), 1496–1498.

Rüsch, N., Zlati, A., Black, G., & Thornicroft, G. (2014). Does the stigma of mental illness contribute to suicidality? *The British Journal of Psychiatry, 205*(4), 257–259.

Saavedra, J., López, M., Gonzáles, S., & Cubero, R. (2016). Does employment promote recovery? Meanings from work experience in people diagnosed with serious mental illness. *Culture, Medicine, and Psychiatry, 40*(3), 507–532.

Sahu, K. K. (2015). Intervening negative impact of stigma on employability of a person with schizophrenia through social case work. *Journal of Psychosocial Rehabilitation and Mental Health, 2*(1), 87–95.

Sakellariou, D., Malfitano, A. P. S., & Rotarou, E. S. (2020). Disability inclusiveness of government responses to COVID-19 in South America: A framework analysis study. *International Journal for Equity in Health, 19*(1), 1–10.

Sanders, C. K., & Scanlon, E. (2021). The digital divide is a human rights issue: Advancing social inclusion through social work advocacy. *Journal of Human Rights and Social Work*, 1–14

Schur, L. A., Ameri, M., & Kruse, D. (2020). Telework after COVID: A "silver lining" for workers with disabilities? *Journal of Occupational Rehabilitation, 30*(4), 521–536.

Seeman, M. V. (2009). Employment discrimination against schizophrenia. *Psychiatric Quarterly, 80*(1), 9–16.

Sharpe, J., & Sharpe, S. (2016). Mental Health in the Caribbean. In J. L. Roopnarine & D. Chadee (Eds.), *Caribbean psychology: Indigenous contributions to a global discipline* (pp. 305–325). American Psychological Association. https://doi.org/10.1037/14753-013

Shaw, W. S., Kristman, V. L., Williams-Whitt, K., Soklaridis, S., Huang, Y. H., Côté, P., & Loisel, P. (2014). The Job Accommodation Scale (JAS): Psychometric evaluation of a new measure of employer support for temporary job modifications. *Journal of Occupational Rehabilitation, 24*(4), 755–765.

Sniatecki, J. L., Pelz, J. A., & Gates, T. G. (2018). Human rights advocacy for students with disabilities: Challenging stigma and promoting opportunity in social work education. *Journal of Human Rights and Social Work, 3*(4), 183–190.

Stein, D., Palk, A., & Kendler, K. (2021). What is a mental disorder? An exemplar-focused approach. *Psychological Medicine, 51*, 894–901.

Stergiou-Kita, M., Mansfield, E., & Colantonio, A. (2014). Injured workers' perspectives on how workplace accommodations are conceptualized and delivered following electrical injuries. *Journal of Occupational Rehabilitation, 24*(2), 173–188.

Stevenson, B. J., Mueller, L., Kelly, M. M., & Rosenheck, R. A. (2021). Correlates of Obtaining Employment among Veterans Receiving Treatment for Severe PTSD in Specialized Intensive Programs. *Psychiatric Quarterly*, 1–14

Stone, D. L., & Colella, A. (1996). A model of factors affecting the treatment of disabled individuals in organizations. *Academy of Management Review, 21*(2), 352–401.

Stuart, H. (2006). Mental illness and employment discrimination. *Current Opinion in Psychiatry, 19*(5), 522–526.

Tavaragi, M. S., & Sushma, C. (2019). Global Burden of Mental Disorders: Quality of Care and Unmet Needs for Treatment of Chronic Mental Illness. In *Chronic Illness and Long-Term Care: Breakthroughs in Research and Practice* (pp. 445–467). IGI Global

Tsang, H. W., Angell, B., Corrigan, P. W., Lee, Y. T., Shi, K., Lam, C. S., Fung, K. M. Corrigan, P., Shi, K., & Jin, S. (2007). A cross-cultural study of employers' concerns about hiring people with psychotic disorder: Implications for recovery. *Social Psychiatry and Psychiatric Epidemiology, 42*(9), 723–733.

Um, Y. J., & Choi, Y. J. (2020). The effect of employment status on people with a mental disability and on daily life satisfaction: The mediating effect of acceptance of disability. *Current Psychology*, 1–8

Wagener, M. N., van Opstal, S. E. M., Miedema, H. S., Brandjes, D. P., Dahmen, R., van Gorp, E. C. M., & Roelofs, P. D. D. M. (2014). Employment-related concerns of HIV-positive people in the Netherlands: Input for a multidisciplinary guideline. *Journal of Occupational Rehabilitation, 24*(4), 790–797.

Wang, P. S., Beck, A. L., Berglund, P., McKenas, D. K., Pronk, N. P., Simon, G. E., & Kessler, R. C. (2004). Effects of major depression on moment-in-time work performance. *American Journal of Psychiatry, 161*(10), 1885–1891.

Ward, A., Moon, N., & Baker, P. M. (2012). Functioning, capability and freedom: A framework for understanding workplace disabilities. *Employee Responsibilities and Rights Journal, 24*(1), 37–53.

Wehmeyer, M. L., Davies, D. K., Stock, S. E., & Tanis, S. (2020). Applied cognitive technologies to support the autonomy of people with intellectual and developmental disabilities. *Advances in Neurodevelopmental Disorders, 4*(4), 389–399.

Wheat, K., Brohan, E., Henderson, C., & Thornicroft, G. (2010). Mental illness and the workplace: Conceal or reveal? *Journal of the Royal Society of Medicine, 103*(3), 83–86.

World Health Organization (WHO). (2021). *Comprehensive mental health action plan 2013–2030*. World Health Organization. https://apps.who.int/iris/handle/10665/345301. License: CC BY-NC-SA 3.0 IGO.

Yoshimura, Y., Bakolis, I., & Henderson, C. (2018). Psychiatric diagnosis and other predictors of experienced and anticipated workplace discrimination and concealment of mental illness among mental health service users in England. *Social Psychiatry and Psychiatric Epidemiology, 53*(10), 1099–1109.

CHAPTER 6

Neurodiversity in the Anglophone Caribbean

Introduction

The term neurodiversity is not one which is used in popular discourse in the Caribbean region, though the conditions which are classified as such are widely recognised. These include but are not limited to the cognitive disabilities of Dyslexia, Dyscalculia, Dyspraxia/Developmental Co-ordination Disorder (DCD), Autistic Spectrum Disorder (ASD), Asperger's Syndrome, Tourette's Syndrome and Attention Deficit Hyperactivity Disorder (ADHD) (Dalton, 2013; Graby, 2015; Krzeminska et al., 2019). Persons who are neurodivergent face challenges with social acceptance and equal access to employment, education and access to necessary goods and services (Graby, 2015; Jaarsma & Welin, 2012). Failure of employers and societies to recognise and accommodate these differences could result in challenges for this marginalised group, in securing suitable long-term employment, but they could also face challenges within other aspects of society, particularly, where any deviation from neurotypical cognition is viewed as less desirable and equated with diminished abilities or incorrectly identified as mental illnesses. The implicit bias against persons with atypical cognitive processes could result in the perception that the employment and retention of such persons is unlikely to add value to the workplace, and as such, the benefits associated

J. H. Stephenson and N. Persadie, *Disability in the Workplace*, Palgrave Explorations in Workplace Stigma,
https://doi.org/10.1007/978-3-031-19340-8_6

with any accommodations which they may require, may not be justified by their costs (Krzeminska et al., 2019).

Notwithstanding this, Doyle (2020) has outlined advantages which can be derived from the employment of individuals with developmental disorders, including creativity, hyper-focus, enhanced memory and comprehension, innovation, visual-spatial skills and attention to detail, *inter alia*. Hence, Caribbean workplaces can benefit from the gainful employment of such individuals, their unique talents and the insights and perspectives which they can contribute. Within the Caribbean, there are no laws, or regulatory guidelines which compel neurodivergent employees to disclose their diagnosis and indeed persons may withhold this information, for fear that it might be disadvantageous to their growth and development within the organisation. There are several modifications to human resource practices, (*which are not cost prohibitive*), which workplaces may adopt, with a view of ameliorating the deleterious effect of the typical workplace, on neurodivergent employees and organisational stakeholders. There is a paucity of literature on neurodiversity in the Caribbean and consequently, this chapter critically analyses whether and the extent to which neurodiversity is understood and accommodated by contemporary Caribbean workplaces, with a view of facilitating the optimal contribution of this marginalised group.

Autism Spectrum Disorders

Autism spectrum disorders (ASD) refer to a category of developmental disabilities characterised by difficulties in social interaction, communication, restricted behaviour, compulsive, repetitive behaviour, have challenges adapting to change, are interested in atypical objects and have either heightened or decreased reactions (of one of their senses) (Bewley & George, 2016; Ekblad, 2013; Hendricks, 2010; Jaarsma & Welin, 2012; Scott et al., 2017; Solomon, 2020). In a broader sense, ASD is a neurodevelopmental disorder, which are disorders that adversely affect one's neurological development (Bishop, 2010). One's neurological development is important for performance and functioning (including intellectual functioning, reading, social skills, memory, attention, focus). This spectrum of disorders includes Dyslexia, Dyscalculia, Dysgraphia, Developmental Co-ordination Disorder (DCD), Tourette's Syndrome, Autistic Spectrum Disorder (ASD), Asperger's Syndrome, Attention Deficit Hyperactivity Disorder (ADHD), neurological illness or brain injury (Doyle et al., 2020). Individuals so diagnosed, are referred to collectively as a neurodiverse group to reflect their atypical neurological development (Doyle et al., 2020; Jaarsma & Welin, 2012).

Within the Anglophone Caribbean, knowledge about neurodiversity among the populous is limited and as a result, societal understanding, in relation to the causes, symptoms and potential treatments, appropriate for neurominorities, is narrow at best, and prevailing stereotypes are relied on. As with all disabilities, the nature and severity of ASD will vary along with each person who has been so clinically diagnosed. According to the American Diagnostic and Statistical Manual of Mental Disorders (2013), published by the American Psychiatric Association (APA) the diagnostic criteria for autism spectrum disorder (ASD) are:

> A. "Persistent deficits in social communication and social interaction across multiple contexts. Examples: - *Deficits in social-emotional reciprocity, Deficits in nonverbal communicative behaviors used for social interaction, Deficits in developing, maintaining, and understanding relationships*".
>
> B. "Restricted, repetitive patterns of behavior, interests, or activities, as manifested by at least two of the following, currently or by history: *Stereotyped or repetitive motor movements, use of objects, or speech; Insistence on sameness, inflexible adherence to routines, or ritualized patterns of verbal or nonverbal behavior; Highly restricted, fixated interests that are abnormal in intensity or focus; Hyper- or hypo reactivity to sensory input or unusual interest in sensory aspects of the environment*".
>
> C. "Symptoms must be present in the early developmental period (but may not become fully manifest until social demands exceed limited capacities or may be masked by learned strategies in later life)".
>
> D. "Symptoms cause clinically significant impairment in social, occupational, or other important areas of current functioning".
>
> E. "These disturbances are not better explained by intellectual disability (intellectual developmental disorder) or global developmental delay. *Intellectual disability and autism spectrum disorder frequently co-occur; to make comorbid diagnoses of autism spectrum disorder and intellectual disability, social communication should be below that expected for general developmental level*". American Diagnostic and Statistical Manual of Mental Disorders (2013)

ASD and Employment

Due to its nature, ASD is regarded as an invisible disability, since it is not immediately obvious that an employee has been so diagnosed. In fact, a neurominority employee would typically need to spend some time in the presence of other colleagues in order to observe any atypical behaviours or mannerisms to become evident (Ohl et al., 2017; Solomon, 2020). It has been argued that (Graby, 2015; Ne'eman & Pellicano, 2022; Radulski, 2022), neurominorities should be viewed through a lens of the social model of disability, which would require an accommodation of their atypical tendencies and behaviours, and from the perspective of the organisation, such employees should be valued for their attendant benefits, rather than rejecting members of this group and viewing them as an anomaly, in need of a cure, after which neuro-normative behaviours would emerge (Doyle, 2020; Jenkins, 2014). Indeed, where organisations espouse inclusive employment policies, this should be comprehensive, and as such should not disregard the potential contribution of employees who are not neurotypical. This would require a comprehensive evaluation of the benefits associated with neurodivergent employees, which include creativity, consistency, detail-oriented, good work ethic, reliable, transparent, efficient, just as productive as employees without ASD, high levels of patience for repetitive work, *inter alia* (Bewley & George, 2016; Harris et al., 2020; Krzeminska et al., 2019; Scott et al., 2017; Solomon, 2020). Collectively, these are desired employee attributes for any organisation concerned with being successful and sustainable, and as such, provide organisation with a further incentive to actively pursue employment diversity and inclusion (Scott et al., 2017; Solomon, 2020).

Notwithstanding this research supporting the benefits of employing persons with ASD, some organisational managers remain unconvinced of their potential contribution and rely on prevailing wisdom (not grounded in facts), in relation to challenges associated with neurodivergent employees, which results in these individuals not being considered for vacancies and limited in relation to any developmental opportunities. The challenges are said to include, excessive honesty (Austin & Pisano, 2017), lower speech and language abilities, the presence of maladaptive behaviours, lack of empathy, lack of drive, inability to appropriately socially engage with organisational members; difficulty in understanding directions, and inability to adapt to change (Bury et al., 2022; Doyle et al., 2020; Jenkins, 2014; Ohl et al., 2017; Solomon, 2020).

Acceptance of these potential challenges of employees with ASD, suggests that organisations view neurodiverse employees as a homogeneous group, instead of considering each employee (and applicant) as unique and assessing them on their own merit (Maria Szulc et al., 2021; Mellifont, 2022). Any attempt to do so could result in the loss of the services of an employee or group of employees, which could provide the organisation with a competitive advantage. Developmental disorders falling into the category of ASD, represent individuals with a spectrum of needs and abilities, specifically, as it relates to their nature and severity of the diagnosed disorder, therefore, it would be injudicious for organisations to make generic generalisations about the likely organisational outcomes of all persons with ASD (Bishop, 2010; Santuzzi & Keating, 2022; Tomczak, 2022). The consequence of which could be failure to "acquire" a performance boosting asset which could potentially be beneficial to the organisation (see Table 6.1).

Further, persons with ASD who are actively seeking employment, but have been denied available opportunities due to the acceptance of stereotypes are then compelled to seek economic and social support elsewhere (including alternative forms of employment like entrepreneurship, gig work, social security funds) (MacLeod et al., 2013; Mawhood & Howlin, 1999; Schur et al., 2017). The absence of employment opportunities has also been found to result in a devalued self-worth, and a diminished sense of accomplishment and competence, particularly, for those persons who have invested the resources into training, education and general upskilling (Berrigan et al., 2020; Krzeminska et al., 2019; Kwon, 2021; Ohl et al., 2017; Scott et al., 2017) The incidence of autism and Asperger's syndrome is lower in the Anglophone (non-Latin Caribbean), relative to other regions (*namely*, South America, Central America, North America, *see* Fig. 6.1), with the exception of the Andean area, which reported the lowest incidence. In the English-speaking Caribbean, across the 19-year period (2000 to 2019) for which PAHO (2021) data is available, there was a reported population average of 53.8 years living with autism and Asperger's syndrome in *2000*; this was followed by a marginal decrease, to an average of 52.7 of years living with autism and Asperger's syndrome in 2010; and over the ensuring 9 year period, in 2019, there was a reported average of 51.8 years living with autism and Asperger's syndrome. Further, in the Caribbean, (as illustrated in the previous chapter), Fig. 5.1 shows the years lived with autism and Asperger's syndrome is considerably lower, relative to other reported disorders

Table 6.1 Work-related challenges and strengths attributed to neurominorities

Attention deficit hyperactivity disorder (ADHD)	*AUTISM*	*Developmental co-ordination disorder (DCD)*	*Dyslexia*
Challenges • Time management • Concentration, attention and self-regulation difficulties • Insomnia, depression, injury and absence • Maintaining employment • Difficulty with teamwork	**Challenges** • Time management, • Concentration and coping with more than one task • Social and communication difficulties • Need for routine	**Challenges** • Difficulties with driving, self-care, organization, • Communication and self-esteem • Processing speed and working memory • Persistence of motor difficulties in operating equipment	**Challenges** • Literacy, memory, organization, communication and self-esteem • Memory, organizational skills, time management, stress management, literacy • Workplace participation in terms of mental functions and social interactions • Cognitive functioning and social self-esteem • Higher incidence of worklessness and incarceration
Strengths • Creative thinking • Visual-spatial reasoning ability • Hyper-focus, passion and courage	**Strengths** • Memory ability, and other 'specialist individual skills' including reading, drawing, music and computation • Innovative thinking and detail observation	**Strengths** • High verbal comprehension ability	**Strengths** • Entrepreneurialism • Creativity and cognitive control • Visual reasoning • Practical skills, visual-spatial skills and story-telling ability

Source Doyle, N. (2020). Neurodiversity at work: a biopsychosocial model and the impact on working adults. *British Medical Bulletin*, *135*(1), 108 (*See also* Bewley & George, 2016; Harris et al., 2020; Hendricks, 2010; Krzeminska et al., 2019; Ohl et al., 2017; Scott et al., 2017; Solomon, 2020).

(including, but not limited to depressive disorders, anxiety disorders, bipolar disorders, schizophrenia, etc.). With challenges in gaining and retaining employment reported for members of this group (see Table 6.1), the responsibility to support this group will invariably be borne by the respective regional Caribbean governments, with allied advocacy or philanthropic groups contributing, insofar as their resources permit.

Persons with ASD want to work and are able to work and be productive, however the incidence of unemployment for this group in the Caribbean, continues to be of concern. The World Bank reported that more than 80% of persons with disabilities in the Caribbean are either

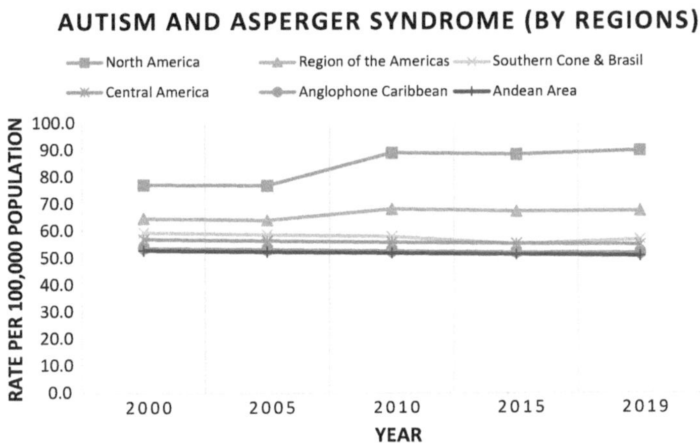

Global Regions	2000	2005	2010	2015	2019
North America	77.3	77.0	89.0	88.4	90.0
Region of the Americas	64.9	64.3	68.3	67.5	67.7
Southern Cone & Brasil	59.7	59.0	58.3	55.4	57.1
Central America, Mexico & Latin Caribbean	57.1	56.5	56.0	55.4	55.0
Non-Latin (Anglophone) Caribbean	53.8	53.3	52.7	52.2	51.8
Andean Area	53.1	52.6	52.0	51.4	50.9

Fig. 6.1 Autism and Asperger syndrome across the non-Latin Caribbean, relative to other region (*Source* Pan American Health Organisation [PAHO]. [2021]. The burden of mental disorders in the Region of the Americas, 2000–2019. Retrieved from: https://www.paho.org/en/noncommunicable-diseases-and-mental-health/enlace-data-portal-noncommunicable-diseases-mental-2)

unemployed or underemployed.[1] Underemployment is not uncommon with persons with developmental disorders (Hendricks, 2010; Ohl et al., 2017; Scott et al., 2017), indeed, notwithstanding their qualifications, persons with ASD are found in food service, customer service, transportation, manufacturing or administrative support roles (Hendricks, 2010; Lorenz et al., 2016; Mavranezouli et al., 2014; Ohl et al., 2017; Solomon, 2020), where they earn significantly less than their similarly qualified colleagues without disabilities. While this employment outcome may be attributed to prevailing stereotypes and stigma associated with this neurodivergent group, the perception of persons with disabilities as having a physical or psychological deficit, instead of re-imagining the challenges they face, by determining what can be done to facilitate their increased participation, is a present and ongoing obstacle faced by PWD within the Caribbean. Inherent in the widespread acceptance of stereotypes and stigmatised attitudes associated with persons with development disorders appears to be the belief that only neuro-normative individuals are capable of productively engaging in work (Bishop, 2010; Schur et al., 2017). Hence, the obstacles which prohibit the active employment participation of neurodivergent individuals, ultimately result in a rejection of the value placed on diversity and inclusion, notwithstanding public statements made to the contrary by organisations (on their websites and published annual reports).

Employment Support for Persons with ASD

Pursuant to an effective intervention strategy to create more employment opportunities for persons with ASD, societies may make modifications to social, cultural and contextual factors, and in so doing provide a catalyst for the active participation and inclusion of persons with ASD in daily life (Hume et al., 2009; LaRue et al., 2022; Wehman et al., 2016). Moreover, relevant accommodations for persons with disabilities (PWD) are permitted by the anti-discrimination legislation enacted in several Caribbean islands. For those islands in the Anglophone Caribbean where such legislation has not yet been passed, the CRPD (for those islands

[1] Underemployment refers to incidents where individuals are employed but they are underutilised, underpaid, overeducated, over skilled and overqualified for the posts they occupy (Mc-Kee-Ryan & Harvey, 2011).

which are signatories[2]) provides guidance in this regard, with the objective of being inclusive to PWD. Some of the organisational changes which can be implemented in short order, to improve employment (***treatment of and***) outcomes for persons with ASD include the following: validating neurodivergent employees' experience, communicating more deliberately and confirming clarity, allowing employees to be autonomous where possible (Harris et al., 2020; Mawhood & Howlin, 1999). In addition, Dreaver et al. (2020), concisely categorised strategies and supports which may result in the effective inclusion of persons with ASD (see Table 6.2), including social, adaptive, cognitive, employment and training support.

As discussed in the previous chapter, technology can be useful in providing support to PWD, to facilitate their ability to function autonomously at work, as it relates to persons with ASD, this would include cognitive technologies (e.g. artificial intelligence and algorithms) (Hendricks, 2010; Wehmeyer et al., 2020). It is useful to note, that organisational support required by persons with ASD should not be used to diminish their contribution and value. Such support is akin to a neurotypical person, requesting a secretary, an assistant or specific software to make them more efficient. Where such requests are made, they are regarded as acceptable, and these employees are often lauded for being forward thinkers and complimented on their improved levels of performance. This same favourable consideration should be extended to requests for support made by neurodivergent employees, to assist them in developing into successful employees and has been found to improve employment outcomes for persons with ASD (Hendricks, 2010; Kwon, 2021; Mawhood & Howlin, 1999). Prior to securing employment, neurodivergent applicants may access the services of a disability employment service (DES) provider, who will render assistance with recruitment and selection, and post-employment. After the applicant has been hired, the DES provider can continue to provide support, training and modifications which may be required by either (or both parties) by acting as a liaison between the employee with ASD and the organisation (Hendricks, 2010; Santuzzi & Keating, 2022; Tomczak, 2022). One further benefit of the engagement of DES support is to obviate the

[2] Caribbean islands which are signatories to the United Nations Convention on the Rights of Persons with Disabilities are Antigua & Barbuda, Barbados, Bahamas, Dominica, Grenada, Guyana, Jamaica, St. Kitts and Nevis; St. Lucia; St. Vincent and the Grenadines; and Trinidad and Tobago.

Table 6.2 Categories of strategies and supports that facilitate successful employment of persons with ASD

Social support	*Adaptive strategies*	*Cognitive supports*	*Employment support services*	*Vocation training support*
Additional supervision for employees with ASD	Written step by step procedures	Reinforce positive behaviour	Job matching support	Personal care training and education
Open honest communication	Written job description	Co-workers model expected behaviour	Initial support and leadership training for managers managing employees with ASD	Transport training
Low number of immediate team members for employee with ASD	Introduce routine and job structure to the workplace	Offer reassurance and encouragement to employees with ASD	ASD training for colleagues	Education about appropriate physical boundaries
Managers and coworkers establish an open door policy and are open minded	Restructure job role to avoid unsuitable tasks	Preparation of ASD employees for new tasks or disruptions via regular feedback and evaluations	Social meetings with managers and employees with ASD	Business writing skills training
Coworkers mentor and support employee with ASD	Establish and define lines of communication	Suggest strategies to overcome stress	Expert external support for employees with ASD	Education about workplace basics (*e.g., shared workspaces*)
Regular communication and support between manager and employee with ASD	Introduce transport options		Open communication between supervisor and support workers	

Social support	*Adaptive strategies*	*Cognitive supports*	*Employment support services*	*Vocation training support*
Employee with ASD is aware of managers expectations	Accommodations to sensory demands of the environment (i.e. dimming lights, blinds, headphones, reducing ambient noise)		One on one support within the workplace for employees with ASD, if necessary	

Source Dreaver, J., Thompson, C., Girdler, S., Adolfsson, M., Black, M. H., & Falkmer, M. (2020). Success factors enabling employment for adults on the autism spectrum from employers' perspective. *Journal of Autism and Developmental Disorders*, *50*(5), 1657–1667

possible influence of stigma or prejudice against this marginalised group, throughout the employment process (Dreaver et al., 2020; Solomon, 2020; Wehmeyer et al., 2020). Table 6.3 offers additional insight as to the range of adjustments that may be useful for neurominorities at work, along with examples of adjustments which might address barriers faced by this group of employees.

Table 6.3 Typical adjustments for neurominorities

Adjustment type	*Adjustment examples*
Work Environment flexibility	Reducing sensory distractions by allowing flexible hours; use of private meeting rooms; noise-cancelling headphones; redesign of shared working space
Schedule flexibility	Avoiding rush hour travel to prevent sensory overload; remote working to avoid sensory overwhelm, improve concentration and reduce social communication demands
Supervisor OR Co-worker support	Additional feedback time with supervisor; differences in instructions provided—more clarity or concreteness given
Support from different stakeholders	Peer mentoring networks within the company; allowing support activities via employee assistance, mental health, or family support throughout the working day; allowing access to stakeholder groups and charities throughout the working day
Executive functions coaching	Workplace coaching to focus on areas such as planning, prioritization, organizational skills using workplace coaching psychology
Training	Adjustments to training provision including sending materials in advance or providing additional induction training
Work-station adjustments	Use of dual screens to improve concentration, whiteboards and other memory aids; standing desks with wobble boards to improve access to movement through the day
Assistive technology and tools	Speech-to-text, text-to-speech software to reduce demands on literacy, handwriting skills and improve concentration; mind mapping software to support shift from overview to detailed thinking; specialist spell checkers designed for dyslexia; planning and memory software

(continued)

Table 6.3 (continued)

Adjustment type	*Adjustment examples*
Literacy coaching	This will be targeted coaching based on the literacy requirements of the role rather than teaching basic skills, such as speed reading, making notes whilst reading, summarizing or structuring and planning written work

Source Doyle, N. (2020). Neurodiversity at work: a biopsychosocial model and the impact on working adults. *British Medical Bulletin*, *135*(1), 108

In addition to the stereotypical perceptions of persons with ASD, a lack of knowledge, fear and potential discomfort which employers have identified as reasons for the low levels of employment for neurodivergent applicants, the assumed costs of accommodation are also cited as a reason for hiring reluctance, by organisations. The accuracy of this assertion has been questioned, as the cost of the adjustment requests typical of neurominorities as outlined in Tables 6.2 and 6.3 are not unreasonable and certainly are unlikely to result in an undue financial burden for the organisation (Carlson & Ehrlich, 2006; Mavranezouli et al., 2014). Indeed, it has been found that (Schur et al., 2017), there is no significant cost variance between employees with ASD and employees who have not been diagnosed with a development disorder in terms of training costs, supervision and employment. Moreover, the lower wages earned by neurodivergent employees effectively offset any additional potential costs incurred as a consequence of hiring them, relative to their neurotypical colleagues (Jenkins, 2014; Solomon, 2020; Szulc et al., 2021). Further, to ensure organisational resources are appropriately used, regarding accommodation costs incurred in relation to neurodivergent employees, it is important for organisations to consult the target employee, before making any decision, regarding the accommodations which might be suitable for their needs.

The Role of Organisational Members and Leaders

The English-speaking Caribbean is largely a patriarchal society (Blank, 2013; Roopnarine, 2012), and this remains evident in the number of men currently holding senior management and executive roles within Caribbean-based organisations. The leadership styles adopted by male leaders are generally authoritative in nature and substance, rather than inclusive or collaborative, where input from team members would be valued. This disparity suggests that the prevailing leadership style would result in managers believing that they have the perfect remedy for any of the organisational challenges faced by neurodivergent employees. Where this decided remedy is pursued, the result may be employee frustration and failure, where the chosen solution fails to result in the anticipated outcomes (Bennett & Gibb, 2022; Houdek, 2022). Thus, it is imperative that neurodivergent employees are directly consulted and their requests actioned, rather than managers making unilateral decisions about the best option for this group. Neurodivergent employees are quite capable of articulating their desires and any accommodations which may be required. Relatedly, the question of accommodation, assumes that the employee's neurodivergent status has been disclosed, and as we have seen (see Chapter 4), this is only likely to be done where the employee does not fear reprisals (bullying, harassment, discrimination) for so doing (Bennett & Gibb, 2022; Djela, 2021; Szulc et al., 2021).

Throughout the neurodivergent employee's tenure with the organisation, the role of the human resource managers and other organisational leaders would be to ensure there is person-job fit, to ensure that the employee's workstation is designed to elicit optimal levels of performance (with minimal distractions), lists of duties and schedule of tasks which are clearly stated, easy access to necessary inputs, and managerial guidance and assistive devices (or other accommodation requests), efficiently offered and easily accessible (Chappel & Somers, 2010; Schall, 2010). Research (Scott et al., 2017) suggests that larger organisations are more likely to be accommodating regarding the support requests made by PWD. This may be a result of easier access to a greater number of useful resources, awareness of and compliance with the mandates contained within prevailing non-discrimination legislation, thus the goal to discharge the responsibilities of the organisation as a reputable corporate citizen (Grougiou et al., 2016; Scott et al., 2017; Udayasankar, 2008).

All employees want to be valued and recognised for their contribution, where this is absent, their levels of organisational commitment and engagement along with levels of job satisfaction are likely to be poor. Where managers and other organisational members cause neurodivergent employees to feel isolated, excluded and harmed by the absence of emotional intelligence when engaging with this cadre of staff, (and instead of contributing to defamatory derogatory gossip, focused on the disorder or the symptoms of their disorder), these marginalised employees are likely to take action to maintain their well-being, to either voluntary or involuntary separated from the organisation (Houdek, 2022; Patton, 2019; Riach & Loretto, 2009). The conclusion of the relationship in this manner is highly undesirable, particularly, as it is possible for neurodivergent employees to be outstanding, efficient and productive employees, where managers make decisions based on clear and convincing evidence, rather than relying on unproven theories (and assumptions) as to probable employment outcomes for persons with developmental disorders (Austin & Pisano, 2017; Stephenson, 2022). A paradigm shift for the inclusion and diversity discourse will occur only where organisations are committed through the zealous pursuit of inclusive employment practices to "*harness the potential of neurodivergent employees to create value for the organisation*" (Krzeminska et al., 2019: 456).

Concluding Remarks

By engaging in selective diversity, organisations are practising the *illusion of inclusion*. Otherwise stated, the concepts of diversity, inclusion, equality and accessibility are relatively new and appear to have been adopted by some organisations, (in name only), to project to relevant stakeholders, a commitment to being on the "right side" of the diversity discourse. However, this faux commitment has resulted in employment policies and practices, which, *prima facie*, are designed to create a diverse cohort of employees, but even a cursory examination of the employees will expose this as an illusion, as the status quo has been maintained, regarding the employee composition. Stereotypes and associated behaviours guided by stereotypes become institutionalised and accepted practice, such that managers may bristle at an accusation of disparate employment practices, because they view themselves and organisations as tolerant and inclusive. However, where organisations interview candidates from many backgrounds, but reject divergent applicants as not being the right fit for the vacancy, such that a pattern emerges of rejected candidates with similar attributes, the authenticity of that assertion is dubious. At its core, the notion of tolerance is offensive, insofar as it suggests that the target of one's tolerance is a burden which has been foisted upon an organisation, without consent, and must now be endured, even where it is fundamentally different from policies and practices believed to be "typical" or "acceptable".

Re-education is necessary, if the espoused changes are to be realised, namely that neuro divergent applicants and employees are assessed using objective job-related criteria, and immutable characteristics are not the primary determining factor as to whether an individual is hired or promoted. Where employment decisions are predicated on the notion that all people are equal, but some are more equal than others, the outcome will inevitably be an exclusionary one. Further, greater levels of resistance by organisation, to suggestions of revising employment policies and practices to ensure or boosts inclusion and diversity, will invariably signal an opportunity to have all employment policies audited by an external party with a view of receiving unbiased, unsanitised feedback regarding areas in which improvement is needed. Such organsations can then be monitored to ensure that the specific, deliberate steps are taken to action the suggested changes, to advance the inclusion agenda. In the Caribbean, we tend to talk about an issue *ad nauseum* before any focused, deliberate action is taken towards change. If this continues unchecked, in 10 years, the employment rate for neurodivergent individuals will remain low across the region. The time is now to convert our written commitment to the CRPD to practice, by taking immediate action to effect organisational change. Evidence is available if employers are interested in reviewing it objectively. As it relates to the CRPD, the signatory jurisdictions should want to take immediate action to effect changes. In the Caribbean region, our resources are not infinite and where people are capable of and willing to work, they should not be prohibited from so doing, and as a consequence, be forced into dependence on the distribution of social security funds or on the largess of charitable advocacy groups, in order to maintain a life of dignity.

References

Allen, S., & Carlson, G. (2003). To conceal or disclose a disabling condition? A dilemma of employment transition. *Journal of Vocational Rehabilitation, 19*(1), 19–30.

Alvarez-Galvez, J., & Rojas-Garcia, A. (2019). Measuring the impact of multiple discrimination on depression in Europe. *BMC Public Health, 19*(1), 1–11.

Austin, R. D., & Pisano, G. P. (2017). Neurodiversity as a competitive advantage. *Harvard Business Review, 95*(3), 96–103.

Bennett, D., & Gibb, Y. K. (2022). Working for Others. In *Entrepreneurship, neurodiversity and gender* (pp. 35–52). Emerald Publishing Limited.

Berrigan, P., Scott, C. W., & Zwicker, J. D. (2020). Employment, education, and income for Canadians with developmental disability: Analysis from the 2017 Canadian survey on disability. *Journal of Autism and Developmental Disorders*, 1–13. https://doi.org/10.1007/s10803-020-04603-3

Bewley, H., & George, A. (2016). *Neurodiversity at work*. National Institute of Social and Economic Research.

Beyer, S., Brown, T., Akandi, R., & Rapley, M. (2010). A comparison of quality of life outcomes for people with intellectual disabilities in supported employment, day services and employment enterprises. *Journal of Applied Research in Intellectual Disabilities, 23*(3), 290–295.

Bishop, D. (2010). Which neurodevelopmental disorders get researched and why? *PLoS ONE, 11*, e15112.

Blank, S. (2013). An historical and contemporary overview of gendered Caribbean relations. *Journal of Arts and Humanities, 2*(4), 1–10.

Brouwers, E. P. (2020). Social stigma is an underestimated contributing factor to unemployment in people with mental illness or mental health issues: Position paper and future directions. *BMC Psychology, 8*(1), 1–7.

Burt, D. B., Fuller, S. P., & Lewis, K. R. (1991). Brief report: Competitive employment of adults with autism. *Journal of Autism and Developmental Disorders, 21*(2), 237–242.

Bury, S. M., Spoor, J. R., Hayward, S. M., & Hedley, D. (2022). Supporting the mental health and well-being of autistic and other neurodivergent employees in the work environment. In *Neurodiversity in the workplace* (pp. 241–266). Routledge.

Carlson, D., & Ehrlich, N. (2006). Sources of payment for assistive technology: Findings from a national survey of persons with disabilities. *Asst Technol., 18*, 77–86.

Chappel, S. L., & Somers, B. C. (2010). Employing persons with autism spectrum disorders: A collaborative effort. *Journal of Vocational Rehabilitation, 32*(2), 117–124.

CIPD (Chartered Institute of Personnel and Development). (2018). Neurodiversity at Work, CIPD (Chartered Institute of Personnel and Development). London: United Kingdom.

Dalton, N. S. (2013). Neurodiversity & HCI. In *CHI'13 Extended abstracts on human factors in computing systems* (pp. 2295–2304). https://doi.org/10.1145/2468356.2468752

Djela, M. (2021). Change of autism narrative is required to improve employment of autistic people. *Advances in Autism, 7*(1), 86–100.

Doyle, N. (2020). Neurodiversity at work: A biopsychosocial model and the impact on working adults. *British Medical Bulletin, 135*(1), 108.

Dreaver, J., Thompson, C., Girdler, S., Adolfsson, M., Black, M. H., & Falkmer, M. (2020). Success factors enabling employment for adults on the autism spectrum from employers' perspective. *Journal of Autism and Developmental Disorders, 50*(5), 1657–1667.

Dyck, E., & Russell, G. (2020). Challenging psychiatric classification: Healthy autistic diversity the neurodiversity movement. In *Healthy minds in the twentieth century* (pp. 167–187). Palgrave Macmillan.

Earnshaw, V. A., Quinn, D. M., Kalichman, S. C., & Park, C. L. (2013). Development and psychometric evaluation of the chronic illness anticipated stigma scale. *Journal of Behavioral Medicine, 36*(3), 270–282.

Ekblad, L. (2013). Autism, personality, and human diversity: Defining neurodiversity in an iterative process using Aspie Quiz. *SAGE Open, 3*(3), 2158244013497722.

Graby, S. (2015). Neurodiversity: Bridging the gap between the disabled people's movement and the mental health system survivors' movement. In *Madness, distress and the politics of disablement* (pp. 231–244). Policy Press.

Grougiou, V., Dedoulis, E., & Leventis, S. (2016). Corporate social responsibility reporting and organizational stigma: The case of "sin" industries. *Journal of Business Research, 69*(2), 905–914.

Hampson, M. E., Watt, B. D., & Hicks, R. E. (2020). Impacts of stigma and discrimination in the workplace on people living with psychosis. *BMC Psychiatry, 20*, 1–11.

Harris, C., van der Vloodt, R. & Maddocks, J. (2020). *Championing neurodiversity and emotional intelligence in the workplace* (Executive Resilience Coaching, white paper). ERC.

Hendricks, D. (2010). Employment and adults with autism spectrum disorders: Challenges and strategies for success. *Journal of Vocational Rehabilitation, 32*(2), 125–134.

Houdek, P. (2022). Neurodiversity in (not only) public organizations: An untapped opportunity? *Administration & Society, 1*, 24.

Hume, K., Loftin, R., & Lantz, J. (2009). Increasing independence in autism spectrum disorders: A review of three focused interventions. *Journal of Autism and Developmental Disorders, 39*(9), 1329–1338.

Jaarsma, P., & Welin, S. (2012). Autism as a natural human variation: Reflections on the claims of the neurodiversity movement. *Health Care Analysis, 20*(1), 20–30.

Jenkins, K. S. (2014). *Assembling autism*. Doctoral Dissertation, City University of New York.

Kapp, S. K., Gillespie-Lynch, K., Sherman, L. E., & Hutman, T. (2013). Deficit, difference, or Both? Autism and Neurodiversity. *Developmental Psychology, 49*(1), 59.

Kirsh, B., Slack, T., & King, C. A. (2012). The nature and impact of stigma towards injured workers. *Journal of Occupational Rehabilitation, 22*(2), 143–154.

Krzeminska, A., Austin, R. D., Bruyère, S. M., & Hedley, D. (2019). The advantages and challenges of neurodiversity employment in organizations. *Journal of Management & Organization, 25*(4), 453–463.

Kwon, C. K. (2021). Resisting ableism in deliberately developmental organizations: A discursive analysis of the identity work of employees with disabilities. *Human Resource Development Quarterly, 32*(2), 179–196.

LaRue, R. H., Manente, C. J., Maraventano, J. C., Budge, J., Butler, C., Hoffmann, M. R., & Kahng, S. (2022). Employment and vocational skills for individuals with autism. In *Handbook of quality of life for individuals with autism spectrum disorder* (pp. 377–395). Springer.

Lattimore, L. P., Parsons, M. B., & Reid, D. H. (2006). Enhancing job-site training of supported workers with autism: A reemphasis on simulation. *Journal of Applied Behavior Analysis, 39*(1), 91–102.

List, T. P. (n.d.) Neurodiversity, ADHD and work: Obstacles and opportunities.

Lorenz, T., Frischling, C., Cuadros, R., & Heinitz, K. (2016). Autism and overcoming job barriers: Comparing job-related barriers and possible solutions in and outside of autism-specific employment. *PLoS ONE, 11*(1), e0147040.

MacLeod, A., Lewis, A., & Robertson, C. (2013). 'Why should I be like bloody R ain M an?!'Navigating the autistic identity. *British Journal of Special Education, 40*(1), 41–49.

Maria Szulc, J., Davies, J., Tomczak, M. T., & McGregor, F. L. (2021). AMO perspectives on the well-being of neurodivergent human capital. *Employee Relations, 43*(4), 858–872.

Mavranezouli, I., Megnin-Viggars, O., Cheema, N., Howlin, P., Baron-Cohen, S., & Pilling, S. (2014). The cost-effectiveness of supported employment for adults with autism in the United Kingdom. *Autism, 18*(8), 975–984.

Mawhood, L., & Howlin, P. (1999). The outcome of a supported employment scheme for high-functioning adults with autism or Asperger syndrome. *Autism, 3*(3), 229–254.

McKee-Ryan, F., & Harvey, J. (2011). "I have a job but…" A review of underemployment. *Journal of Management, 37*(4), 962–996.

Mellifont, D. (2022). COVID-19 related factors affecting the experiences of neurodivergent persons in the workplace: A rapid review. *Work, 71*, 1–10.

Moore, C. B., McIntyre, N. H., & Lanivich, S. E. (2021). ADHD-related neurodiversity and the entrepreneurial mindset. *Entrepreneurship Theory and Practice, 45*(1), 64–91.

Ne'eman, A., & Pellicano, E. (2022). Neurodiversity as politics. *Human Development, 66*(2), 149–157.

Ohl, A., Grice Sheff, M., Small, S., Nguyen, J., Paskor, K., & Zanjirian, A. (2017). Predictors of employment status among adults with autism spectrum disorder. *Work, 56*(2), 345–355.

Pan American Health Organization (PAHO). (2021). The burden of mental disorders in the Region of the Americas, 2000–2019.

Patton, E. (2019). Autism, attributions and accommodations: Overcoming barriers and integrating a neurodiverse workforce. *Personnel Review, 48*(4), 915–934.

Radulski, E. M. (2022). Conceptualising autistic masking, camouflaging, and neurotypical privilege: Towards a minority group model of neurodiversity. *Human Development, 66*(2), 113–127.

Riach, K., & Loretto, W. (2009). Identity work and theunemployed'worker: Age, disability and the lived experience of the older unemployed. *Work, Employment and Society, 23*(1), 102–119.

Roopnarine, J. L. (2012). Father involvement in English-speaking Caribbean families. In *Handbook of father involvement* (pp. 291–314). Routledge.

Sahu, K. K. (2015). Intervening negative impact of stigma on employability of a person with schizophrenia through social case work. *Journal of Psychosocial Rehabilitation and Mental Health, 2*(1), 87–95.

Santuzzi, A. M., & Keating, R. T. (2022). Neurodiversity and the disclosure dilemma. In *Neurodiversity in the workplace* (pp. 124–148). Routledge.

Schall, C. M. (2010). Positive behavior support: Supporting adults with autism spectrum disorders in the workplace. *Journal of Vocational Rehabilitation, 32*(2), 109.

Schur, L., Han, K., Kim, A., Ameri, M., Blanck, P., & Kruse, D. (2017). Disability at work: A look back and forward. *Journal of Occupational Rehabilitation, 27*(4), 482–497.

Scott, M., Jacob, A., Hendrie, D., Parsons, R., Girdler, S., Falkmer, T., & Falkmer, M. (2017). Employers' perception of the costs and the benefits of hiring individuals with autism spectrum disorder in open employment in Australia. *PLoS ONE, 12*(5), e0177607.

Scott, M., Milbourn, B., Falkmer, M., Black, M., Bölte, S., Halladay, A., Lerner, M., Taylor, J. L., & Girdler, S. (2019). Factors impacting employment for people with autism spectrum disorder: A scoping review. *Autism, 23*(4), 869–901.

Smith, M. J., Fleming, M. F., Wright, M. A., Losh, M., Humm, L. B., Olsen, D., & Bell, M. D. (2015). Brief report: Vocational outcomes for young adults with autism spectrum disorders at six months after virtual reality job interview training. *Journal of Autism and Developmental Disorders, 45*(10), 3364–3369.

Solomon, C. (2020). Autism and Employment: Implications for Employers and Adults with ASD. *Journal of Autism & Developmental Disorders, 50*(11), 4209–4217.

Stephenson, J. H. (2022). Efficacy of Anti-Discrimination Legislation – The Case of Autism Spectrum Disorder. In A. E. Hurley-Hanson & C. M. Giannantonio (Eds.), *Generation A (Emerald Studies in Workplace Neurodiversity)* (pp. 141–177). Bingley: Emerald Publishing Limited. https://doi.org/10.1108/978-1-80262-263-820220010

Szulc, J. M., McGregor, F. L., & Cakir, E. (2021). Neurodiversity and remote work in times of crisis: Lessons for HR. *Personnel Review, 2021*, 16–16.

Tomczak, M. T. (2022). How can the work environment be redesigned to enhance the well-being of individuals with autism?. *Employee Relations*, 1–18.

Udayasankar, K. (2008). Corporate social responsibility and firm size. *Journal of Business Ethics, 83*(2), 167–175.

Van Wieren, T. A., Armstrong, A. J., & McMahon, B. T. (2012). Autism spectrum disorders and intellectual disabilities: A comparison of ADA Title I workplace discrimination allegations. *Journal of Vocational Rehabilitation, 36*(3), 159–169.

Wehman, P., Brooke, V., Brooke, A. M., Ham, W., Schall, C., McDonough, J., & Avellone, L. (2016). Employment for adults with autism spectrum disorders: A retrospective review of a customized employment approach. *Research in Developmental Disabilities, 53*, 61–72.

Wehmeyer, M. L., Davies, D. K., Stock, S. E., & Tanis, S. (2020). Applied cognitive technologies to support the autonomy of people with intellectual and developmental disabilities. *Advances in Neurodevelopmental Disorders, 4*(4), 389–399.

Yoshimura, Y., Bakolis, I., & Henderson, C. (2018). Psychiatric diagnosis and other predictors of experienced and anticipated workplace discrimination and concealment of mental illness among mental health service users in England. *Social Psychiatry and Psychiatric Epidemiology, 53*(10), 1099–1109.

CHAPTER 7

Disability, Employment and the Law: A Caribbean Outlook

Introduction

Employment opportunities for persons with disabilities are often limited due to the structural barriers they face throughout the course of having a disability, whether it be from birth or from having acquired one later on. Disability type and severity variably affect employment outcomes. For those born with a disability, they face these barriers from very early on in life, as evidenced by their experiences with educational systems, which ultimately adversely affect their prospects of independence as adults. Limited access to educational opportunities is a fundamental concern for children with disabilities, as they are likely to face limited access to employment opportunities as adults (Aron & Loprest, 2012; Connor et al., 2008; Lavia, 2007) and remain dependent on caregivers. This prevents them from realising their full potential and consequently limits their full and equal participation in society (Jones & Serieux-Lubin, 2018). Persons with disabilities face not only unemployment, but also underemployment even where they are able to secure a job (International Labour Office, 2014). In comparison to their peers without disabilities, they experience significantly higher rates of unemployment and lower rates of employment (Gayle-Geddes, 2015; Morris, 2018), and earn less (Mora et al., 2021), putting them at a serious disadvantage. People with disabilities are more likely than persons without disabilities

J. H. Stephenson and N. Persadie, *Disability in the Workplace*, Palgrave Explorations in Workplace Stigma,
https://doi.org/10.1007/978-3-031-19340-8_7

to experience disadvantage, exclusion and discrimination in the labour market (International Labour Office, 2014), as they face unequal unemployment circumstances when compared to persons without disabilities (Gayle-Geddes, 2015).

Persons with disabilities in the Caribbean face very similar issues, such that individual governments have seen it necessary to legislate the treatment of persons with disabilities in the employment market. Most Caribbean countries have enacted laws to protect the rights of persons with disabilities within employment, education and the provision of goods and services. Discrimination against persons with disabilities in employment can take one of several approaches: discrimination against a person with a disability trying to gain or keep employment; discrimination against a person who sustains a job-related injury and becomes disabled during the course of employment; discrimination against a person who becomes disabled during the course of employment on account of a non-job-related incident and whether the disability is permanent or temporary. This is not an exhaustive list but simply highlights some of the nuances related to disabilities and employment. This chapter will review the legal protections and support provided by individual countries in addressing the challenges faced by persons with disabilities who seek or have employment. This overview is done primarily on the basis of international legal obligations and existing domestic law as it relates to disability in employment to determine how the various Caribbean governments have attempted to address such matters through law.

Disability and Employment

Employment and labour market outcomes for persons with disabilities are bleak, as they are overwhelmingly excluded from the world of work (Mora et al., 2021); this situation is largely attributable to inadequate educational opportunities and/or poor quality of available education and training (Caribbean Development Bank, 2018; UNESCO, 2021), employers' ableist attitudes and beliefs, and workplaces and work cultures that are not disability-friendly (Mora et al., 2021). Many of the challenges faced by persons with disabilities attempting to enter the labour market or retain employment bear many similarities to the issues they face in accessing education. These include inaccessible workplaces and educational and training facilities which lead to educational underachievement; inaccessible and cost-prohibitive transportation; stigma, ignorance and discrimination; and low societal expectations, among others (Ditchman et al., 2016; Gayle-Geddes, 2015; Jones & Serieux-Lubin, 2018; Mickahail & Andrews, 2018; Reynolds, Nicholls, & Alferoff, 2001; UNESCO, 2021). Challenges specific to those seeking or wishing to retain employment include unequal pay and lower wages; employer reluctance to hire persons with disabilities based on the presumed high costs of accommodation; communication challenges; inaccessible physical and non-adaptive working environments; lack of scope for growth, career advancement and better compensation; limited managerial support; employer presumption of limited productivity or unemployability of persons with disabilities; limited employment support and transitional programmes; underemployment; limited rehabilitation; gradual marginalisation of persons who become disabled while in employment; challenges with the job application and interview process; and job design tailored to exclude persons with disabilities, among others (Ditchman et al., 2016; Gayle-Geddes, 2015; International Labour Office, 2014; Mora et al., 2021; Persons, 2018; Reynolds et al., 2001).

It has been reported, however, that the provision of transition services, supported employment and vocational rehabilitation can assist persons with disabilities to secure and maintain employment (see e.g. Griffiths et al., 2016). Such services seem to contribute to better financial gain, wider social integration, increased worker satisfaction and higher self-esteem (Howlin et al., 2005). On the employer side, sensitisation programmes would assist employers in understanding how to accommodate persons with disabilities in the workplace and that accommodations are not necessarily cost prohibitive; understanding individual needs leads to a positive, productive and purposeful working environment for employees at all levels (Griffiths et al., 2016; Hurley-Hanson et al., 2020; Nachmias & Caven, 2018). It would also help employers understand the advantages of employing persons with disabilities. Benefits of a diverse workforce which encompasses persons with disabilities include competitive advantage; resolving complex business and organisational issues; increased, strong interpersonal relationships; higher productivity rate; and better ability to meet organisational goals (Mickahail & Andrews, 2018; Nachmias & Caven, 2018). It would also have the ultimate effect of dispelling negative stereotypes.

Given the numerous challenges noted above, it is not surprising that governments often turn to law as a means of redressing social issues. An enabling legal and policy environment can help with some of the challenges faced by persons with disabilities. In the case of disability, they can focus on non-discrimination, which can protect persons with disabilities from unequal treatment in employment, for example; or prohibiting discrimination on certain grounds, such as disability (International Labour Office, 2014). Laws that emphasise non-discrimination commonly include a number of protected grounds with disability being one where it is included (International Labour Office, 2014). The International Labour Office (2014) has noted that such provisions are likely to have the greatest practical impact on opportunities for disabled jobseekers and workers. Laws designed to protect and promote the rights of persons with disabilities can take the form of a comprehensive law that applies to different groups within the population or they can be disability-specific and address employment as one of several areas affecting persons with disabilities. Such laws may promote equality in terms of identical treatment; equality of opportunity, which provides for equal chances, but not necessarily equal results; or equality of results, where securing the same outcomes for all is fundamentally important (International Labour Office, 2014). This last approach can be used as an indicator of the effectiveness of measures taken to achieve equality of opportunity (International Labour Office, 2014). Some countries may choose to legislate the adoption of affirmative action measures for persons with disabilities, such as quotas, which are aimed at helping vulnerable and marginalised groups overcome structural disadvantages they experience (International Labour Office, 2014).

Disability, Employment and the Law in the Anglophone Caribbean

Twelve independent English-speaking Caribbean countries form the basis of this study: Antigua and Barbuda, The Bahamas, Barbados, Belize, Dominica, Grenada, Guyana, Jamaica, St. Kitts and Nevis, St. Lucia, St. Vincent and the Grenadines, and Trinidad and Tobago. All countries listed here are Parties to the Convention on the Rights of Persons with Disabilities (see Table 7.1) which prohibits discrimination against persons with disabilities regarding employment and promotes their equal participation and access to employment and training opportunities (art 27). It further provides that persons with disabilities should have access to public sector and private sector employment where appropriate policies and measures are implemented and where reasonable accommodations are made.

Many of the international conventions dealing with employment were issued by the International Labour Office. The two included here specifically address persons with disabilities. Article 5 of the ILO Discrimination (Employment and Occupation) Convention, 1958 (No. 111) promotes the use of special measures to meet the particular requirements of persons who, for reasons such as disablement, are generally recognised to require special protection or assistance, and which shall not be deemed to be discrimination (International Labour Organization, 2017a). All 12 countries are Parties to the Convention, as shown in Table 7.1.

Article 1(2) of the ILO Vocational Rehabilitation and Employment (Disabled Persons) Convention, 1983 (No. 159) (International Labour Organization, 2008) identifies the purpose of vocational rehabilitation to enable a disabled person to secure, retain and advance in suitable employment and thereby to further such person's integration or reintegration into society; therefore, this convention focuses solely on persons with

Table 7.1 Signatory/Accession/Ratification Status of Anglophone Caribbean Countries to three Conventions addressing Disability and Employment

Caribbean island states	*CRPD*	*C111*	*C159*
	Date of signature/accession (a)		
Antigua and Barbuda	2007	1983	–
Barbados	2007	1974	–
Belize	2011	1999	–
Dominica	2007	1983	–
Grenada	2010	2003	–
Guyana	2007	1975	–
Jamaica	2007	1975	–
St. Kitts and Nevis	2019	2000	–
St. Lucia	2011	1983	–
St. Vincent and the Grenadines	2010(a)	2001	–
The Bahamas	2013	2001	–
Trinidad and Tobago	2007	1970	1999

CRPD: Convention on the Rights of Persons with Disabilities
C111: ILO Discrimination (Employment and Occupation) Convention, 1958
C159: ILO Vocational Rehabilitation and Employment (Disabled Persons) Convention, 1983
Source Compiled by author from United Nations (2014); International Labour Organization (2017b, 2017c)

disabilities and their relationship with employment. Article 4 emphasises equality of opportunity and treatment and the use of special measures to ensure these are met and are guaranteed by law (Article 6) and the provision of training (Article 7), employment services (Article 8) and rehabilitation counsellors (Article 9). Of the twelve countries under study here, only Trinidad and Tobago is a party to this Convention (see Table 7.1).

Laws of each of the countries were reviewed at the domestic level as they relate to the intersection of disability and employment, and equality in jurisdictions that have enacted such laws. It should be noted that some of the country's laws were not easily available or accessible and therefore could not be reviewed or included. This section provides a review of the domestic legal framework of each of the twelve countries under study as it relates to dealing with disability and employment. This review will help in understanding how specific laws provide (or not) for persons with disabilities in the workplace in the Anglophone Caribbean.

Antigua and Barbuda

Antigua and Barbuda is one of four Caribbean countries with legislation that addresses disability (see Table 7.2). The *Disabilities and Equal Opportunities Act* (2017) specifically protects persons with disabilities from any form of discrimination on the basis of disability (s 14). Section 20 prohibits an employer from discriminating against a person with a disability as it relates to recruitment, promotion, equal opportunities and equal pay, continuance of employment and union rights. The employer is required to make reasonable accommodations to facilitate the work of a person with disabilities (s 20(2)) and must redeploy persons with disabilities as required by any change in that person's circumstance (s 21), once it does not cause undue hardship to the employer. This is complemented by the right of a person with disabilities to education and training without discrimination and on the basis of equal opportunity (s 17).

The other three pieces of legislation that apply to employment and disability are the *Labour Code*, Cap. 27, the *Social Security Act*, Cap. 408, and the *Workmen's Compensation Act*, Cap. 475. The Labour Code makes allowances for reasonable breaks in employment on account of physical

Table 7.2 Anglophone Caribbean Countries with legislation for disability, equal opportunities, non-discrimination and special measures in employment

Caribbean countries	*LAW*			
	Disability	*Equal opportunities*	*Non-discrimination*	*Special measures*
Antigua and Barbuda	✓	✓	✓	
Barbados		✓	✓	✓
Belize				✓
Dominica				
Grenada			✓	✓
Guyana	✓	✓	✓	✓
Jamaica	✓		✓	
St. Kitts and Nevis				
St. Lucia		✓	✓	✓
St. Vincent and the Grenadines				
The Bahamas	✓	✓	✓	✓
Trinidad and Tobago		✓	✓	

Source Compiled by author from the laws of each country

disability (s C2(2)); the *Social Security Act* makes provisions for the enactment of regulations to deal with disablement benefits; and the *Workmen's Compensation Act* addresses disability payments.

Barbados

Barbados does not have any disability legislation or formal policy nor is there a single, comprehensive repository of laws available online. Employment matters are addressed through a number of pieces of legislation, three of which address disability benefits (*Casual Employees Pensions Act*, Cap. 20; *National Insurance and Social Security Act*, Cap. 47; *Occupational Pension Benefits Act*, Cap. 350B); one of which requires notification of accidents at work that cause disablement (*Accidents and Occupational Diseases (Notification) Act*, Cap. 338); and one of which relates to the safety, health and welfare of employees at work (*Safety and Health at Work*

Act, Cap. 356) but does not address disability in any way. The *Factories Act*, Cap. 347 makes no mention of disability in any way.

Disability is addressed in two key pieces of employment legislation. The *Employment (Prevention) of Discrimination Act*, 2020 seeks to protect persons from discrimination related to employment. Section 3(2)(p) identifies disability as a ground of discrimination. Sections 4–7 address the prevention of discrimination against persons in relation to job creation and recruitment, employment and medical testing as a precondition for employment (ss 4–6). The employer is required to make reasonable adjustments for employees with disabilities at their request (s 7), except where doing so will create unjustifiable hardship for the employer (s 9). Section 10 permits the employer to adopt measures to promote equality of opportunity for disadvantaged groups as necessary without such action being deemed discriminatory. *The Employment Rights Act*, 2012–9 works in harmony with, but in deference to, the *Employment (Prevention) of Discrimination Act*, prohibiting the dismissal of an employee who is or was disabled regardless of how the disability resulted where the employer could have offered alternative employment (s 30(1)(c)(vii)).

Belize

Belize has incorporated all ILO conventions which it has ratified into its local law through the *International Labour Organization Conventions Act*, Cap. 304:01. This means that all provisions relating to the ILO Discrimination (Employment and Occupation) Convention, 1958 have the force of law in Belize; however, there is no separate or specific disability legislation. The *Labour Act*, Cap. 297 prohibits the dismissal of an employee due to disability. The *Social Security Act*, Cap. 44 and the *Workmen's Compensation Act*, Cap. 303 provide for disablement benefits.

Dominica

Dominica has no disability legislation or formal policy. There are some four pieces of legislation which address employment, one of which makes provisions for the enactment of regulations to deal with disablement benefits (*Social Security Act*, Cap. 31:01); and another which requires notification of accidents at work that cause disablement (*Accidents and Occupational Diseases (Notification) Act*, Cap. 89:51). The *Employment Safety Act*, Cap. 90:08 makes no reference to disability whatsoever. There is a *Labour Standards Act*, Cap. 89:05, dated 1977, which addresses "handicapped person[s]" who, for the purposes of gainful employment, the Labour Commissioner may authorise the employment of said person "at a wage lower than the minimum wage" (s 7), except where a minimum wage for a particular occupation or category has been fixed by law (s 8).

Grenada

Grenada's *Employment Act*, Cap. 89 prohibits discrimination against an employee on several grounds, including disability (s 26(1)), and allows for special measures to be implemented to better the conditions of disadvantaged individuals (s 26(2)). The Act further notes the invalidity of disability as a reason for dismissal or disciplinary action (s 74(2)(a)). The *Labour Relations Act*, Cap. 157A, which allows for freedom of association, prohibits discrimination against a member on several grounds, including disability, and also promotes the implementation of special measures for disadvantaged individuals (s 28).

The *National Insurance Act*, Cap. 205 and the *Social Security (OECS Convention) Act*, Cap. 307A provide for disablement benefits while the *Social Security (CARICOM Agreement) Act*, Cap. 307A provides for disablement pensions.

Guyana

Guyana is another country of the group of four with disability legislation (see Table 7.2). The *Persons with Disabilities Act*, Cap. 36:05 was enacted to honour the country's obligations under the Convention on the Rights of Persons with Disabilities. The Act provides for equal access to opportunities for employment on the same terms, conditions and compensation packages as a person who does not have a disability (s 8(1), (3)). Discrimination by employers is prohibited in job advertisements, recruitment, classification of posts, determination of compensation packages, candidate selection and provision of employment-related facilities (s 8(2)). This is supported by the right of a person with disabilities to access vocational training, skills development and training programmes which are to be provided by the government (s 12). The *Persons with Disabilities Act* is complemented by the provision of the *Prevention of Discrimination Act*, Cap. 99:08 which prohibits discrimination on a variety of grounds, including disability. Discrimination by employers is prohibited as it relates to recruitment and selection; training and apprenticeship; terms and conditions of employment; health and safety measures; provision of employment-related facilities; access to employment-related training, benefits or services; retrenchment or dismissal; or subjecting the employee to any other disadvantage (s 5). The Act allows for special measures to promote equality of opportunity in employment without such action being deemed discriminatory (s 7).

The *Occupational Safety and Health Act*, Cap. 99:06 addresses disability only inasmuch as it requires notification of accidents at work that cause disablement (s 69). The *National Insurance and Social Security Act*, Cap. 36:01 provides for disablement benefits.

Jamaica

Jamaica is one of the four Caribbean countries that has a dedicated law addressing disability (see Table 7.2). *The Disabilities Act* (2014) promotes, protects and ensures the full and equal enjoyment by persons with disabilities of privileges, interests, benefits and treatment on an equal basis with others. The Act protects job applicants and employees from discrimination on the basis of disability in relation to the terms of employment; opportunities at work for training, transfer, promotion; and dismissal (s 29). The employer is required to make reasonable adjustments to accommodate an employee with disabilities (s 30) or redeploy that employee as required by any change in that person's circumstance, once it does not cause undue burden to the employer (s 31). This is complemented by the right of a person with disabilities to education and training without discrimination (s 26).

The Factories Act addresses disability only inasmuch as it requires notification of accidents at work that cause disablement (s 21). *The National Insurance Act* makes provisions for disablement pensions and *The Workmen's Compensation Act* provides for disability payments.

St. Kitts and Nevis

St. Kitts and Nevis does not have any disability legislation or formal policy. There are some four pieces of legislation which address employment, one of which provides for disablement benefits (*Social Security Act*, Cap. 22.10); and two which require notification of accidents at work that cause disablement (*Accidents and Occupational Diseases (Notification) Act*, Cap. 9:01 and the *Labour Act*, Cap. 18.18). The *Factories Act*, Cap. 18.12 makes no mention whatsoever of disability.

St. Lucia

St. Lucia has a *Labour Act*, Cap. 16.04 which has repealed a number of other pieces of legislation relating to employment and addresses it comprehensively. The Act prohibits an employer from discriminating against applicants and employees on numerous grounds, including disability, in respect of "recruitment, training, work facilities or service, promotion, terms and conditions of employment or benefit arising out of the employment relationship" (s 7(1)). The Act also allows for special measures to be implemented to better the conditions of disadvantaged individuals (s 7(2)). Employers are required to reasonably accommodate persons with disabilities in employment and the workplace. The Act prohibits dismissal or disciplinary action on the basis of disability (s 131(1)(a)). There is a requirement to give notification of accidents at work that cause disablement (s 246), previously the remit of the *Employees (Occupational Health and Safety) Act*. Part V of the Act incorporates the relevant provisions of the former *Equality of Opportunity and Treatment in Employment and Occupation Act* and prohibits discrimination which would "impair equality of opportunity or treatment in occupation or employment" on the basis of disability, among multiple other grounds (s 267). Specifically, discrimination by employers is prohibited as it relates to recruitment and selection; training; terms and conditions of employment; safety and health measures; provision of employment-related facilities; access to employment-related training, benefits or services; retrenchment or dismissal; or subjecting the employee to any other disadvantage (s 268). This is complemented by the right of a person with disabilities to technical vocational training without discrimination (s 276). The *National Insurance Corporation Act*, Cap. 16.01 provides for disablement benefits.

St. Vincent and the Grenadines

St. Vincent and the Grenadines does not have any disability legislation or formal policy nor is there a single, comprehensive repository of laws available online. In fact, laws were not easily accessible or available for review.

The *Protection of Employment Act* (2003) deals with unfair dismissal and severance pay; disability is not included as one of the grounds for which an employee may not be terminated (s 16). The *Factories Act*, Cap. 335 makes no mention whatsoever of disability. The *National Insurance Act*, Cap. 296 and *National Insurance (Employment Injury Benefits) Regulations*, 1997 provide for disablement benefits.

The Bahamas

The Bahamas is one of the group of four countries with legislation that addresses disability (see Table 7.2). The *Persons with Disabilities (Equal Opportunities) Act*, 2014 was enacted to honour the country's obligations under the Convention on the Rights of Persons with Disabilities. The Act provides for equal access to opportunities for employment on the same terms, conditions and compensation packages as employees without disabilities (s 14). Interestingly, the Act legislates a quota of one per cent of persons with disabilities to be employed where there are more than one hundred employees (s 14(3)). The Act mandates the design and implementation of vocational training skills, development and training programmes to develop the skills of persons with disabilities (s 15). Discrimination by employers is prohibited in job advertisements, recruitment, creation and abolition of posts, determination of compensation packages, candidate selection and provision of employment-related facilities (s 16(1)). Employers are required to make reasonable accommodations for persons with disabilities (s 16 (7)). This is complemented by a right of a person with disabilities to access quality education and training (ss 31–32).

Despite the very progressive approach of the *Persons with Disabilities (Equal Opportunities) Act*, the *Employment Act*, Cap. 321A permits employers to hire a person with disabilities at a lesser rate of pay where that person cannot be accommodated without undue hardship (s 7). The *National Insurance Act*, Cap. 350 provides for disablement benefits.

Trinidad and Tobago

Trinidad and Tobago has no disability legislation but does have a national policy on persons with disabilities which fully supports the enactment of relevant legislation to address employment matters, among other areas of concern (Ministry of Social Development and Family Services, 2019).

The country has an *Equal Opportunities Act*, Ch. 22:03 which prohibits certain kinds of discrimination and promotes equality of opportunity. The Act specifically prohibits discrimination in relation to employment (s 4(a)) on a number of grounds including disability. Such discrimination applies to applicants in the recruitment and selection process, and terms and conditions of employment (s 8); it also applies to employees in relation to the terms and conditions of their employment, access to opportunities for promotion, transfer or training, and dismissal (s 9). Persons' right to vocational training complement these protections (s 10). Nevertheless, where meeting these requirements poses unjustifiable hardship to the employer or presents an unreasonable possibility of risk of injury to others or to the person with the disability, these requirements no longer apply (s 14).

The *National Insurance Act*, Ch. 32:01 provides for disablement benefits, grants and pensions and the *Workmen's Compensation Act*, Ch. 88:05 provides for disability payments. Under the *Occupational Safety and Health Act*, Ch. 88:08, a notice of injury leading to disability is required under section 46A.

Discussion

All legislation under review examines how legislation from each country addresses disability, employment, equal opportunities and non-discrimination in employment, and any special measures included for hiring persons with disabilities (see Table 7.2).

As noted above, legislation enacted to protect persons with disabilities from discrimination or promote their right to equal opportunities generally takes one of two forms: a comprehensive law that prohibit discrimination on various grounds or status, such as disability, and therefore applies to various disadvantaged or marginalised groups. Laws such as the *Equal Opportunities Act* of Trinidad and Tobago or the *Prevention of Discrimination Act* of Guyana would fall into this first category. The second form such legislation takes is disability-specific laws that also prohibit discrimination and generally promotes the provision of equal opportunities, sometimes through the implementation of temporary, special measures, in a variety of social areas, including employment. Examples of laws falling into this second category include the *Disabilities and Equal Opportunities Act* of Antigua and Barbuda; the *Persons with Disabilities* Act of Guyana; *The Disabilities Act* of Jamaica; and *The Persons with Disabilities (Equal Opportunities) Act* of The Bahamas. A third category exists that specifically prohibits discrimination in employment against persons of differing characteristics, including disability. Such legislation includes the *Employment (Prevention) of Discrimination Act* of Barbados; the *Employment Act* of Grenada; and the *Labour Act* of St. Lucia. Belize has incorporated various ILO conventions into its domestic law through the *International Labour Organization Conventions Act*, therefore, the principles and provisions of any of the employment conventions which address disability, such as the *Discrimination (Employment and Occupation) Convention*, 1958 (No. 111) must be implemented. Table 7.3 summarises the three types of laws enacted in each country. Dominica, St. Kitts and Nevis, and St. Vincent and the Grenadines have no legislation of any of the three types (see Table 7.3). In other cases, legislation makes financial provisions for employment-related disability through disablement benefits, grants or pensions.

Six countries' legislation includes provisions for the adoption of special, temporary measures, as a form of affirmative action, with the goal of promoting equality of opportunity in employment (Barbados, Belize, Grenada, Guyana, St. Lucia, The Bahamas). Interestingly, section 10(3)

Table 7.3 Anglophone Caribbean Countries with disability legislation addressing employment matters that is comprehensive, disability-specific or employment-specific

Caribbean countries	*LAW*		
	Comprehensive	*Disability-specific*	*Employment-specific*
Antigua and Barbuda		✓	
Barbados			✓
Belize			✓
Dominica			
Grenada			✓
Guyana	✓	✓	
Jamaica		✓	
St. Kitts and Nevis			
St. Lucia			✓
St. Vincent and the Grenadines			
The Bahamas		✓	
Trinidad and Tobago	✓		

Source Compiled by author from the reviews of the laws of each country

of the *Persons with Disabilities (Equal Opportunities) Act* of The Bahamas mandates a quota: "Every employer having more than one hundred employees shall employ not less than one percent of qualified persons with disabilities". This is the only country in the Anglophone Caribbean to legislate a quota requirement as part of its special measures. Whether this is implemented by employers or enforced by the government is unclear. Additionally, while an undoubtedly positive inclusion, the effectiveness and need for disability quotas in employment (legislation) are questioned in the context of wider anti-discrimination policy and legal approaches (Sargeant et al., 2016).

Caveats to these positive provisions include unjustifiable or undue hardship to employers, inherent requirements of the job and substantial risk to self (employees with disabilities) or unreasonable risk to others, however, it is not clear how "unjustifiable" or "undue" are quantified. The Equal Opportunity Commission of Trinidad and Tobago, which works towards the elimination of discrimination and the promotion of equality and good relations between persons of different statuses, has created guidelines for employers on disability that can help answer this (Equal Opportunity Commission of Trinidad and Tobago, 2018). "Unjustifiable hardship" is an action that requires significant or considerable difficulty or expense in the implementation of reasonable accommodation. The effectiveness of the accommodation and the extent to which it would seriously disrupt the operation of the business must be taken into consideration in carrying out this assessment (Equal Opportunity Commission of Trinidad and Tobago, 2018). While this does not provide an actual means of quantification, it must be that the cost–benefit analysis of providing the reasonable accommodation will prove that the measure is not cost-effective. Presumably, the results of any such assessment will differ based on the size of the employer, number of disabled workers already employed, public funding available and length of the envisaged employment contract (International Labour Office, 2014.) The assessment must also consider the impact of providing or not providing the measure to the employee (Department of Labour, South Africa, n.d.), particularly, as such measures are meant to provide redress to employees with disabilities.

In addition to these laws, legislation related to work in factories, as addressed in the *Factories Acts*, is often updated and replaced by occupational safety and health legislation, which provide for the safety, health and welfare of persons employed, ordinarily deals with disability even if only as it concerns the notification of accidents that result in disability. Of the four countries with such legislation, only the *Factories Act* of Jamaica includes a provision for notification. Where occupational safety and health legislation has been enacted, notification requirements exist for Jamaica and Trinidad and Tobago only. St. Lucia adopted a *Labour Act* which comprehensively codifies employment matters; it is here that the notification of accidents that result in disability is required.

Not all aspects of laws addressing disability and employment are positive. The *Employment Act* of the Bahamas permits employers to hire a person with disabilities at a lesser rate of pay where that person cannot be accommodated without undue hardship (s 7). The law in Dominica is written in a much more unfortunate, even offensive, manner. The *Labour Standards Act*, dated 1977, not only authorises the payment of wages "at a wage lower than the minimum wage" (s 7) but addresses persons with disabilities as "handicapped person[s]". This terminology is considered offensive, inappropriate and outdated (International Labour Office, 2014); the date of the Act makes it 45-years old, but it needs to be amended and updated as a matter of urgent political correctness.

Conclusion

Most countries of the Anglophone Caribbean have found it necessary to enact laws that protect and promote the rights of persons with disabilities in employment, whether through disability-specific legislation that prohibits discrimination against persons in different spheres of socio-economic activity, including employment, or employment-specific legislation that also prohibits discrimination against persons with disabilities and other specific characteristics and promotes access to equal opportunities in employment. Two countries have taken an even more progressive approach by adopting comprehensive laws that prohibit discrimination on various grounds or status, such as disability, seeking to ameliorate the position of disadvantaged groups. The adoption of special, temporary measures forms part of the laws of half the countries under study as a form of affirmative action, with the goal of promoting equality of opportunity in employment to "redress the effects of past discrimination" against historically disadvantaged groups (International Labour Office, 2014), such as persons with disabilities. The requirement to implement such measures can be waived in cases of unjustifiable hardship or burden to the employer. Remarkably, one country has chosen to legislate a disability quota for employers of a certain size. Conversely, there are three countries that do not cater in any practical way to the advancement of persons with disabilities in the area of employment. Two countries have what can only be referred to as regressive legislative provisions that permit the payment of lower wages to persons with disabilities, in one case where it is in the "best interest" of that person to be so employed and, in the other, where the employment of persons with disabilities will result in undue hardship to the employer. This seems like one instance where the application of the principle of undue hardship should not be permitted. Other laws dealing with disability in employment focus on financial compensation.

Despite all these legislative advancements, for the most part, lower rates of employment are persistent for persons with disabilities in the Caribbean largely due to their exclusion from quality education in addition to general societal and employer stigma and discrimination. It is only through public and workplace sensitisation, formal and informal education and training that such attitudes can change. This can be achieved through law by mandating such education and training for employers and employees alike. Access to quality education, training and lifelong learning opportunities, which is already problematic for persons with disabilities, from early childhood into adulthood, provides a key to such persons being able to realise their full potential in the workplace and participate in and contribute to society on their own terms.

References

Aron, L., & Loprest, P. (2012). Disability and the education system. *The Future of Children*, *22*(1), 97–122.

Caribbean Development Bank. (2018). Technical Assistance–Disability Assessment in Borrowing Member Countries. Paper BD 16/18. Bridgetown: Caribbean Development Bank..

Connor, D., Gabel, S., Gallagher, D., & Morton, M. (2008). Disability studies and inclusive education—implications for theory, research, and practice. *International Journal of Inclusive Education*, *12*(5–6), 441–457. https://doi.org/10.1080/13603110802377

Department of Labour, South Africa. (n.d.). *Technical Assistance Guidelines on the Employment of Persons with Disabilities*. Department of Labour. Available from http://aut2know.co.za/wp/wp-content/uploads/Technical-Assistance-Guidelines-on-the-employment-of-people-with-disabilities.pdf.

Ditchman, N., Kosyluk, K., Lee, E., & Jones, N. (2016). How stigma affects the lives of people with intellectual disabilities: An overview. In K. Scior &

S. Werner (Eds.), *Intellectual disability and stigma* (pp. 31–48). Palgrave Macmillian. https://doi.org/10.1057/978-1-137-52499-7_3.

Equal Opportunity Commission of Trinidad and Tobago. (2018). *Guidelines for employers on disability in Trinidad and Tobago.* Equal Opportunity Commission of Trinidad and Tobago.

Gayle-Geddes, A. (2015). *Disability and inequality: Socioeconomic imperatives and public policy in Jamaica.* Palgrave MacMillan.

Gjaltema, T., Gonzales, C., & Ebbeson, L. (2011). *An analysis of the status of implementation of the convention on the rights of persons with disabilities in the Caribbean.* ECLAC – Studies and Perspectives Series – The Caribbean – No. 15. UN ECLAC.

Griffiths, A. J., Giannantonio, C. M., Hurley-Hanson, A. E., & Cardinal, D. N. (2016). Autism in the workplace: Assessing the transition needs of young adults with autism spectrum disorder. *Journal of Business and Management, 22*(1), 5–22.

Heron, R., & Murray, B. (2003). *Assisting disabled persons in finding employment: A practical guide.* International Labour Office.

Howlin, P., Alcock, J., & Burkin, C. (2005). An 8 year follow-up of a specialist supported employment service for high-ability adults with autism or Asperger syndrome. *SAGE Publications and the National Autistic Society, 9*(5), 533–549. https://doi.org/10.1177/1362361305057871

Hurley-Hanson, A. E., Giannantonio, C. M., & Griffiths, A. J. (2020). *Autism in the workplace: Creating positive employment and career outcomes for generation A.* Palgrave.

International Labour Office. (2008). *ILO Vocational Rehabilitation and Employment (Disabled Persons) Convention (No. 159) and Recommendation (No. 168); United Nations Convention on the Rights of Persons with Disabilities.* International Labour Office.

International Labour Office. (2014). *Achieving equal employment opportunities for people with disabilities through legislation: Guidelines.* International Labour Office.

International Labour Organization. (2017a). Discrimination (Employment and Occupation) Convention, 1958 (No. 111). Retrieved April 08, 2021, from https://www.ilo.org/dyn/normlex/en/f?p=normlexpub:12100:0::no::p12100_ilo_code:c111

International Labour Organization. (2017b). Ratifications of C111 - Discrimination (Employment and Occupation) Convention, 1958 (No. 111). https://www.ilo.org/dyn/normlex/en/f?p=1000:11300:0::no:11300:p11300_instrument_id:312256

International Labour Organization. (2017c). Ratifications of C159 - Vocational Rehabilitation and Employment (Disabled Persons) convention, 1983 (No.

159). https://www.ilo.org/dyn/normlex/en/f?p=normlexpub:11300:0::no::p11300_instrument_id:312304
Jones, F., & Serieux-Lubin, L. (2018). *Disability, human rights and public policy in the Caribbean: A situation analysis*. ECLAC – Studies and Perspectives Series – The Caribbean – No. 64. UN ECLAC. Retrieved April 05, 2021, from https://www.cepal.org/sites/default/files/publication/files/43306/S1701279_en.pdf
Lavia, J. (2007). Girls and special education in the Caribbean. *Support for Learning, 22*(4), 189–196.
Morris, F. (2018). An inclusive, equitable and prosperous Caribbean: The case of persons with disabilities. *Social and Economic Studies, 67*(4), 95–119.
Mickahail, B., & Andrews, K. (2018). Embracing people with special needs and disabilities. In C. T. E. de Aquino & R. W. Robertson (Eds), *Diversity and inclusion in the global workplace: Aligning initiatives with strategic business goals* (pp. 139–152). Palgrave Macmillan.
Ministry of Social Development and Family Services, Government of Trinidad and Tobago. (2019). National Policy on Persons with Disabilities. Ministry of Social Development and Family Services.
Mora, G., Elena, M., Orellana, S., & Freire, G. (2021). *Disability inclusion in Latin America and the Caribbean: A path to sustainable development*. World Bank.
Nachmias, S., & Caven, V. (2018). Introduction to 'hidden' inequalities in the workplace. In S. Nachmias & V. Caven (Eds.), *Hidden inequalities in the workplace: A guide to the current challenges, issues and business solutions* (pp. 1–16). Palgrave Macmillian.
Pegus, C. (2007). *Review and analysis of compliance of the National Labour Legislation of Saint Vincent and the Grenadines with CARICOM Model Labour Laws*. Available from https://www.ilo.org/wcmsp5/groups/public/---americas/---ro-lima/---sro-port_of_spain/documents/projectdocumentation/wcms_305929.pdf
Persons, H. (2018). *Persons with disabilities in Trinidad & Tobago: A situational analysis*. Commonwealth of Learning.
Reynolds, G., Nicholls, P., & Alferoff, C. (2001). Disabled people, (re)training and employment: A qualitative exploration of exclusion. In M. Noon & E. Ogbonna (Eds.), *Equality, diversity and disadvantage in employment* (pp. 190–207). Palgrave Macmillan.
Sargeant, M., Radevich-Katsaroumpa, E., & Innesti, A. (2016). Disability quotas: Past or future policy? *Economic and Industrial Democracy, 1–18*. https://doi.org/10.1177/0143831X16639655
UNESCO. (2021). *Training manual for the meaningful inclusion of persons with disabilities*. UNESCO.

United Nations. (2014). *Status of ratification interactive dashboard*. United Nations Human Rights, Office of the High Commissioner. Available from https://indicators.ohchr.org/

Laws

Antigua and Barbuda

Disabilities and Equal Opportunities Act, 2017. Available from http://laws.gov.ag/wp-content/uploads/2019/04/No.-32-of-2017-Disabilities-and-Equal-Opportunities-Act-2017.pdf

The Antigua and Barbuda Labour Code, Cap. 27. Available from http://laws.gov.ag/wp-content/uploads/2018/08/cap-27.pdf

The Social Security Act, Cap. 408. Available from http://laws.gov.ag/wp-content/uploads/2018/08/cap-408.pdf

The Workmen's Compensation Act, Cap. 475. Available from http://laws.gov.ag/wp-content/uploads/2018/08/cap-475.pdf

Barbados

Accidents and Occupational Diseases (Notification) Act, Cap. 338. Available from http://www.barbadosparliament-laws.com/en/ShowPdf/338.pdf

Casual Employees Pensions Act, Cap. 20. Available from http://www.barbadosparliament-laws.com/en/ShowPdf/20.pdf

Employment (Prevention) of Discrimination Bill, 2020. Available from https://www.barbadosparliament.com/uploads/bill_resolution/06948a67143d62e36c426fbd077e1055.pdf

Employment Rights Act, 2012–9. Available from https://www.ilo.org/dyn/natlex/docs/ELECTRONIC/94144/110398/F-749620620/BRB94144.pdf

Factories Act, Cap. 347. Available from http://www.barbadosparliament-laws.com/en/ShowPdf/347.pdf

National Insurance and Social Security Act, Cap. 47. Available from http://www.barbadosparliament-laws.com/en/ShowPdf/47.pdf

Occupational Pension Benefits Act, Cap. 350B. Available from http://www.barbadosparliament-laws.com/en/ShowPdf/350B.pdf

Safety and Health at Work Act, Cap. 356. Available from http://www.barbadosparliament-laws.com/en/ShowPdf/356.pdf

Belize

International Labour Organization Conventions Act, Cap. 304:01. (Revised Edition 2020). Available from https://www.agm.gov.bz/wp-content/uploads/2021/11/Cap.-304.01-International-Labour-Organization-Conventions-Act.pdf

Labour Act, Cap. 297. (Revised Edition 2020). Available from https://www.agm.gov.bz/wp-content/uploads/2022/05/Cap.-297-Labour-Act.pdf

Social Security Act, Cap. 44. Available from https://www.agm.gov.bz/wp-content/uploads/2021/11/Cap.-44-Social-Security-Act.pdf

Workmen's Compensation Act, Cap. 303. (Revised Edition 2020). Available from https://www.agm.gov.bz/wp-content/uploads/2021/11/Cap.-303-Workmens-Compensation-Act.pdf

Dominica

Accidents and Occupational Diseases (Notification) Act, Cap. 89:51. Available from https://www.dominica.gov.dm/laws/chapters/chap89-51.pdf

Employment Safety Act, Cap. 90:08. Available from https://www.dominica.gov.dm/laws/chapters/chap90-08.pdf

Labour Standards Act, Cap. 89:05. Available from https://www.dominica.gov.dm/laws/chapters/chap89–05.pdf

Social Security Act, Cap. 31:01. Available from https://www.dominica.gov.dm/laws/chapters/chap31-01.pdf

Grenada

Employment Act, Cap. 89. Available from https://laws.gov.gd/

Labour Relations Act, Cap. 157A. Available from https://laws.gov.gd/

National Insurance Act, Cap. 205. Available from https://laws.gov.gd/

Social Security (CARICOM Agreement) Act, Cap. 307A. Available from https://laws.gov.gd/

Social Security (OECS Convention) Act, Cap. 307A. Available from https://laws.gov.gd/

Guyana

Equal Rights Act, Cap. 38:01. Available from https://mola.gov.gy/sites/default/files/Cap.%203801.pdf

Labour Act, Cap. 98:01. Available from https://mola.gov.gy/sites/default/files/Cap.%209801.pdf

Persons with Disabilities Act, Cap. 36:05. Available from https://mola.gov.gy/sites/default/files/Cap.%203605%20Person%20with%20Disabilities.pdf

Prevention of Discrimination Act, Cap. 99:08. Available from https://mola.gov.gy/sites/default/files/Cap.%209908.pdf

National Insurance and Social Security Act, Cap. 36:01. Available from https://mola.gov.gy/sites/default/files/Cap.%2036.01%20National%20Insurance%20%26%20Social%20Security.pdf

Occupational Safety and Health Act, Cap. 99:06. Available from https://mola.gov.gy/sites/default/files/Cap.%209906.pdf

Jamaica

The Disabilities Act, 2014. Available from https://japarliament.gov.jm/attachments/341_The%20Disabilities%20bill%202014%20No.13.pdf

The Factories Act, last amended 2009. Available from https://laws.moj.gov.jm/library/statute/the-factories-act

The National Insurance Act, last amended 2016. Available from https://laws.moj.gov.jm/library/statute/the-national-insurance-act

The Workmen's Compensation Act. Available from https://laws.moj.gov.jm/library/statute/the-workmens-compensation-act

St. Kitts and Nevis

Accidents and Occupational Diseases (Notification) Act, Cap. 9.01. Available from https://aglcskn.info/wp-content/documents/Act02and09TOC/Ch-09_01-Accidents-Occupational-Diseases-Notification-Act.pdf

Factories Act, Cap. 18.12. Available from https://aglcskn.info/documents/Act02and09TOC/Ch%2018.12%20Factories%20Act.pdf

Labour Act, Cap. 18.18. Available from https://aglcskn.info/wp-content/documents/Act02and09TOC/Ch-18_18-Labour-Act.pdf

Social Security Act, Cap. 22.10. Available from https://aglcskn.info/wp-content/documents/Act17TOC/Ch-22_10-Social-Security-Act.pdf

St. Lucia

Employees (Occupational Health and Safety) Act, Cap. 16.02. Available from https://www.govt.lc/media.govt.lc/www/resources/legislation/EmployeesOccupationalHealthandSafetyAct.pdf

Equality of Opportunity and Treatment in Employment and Occupation Act, Cap. 16.14. Available from https://www.ilo.org/wcmsp5/groups/public/---ed_protect/---protrav/---ilo_aids/documents/legaldocument/wcms_127741.pdf

Labour Code, 2006. Available from https://www.govt.lc/media.govt.lc/www/resources/legislation/SaintLuciaLabourCode2006.pdf

National Insurance Corporation Act, Cap. 16.01. Available from https://www.ilo.org/dyn/natlex/docs/ELECTRONIC/60635/128159/F781131238/LCA60635%202005.pdf

St. Vincent and the Grenadines

Factories Act, Cap. 335 (Revised Edition 1990). Available from https://www.ilo.org/dyn/legosh/en/f?p=14100:1100:0::NO::P1100_ISO_CODE3,P1100_SUBCODE_CODE,P1100_YEAR:VCT,,2015

National Insurance Act, Cap. 296. Available from https://www.ilo.org/dyn/natlex/docs/ELECTRONIC/54275/88412/F1313009582/VCT54275%202007.pdf

National Insurance (Employment Injury Benefits) Regulations, 1997. Available from https://www.ilo.org/dyn/natlex/natlex4.detail?p_lang=en&p_isn=54275

Protection of Employment Act, 2003. Available from https://www.ilo.org/dyn/natlex/docs/ELECTRONIC/80807/87478/F414224706/VCT80807.pdf

The Bahamas

Employment Act, Cap. 321A. Available from http://laws.bahamas.gov.bs/cms/images/legislation/principal/2001/2001-0027/EmploymentAct_1.pdf

National Insurance Act, Cap. 350. Available from http://laws.bahamas.gov.bs/cms/images/LEGISLATION/PRINCIPAL/1972/1972-0021/NationalInsuranceAct_1.pdf

Persons with Disabilities (Equal Opportunities) Act, 2014. Available from http://laws.bahamas.gov.bs/cms/images/LEGISLATION/PRINCIPAL/2014/2014-0031/PersonswithDisabilitiesEqualOpportunitiesAct2014_1.pdf

Trinidad and Tobago

Equal Opportunities Act, Ch. 22:03. (Revised Laws of Trinidad and Tobago, 2016). Available from https://agla.gov.tt/downloads/laws/22.03.pdf

National Insurance Act, Ch. 32:01. (Revised Laws of Trinidad and Tobago, 2016). Available from https://agla.gov.tt/downloads/laws/32.01.pdf

Occupational Safety and Health Act, Ch. 88:08. (Revised Laws of Trinidad and Tobago, 2016). Available from https://agla.gov.tt/downloads/laws/88.08.pdf

Workmen's Compensation Act, Ch. 88:05. (Revised Laws of Trinidad and Tobago, 2016). Available from https://agla.gov.tt/downloads/laws/88.05.pdf

CHAPTER 8

Disability, Employment and the Law: Lessons for Caribbean Countries from Australia and the United Kingdom

Introduction

Employment opportunities for persons with disabilities are limited due to a variety of factors, starting with limited access to (quality) education as children which leaves them unprepared for employment, ultimately leading to poor workforce participation when they become of age to enter the workforce. At this stage, attitudinal, physical and structural barriers compound the effect of exclusion in the workplace. Statistically, it is challenging to indicate how many persons with disabilities are excluded from employment, as data on persons with disabilities in employment is often not collected on a country-level basis, particularly in developing countries. The Central Statistical Office of Trinidad and Tobago (2022), for example, in its Continuous Sample Survey of Population provides data on Labour Force Characteristics. Collected data and categories include employment data related to age, sex, employment status, industrial group, occupational group, type of worker and educational attainment (Central Statistical Office of Trinidad and Tobago, 2022). Separately, the Survey notes the "Economically Inactive Population (Out of the Labour Force)" which includes "The Disabled", among six other categories: there are no country-level employment data for persons with disabilities (Central Statistical Office of Trinidad and Tobago, 2022). On a global level, data on persons with disabilities in employment is

J. H. Stephenson and N. Persadie, *Disability in the Workplace*, Palgrave Explorations in Workplace Stigma,
https://doi.org/10.1007/978-3-031-19340-8_8

also difficult to obtain (United Nations, n.d. [a]). The International Labour Organization, however, estimates that globally almost two-thirds of persons with disabilities of working age are outside the labour force and are two times less likely to be employed than persons without disabilities (Stoevska, 2020). Even when they are able to secure employment, persons with disabilities are often underemployed (International Labour Office, 2014) and receive lower wages than their co-workers (Handicap International, 2016; Mora et al., 2021; World Economic Forum, 2022).

In light of the challenges faced by persons with disabilities in seeking and retaining employment, many countries have adopted legislative measures to protect and/or promote the rights of persons in this marginalised group. Over one hundred and twenty (120) countries have enacted legislation with a view to abolishing "discrimination against persons with disabilities and eliminate barriers towards the full enjoyment of their rights and their inclusion in society" (United Nations, n.d. [b]). As noted in Chapter 7, most English-speaking Caribbean countries have adopted similar legislation, embodying principles of equality and/or non-discrimination (see Table 7.3). Notably, these are all very recent additions to the statute books of each country, the earliest having been enacted in the year 2000. While similar legislation has been recently adopted in other jurisdictions, implementation of the law may have evolved differently and more quickly. In doing so, the effectiveness of the legislation would have been highlighted and recommendations for improvements suggested. Such recommendations concerning the effectiveness of the laws could provide insight into improving the effectiveness of the laws of the relevant English-speaking Caribbean countries. Consequently, this chapter considers the experience of two common law jurisdictions, namely the United Kingdom and Australia, in the implementation of their respective disability or equal rights legislation as it relates to the employment of persons with disabilities and lessons which can be learned from their experiences.

Equality, Non-discrimination and Disability Legislation

International human rights legal instruments embody the principles of equality and non-discrimination. Post-1945, these principles took on urgent and global significance and form key part of The Universal Declaration of Human Rights which states that "[a]ll human beings are born free and equal in dignity and rights" (United Nations, 1948, Art 1) and that these rights are to be enjoyed without "distinction of any kind, such as race, colour, sex, language, religion, political or other opinion, national or social origin, property, birth or other status" (United Nations, 1948, Art 2). Unsurprisingly, these principles also feature in the Convention on the Rights of Persons with Disabilities. Article 5 of the Convention is dedicated to addressing legal equality and non-discrimination where it declares all persons equal in relation to the law; prohibits discrimination on the basis of disability and provides for legal protections; allows for reasonable accommodation to be provided to promote equality and eliminate discrimination; and deems the implementation of special measures to achieve equality of persons with disabilities to be non-discriminatory (United Nations, 2008).

Equality and non-discrimination are inextricably related, such that they are deemed interchangeable (see MacNaughton, 2009), "two labels for a single general principle" (Wouters & Schmitt, 2017), "twin principles" (Casolari, 2017), synonymous (Zaccaroni, 2017) and equivalents (McDonnell, 2017). Equality and non-discrimination are considered to be positive and negative statements of the same principle where one is treated equally when one is not discriminated against and one is discriminated against when one is not treated equally (Besson, 2005). Whereas equality places a positive duty on the part of States to promote measures that advance equality, non-discrimination is a negative duty of restraint designed to suppress acts of unequal treatment of persons by the State (Stephenson et al., 2020). Non-discrimination as a principle is certainly not without its challenges as it embraces the notion of difference which means that legal systems must "determine what kinds of differences it will acknowledge as justifying different treatment and what kinds it will deny" (Ambrosini, 2017) as the law "prohibits both treating similar situations differently and treating different situations in the same way unless there are objective reasons for such treatment" (Wouters & Schmitt, 2017).

The concepts of equality and non-discrimination are key to disability legislation as they reflect the principle that persons with disabilities are equal human beings, entitled to equal treatment and equal opportunities in employment matters (International Labour Office, 2014). Non-discrimination legislation is designed to protect and promote the rights of persons with disabilities; it can take the form of a comprehensive law that applies to different groups within the population, including persons with disabilities, or can be disability-specific and address employment as one of several areas affecting persons with disabilities (International Labour Office, 2014). As noted in Chapter 7, such laws may promote equality in terms of identical treatment; equality of opportunity, which provides for equal chances, but not necessarily equal results; or equality of results, where securing the same outcomes for all is key (International Labour Office, 2014). Regardless of the form that non-discrimination legislation may take, special measures are often contemplated by disability legislation and usually manifest as provisions for affirmative action or positive discrimination. They are required in instances in which an individual must be treated differently in order to protect his or her right to equality (Persadie, 2012). Such measures seek to promote equality of opportunity by providing preferential treatment to groups of historically disadvantaged persons, such as persons with disabilities, to compensate for the structural disadvantages they have faced (International Labour Office, 2014). In legislative provisions, they are often meant to be temporary until such time that they are no longer required. As noted in the preceding paragraph, the subjectivity of the non-discrimination approach creates the potential for challenges in its application.

Disability, Employment and the Law in the Caribbean, Australia and the United Kingdom

Non-discrimination legislation is a rights-based approach to disability often modelled on equal opportunities approaches (Degener & Quinn, 2021). Enacted to protect persons with disabilities from discrimination or promote their right to equal opportunities, non-discrimination legislation generally takes one of two forms: comprehensive laws that prohibit discrimination on various grounds or status, such as disability, with applicability to various historically disadvantaged and socially excluded groups. Disability-specific legislation is the second main form; these laws also prohibit discrimination and generally promote the provision of equal opportunities to this historically disadvantaged group, sometimes through the implementation of temporary, special measures, in a variety of social areas, including employment. Employment-specific legislation provides a third category and these laws specifically prohibit discrimination in employment against persons of differing characteristics, including disability. As legislation designed to promote and protect the rights of persons with disabilities in employment in the English-speaking Caribbean are fairly limited in scope and number, all three categories are used to form the basis of the review: equality legislation, disability-specific legislation and employment-specific legislation. Australia and the United Kingdom are used as developed-country, common-law comparators to provide a basis for comparative review, as their legal systems and statutory provisions are similar to what obtains in the majority of English-speaking Caribbean states, but are much wider in scope. The review will focus on the *Disability Discrimination Act* (1992) and the *Fair Work Act* (2009) of Australia which both address the employment of persons with disabilities. For the United Kingdom, the *Equality Act* (2010) is the key piece of legislation that addresses these matters. These three pieces of legislation are comprehensive and, as such in this chapter, only specific employment and disability-related provisions are reviewed, after which best practices are highlighted, with a view of providing recommendations and guidance to the islands of the English-speaking Caribbean.

The Caribbean

Labour force participation rates differ significantly between persons with disabilities and persons without disabilities, as estimated by the International Labour Organization (Stoevska, 2020). While data for persons with disabilities in relation to employment may be unavailable for Caribbean countries (Seetahal & Charran, 2018), the World Bank estimates that there are some 85 million persons with disabilities in Latin America and the Caribbean, representing nearly 15% of the total population (World Bank, 2021). Persons with disabilities in the Caribbean are often excluded from labour markets due to physical, legal and attitudinal barriers to employment that restrict job and career prospects, and wages earned (Mora et al., 2021; see also Chapter 7). In comparison to persons without disabilities, they experience significantly higher rates of unemployment, lower rates of employment (Jones & Serieux-Lubin, 2018) and also underemployment even where they are able to secure a job (International Labour Office, 2014).

Law has been enacted in various Caribbean countries in an attempt to redress the challenges faced by persons with disabilities in relation to employment. Five countries in the English-speaking Caribbean have equal rights and disability-specific legislation which protect and promote the rights of persons with disabilities in employment, as seen in Table 7.3 of the previous chapter. Antigua and Barbuda, Guyana, Jamaica and The Bahamas have enacted disability-specific legislation while Guyana and Trinidad and Tobago have passed equal rights legislation; Guyana has both. Four other countries—Barbados, Belize, Grenada, St. Lucia—have employment-specific legislation which protects certain grounds, including disability, against discrimination. Each piece of legislation addresses different areas in disability in employment; Table 8.1 identifies fifteen (15) main areas combined across the legislative provisions of each of the nine countries. Three countries have no laws of any type identified. The provisions in Table 8.1 are designed to provide various protections or equal opportunities to persons with disabilities in the workplace. Protections for persons with disability in employment include protection against disciplinary action, retrenchment or termination on account of their disability; the right to alternative employment or redeployment where they are no longer able to continue in their current positions; the right to return to work, particularly in the event of disability occurring at the workplace, requiring the employee to seek extended medical attention; the right to health and safety measures; the right to be reasonably accommodated at work; and the right not to be medically tested or questioned about health conditions as a precondition for employment. Equal opportunities include the right to fair and equitable recruitment and selection practices; the right to equal pay and benefits in compensation packages; the right to employment-related education and training; the right to promotions, transfers or other employment opportunities; the right to employment-related facilities; the right to equal terms and conditions of employment as their colleagues; and the right for special measures to be taken to promote equality of opportunity at work. In the majority of cases, an undue or unjustifiable hardship or burden provision exists to protect the right of the employer where reasonable steps cannot be taken to accommodate persons with disabilities in the workplace.

While not deemed best practices, the Equal Opportunity Commission of Trinidad and Tobago, which works towards the elimination of discrimination and the promotion of equality and good relations between persons of different statuses, has created guidelines for employers on disability (Equal Opportunity Commission of Trinidad and Tobago, 2018) based on its statutory duty (s 27(1)(f) of the *Equal Opportunity Act*). It is quite comprehensive and spans the gamut of human resource practices, from recruitment, advertisement, selection, interview, placement,

Table 8.1 A comparison of provisions contained in the equality and disability-specific legislation in relation to employment matters of Anglophone Caribbean Countries

	*Areas of employment addressed**														
	AE	*CE*	*CP*	*DA*	*EF*	*ET*	*HS*	*MT*	*PT*	*RA*	*RS*	*SM*	*TC*	*UH*	*UT*
Antigua and Barbuda	✓	✓	✓			✓			✓	✓	✓			✓	
Barbados	◇							✓		✓	✓	✓		✓	
Belize												✓			
Grenada				✓								✓			
Guyana			✓		✓	✓	✓				✓	✓	✓		✓
Jamaica	✓					✓			✓	✓			✓	✓	✓
St Lucia				✓	✓	✓	✓		✓	✓	✓	✓	✓	✓	✓
The Bahamas			✓		✓	✓				✓	✓	✓	✓	✓	
Trinidad and Tobago						✓			✓		✓		✓	✓	✓

AE: Alternative employment or redeployment
CE: Continuance of Employment
CP: Compensation packages
DA: Disciplinary action
EF: Employment-related facilities
ET: Employment-related education and training
HS: Health and safety measures
◇ - provision exists elsewhere
MT: Medical testing as precondition for employment
PT: Promotion or transfer
RA: Reasonable accommodations or adjustments
RS: Recruitment and Selection
SM: Special measures
TC: Terms and conditions of employment
UH: Undue or unjustifiable hardship or burden
UT: Unfair termination or retrenchment
*Some of the areas have been grouped together where practicable, for example, recruitment and selection includes job creation, job advertisements, the interview process, and candidate selection, such that the legislative provision itself may be more detailed than the area created in the table.
Source Compiled by author from the reviews of the laws of each country

employee induction, training, career advancement and termination. This is all prefaced by encouragement to employers to adopt strategies for managing disability in the workplace by providing reasonable accommodation to jobseekers with disabilities, equal opportunities for employees with disabilities and job retention by employees who acquire a disability.

Australia

Australian workforce participation rates for persons with disabilities are also low, with a near 30% gap between this group and persons without disabilities (Allen, 2018; Devine et al., 2021; Raymond et al., 2019; Scott, 2016). Barriers to employment of persons with disabilities in Australia are very similar to what is experienced in the Caribbean: they are multifaceted, intertwining individual-level socio-demographic characteristics with vocational, non-vocational and structural barriers to gaining and maintaining work (Devine et al., 2021); more specifically, they include discriminatory recruitment practices, lower wages paid, employer lack of understanding of disability in the workplace and consequent unwillingness to make adjustments to accommodate a disability (Allen, 2018; Gray, 2020) based on the presumed cost-prohibitive nature of making such accommodations (Scott, 2016). These challenges are reinforced by pervasive myths, assumptions and stereotypes about persons with disabilities (Ruhindwa et al., 2016; Scott, 2016), as well as a lack of resources generally to meet basic needs (Devine et al., 2021).

Two pieces of legislation have been enacted to address this matter: the *Disability Discrimination Act* (1992) and the *Fair Work Act* (2009). The *Disability Discrimination Act* ("DDA") is a large statutory instrument, containing some 132 provisions. It prohibits discrimination in employment (ss 15–21B) as well as seven other named areas (ss 22–28). The DDA allows for the creation of disability standards in relation to any of the named areas (ss 31–34) and gives it regulatory powers (s 132), both of which allow for dealing with any matter in the Act with greater specificity. Scott (2016) notes that this ability to develop disability standards holds the possibility of addressing labour market disadvantages experienced by persons with disabilities, as standards will move away from the open-ended nature of the DDA by ensuring that employers are clear about their legal obligations towards employees with disabilities. Section 15 prohibits discrimination against persons with disabilities in the recruitment and selection process, terms and conditions of employment, training and employment opportunities and dismissal. Sections 16–21 contain provisions not present in the majority of Caribbean legislation: it prohibits discrimination against persons with disabilities who are commission agents, contract workers and partners. Qualifying bodies (professional bodies), organisations registered under the *Fair Work Act*, and employment agencies are prohibited from discriminating against persons with disabilities. Exceptions are permitted for inherent requirements of job positions and unjustifiable hardship to employers (ss 21A–21B).

The *Fair Work Act* is phenomenally large, with some 800 provisions and five schedules, split into two volumes. The Act defines disability broadly, increased substantially the penalties for non-compliance and created a state institution to enforce disability rights (Harpur et al., 2012). The purpose of the Act is to provide a "balanced framework for cooperative and productive workplace relations that promotes national economic prosperity and social inclusion for all Australians" (s 3). It seeks to do this by providing workplace relations laws that are fair; ensuring fair, relevant and enforceable minimum terms and conditions and minimum wages; allowing for work-life balance through flexible work arrangements; preventing discrimination and protecting against unfair treatment and discrimination; providing accessible and effective dispute resolution and compliance mechanisms; promoting collective bargaining; and giving special consideration to small- and medium-sized businesses. Disability is one of 13 protected characteristics of an employee that is protected from discrimination and adverse action. Adverse action is taken by an employer against an employee if the employer: (a) dismisses the employee; or (b) injures the employee in his or her employment; or (c) alters the position of the employee to the employee's prejudice; or (d) discriminates between the employee and other employees of the employer (s 342). For prospective employees, a prospective employer takes adverse action against a prospective employee if the prospective employer: (a) refuses to employ the prospective employee; or (b) discriminates against the prospective employee in the terms or conditions on which the prospective employer offers to employ the prospective employee.

Unlike traditional disability discrimination legislation, the *Fair Work Act* adopts a different approach. Disability discrimination laws define discrimination (Allen, 2018) whereas the *Fair Work Act* addresses "workplace rights" in Division 3 which does not include a definition of discrimination but confers on persons the benefits of any workplace law, the right to take legal action and make a complaint or inquiry (s 341(1)).

Coercion and undue influence or pressure in relation to these rights are prohibited. Division 5 addresses discrimination but without defining the term. Neither does the Act define disability, but refers only to "physical and mental disability". Both terms—discrimination and disability—are left to be interpreted by the courts and they have done so narrowly (Allen, 2018). Moreover, the law does not require the employer to make reasonable adjustments for employees with disabilities (Allen, 2018; Harpur et al., 2012), but this can be addressed through the DDA. One very clear positive feature is that the Act reverses the burden of proof such that the employer must prove that it did not take an adverse action against the employee in his exercise of a workplace right; anti-discrimination laws ordinarily place the burden on the employee (Allen, 2018; Harpur et al., 2012). This forms part of the strong enforcement mechanisms contained in the Act (Allen, 2018).

In addition, the *Fair Work Act* creates National Employment Standards which are minimum standards that relate to: (a) maximum weekly hours (Division 3); (b) requests for flexible working arrangements (Division 4); (c) parental leave and related entitlements (Division 5); (d) annual leave (Division 6); (e) personal/carer's leave and compassionate leave (Division 7); (f) community service leave (Division 8); (g) long service leave (Division 9); (h) public holidays (Division 10); (i) notice of termination and redundancy pay (Division 11); and (j) Fair Work Information Statement (Division 12). Implementation of the standards, which provide specificity to the general provisions created in both pieces of legislation, and research conducted on inclusionary workplaces practices to facilitate persons with disabilities have produced best practice guidelines. Only two will be reviewed here: one with general applicability and one specific to workplace adjustments (or accommodations). The Fair Work Ombudsman, a creation of the *Fair Work Act*, who is mandated with promoting and monitoring compliance with this Act, and providing education, assistance and advice to employees, employers, outworkers, outworker entities and organisations (Part 5–2, Fair Work Act) has produced one such guide. To the benefit of persons with disabilities, while not specifically written for them, the guide covers flexible working arrangements, consultation and cooperation in the workplace, use of individual flexibility arrangements, managing underperformance and effective dispute resolution, among other areas (Fair Work Ombudsman, 2022).

The Centre for Workplace Leadership has also produced some best practices based on research it conducted on implementing reasonable adjustments in the workplace (Raymond et al., 2019). Their research indicated that effective reasonable adjustments can be formal or informal, but recommend formal processes; feedback processes after the adjustments are made is limited and the effectiveness of the measures needs to be understood; reasonable adjustments for invisible disabilities, such as mental illness, are underrepresented, therefore increased knowledge and understanding around, and inclusion of individuals with, both visible and invisible disabilities are required; the recruitment and interview process needs to be more accessible and inclusive; continuous learning is necessary for managers to ensure access and inclusion; and funding for reasonable adjustments should come out of a central, rather than departmental, fund (Raymond et al., 2019). While legislative provisions and standards set thresholds for behaviour towards persons with disabilities in employment, it is only through implementation that the effectiveness of such provisions can be determined and recommendations made.

The United Kingdom

Unemployment statistics for persons with disabilities in the United Kingdom ("UK") fare no better than those found in Australia; there is also a near 30% gap between this group and persons without disabilities in employment (Office for National Statistics, 2021; Powell, 2021). Similarly, barriers exist across all spheres of life for persons with disabilities including, but not limited to, accessing educational and employment opportunities (Barnes & Mercer, 2005). Barriers confronting persons with disabilities seeking employment reflect those found elsewhere: lower rates of employment; lower wages; underemployment; stigma; issues related to access and support; difficulty with transport; employer belief in their inability to perform in the workplace; lack of awareness and knowledge; presumed higher costs for accommodations required; and possible litigation (Barnes & Mercer, 2005; Bell & Heitmueller, 2009; Coleman et al., 2013; Corby et al., 2019).

The *Equality Act* (2010) is the primary piece of legislation that addresses the rights of persons with disabilities in the UK (Haves, 2018). This is another massive statutory instrument containing some 218 sections and 28 schedules, consolidating nine major pieces of legislation and some 100 statutory instruments (Ashtiany, 2011). Among many of its parts and chapters, it addresses protected characteristics, prohibited conduct, employment, equality of terms, education, enforcement and, importantly, the advancement of equality (*Equality Act*, 2010). The application of the law is specific to nine protected characteristics, including disability. Sections 13–19 address discrimination, including on the basis of disability. In terms of employment, the Act prohibits discrimination against (and victimisation of) employees and applicants with respect to employment offers; terms of employment; opportunities for promotion, transfer or training or for receiving any other benefit, facility or service; and dismissal (s 39). Subsection (5) places a duty on employers to make reasonable adjustments. Specific to persons with disabilities, section 20 of the Act imposes a duty on persons to make reasonable adjustments to facilitate persons with disabilities who are placed at a substantial disadvantage with respect to a workplace provision, criterion or practice; physical feature; or the non-provision of an auxiliary aid relative to fellow employees without disabilities so as to help them avoid the disadvantage. A similar duty is not imposed for any other protected characteristic (Griffiths, 2015) in light of the recognition that disability discrimination is asymmetrical, such that measures to achieve equality include a duty to make reasonable adjustments for persons with disabilities (Hepple, 2010). While recruiters may enquire into a job applicant's health or disability, such enquiries are very heavily circumscribed by section 60 so as to avoid any discriminatory behaviour (Stephenson et al., 2020), a key addition to the law (Lawson, 2011). There are six schedules dedicated to the duty to make adjustments, with Schedule 8 focusing on work and Schedule 9 identifying exceptions. The Act also allows for regulations to be made as it relates to adjustments. Sections 41–48 contain provisions not present in the majority of Caribbean legislation: it prohibits discrimination against persons with disabilities who are contract workers, partners and attorneys. Qualifying bodies (professional bodies), employment service providers, trade organisations and local authorities are prohibited from discriminating against persons generally, including those with disabilities (ss 53–59). With respect to the burden of proof, the Act takes a different approach to the *Fair Work Act*: while the burden of proving discrimination rests with the person experiencing the discriminatory behaviour, there is now a focus on alternative approaches, such as the proactive duties to promote or achieve equality (Fredman, 2011), as seen in the public sector duty addressed below.

An interesting inclusion is the imposition of a public sector equality duty to (a) eliminate discrimination and any other conduct prohibited by or under the Act; (b) advance equality of opportunity between persons who share a relevant protected characteristic and persons who do not share it; and (c) foster good relations between persons who share a relevant protected characteristic and persons who do not share it (s 149(1)), with the exception of one. It specifically recognises that the "steps involved in meeting the needs of disabled persons that are different from the needs of persons who are not disabled include, in particular, steps to take account of disabled persons' disabilities" (s 149(4)), noting also that this may involve treating some persons more favourably than others (s 149(6)). The Act further encourages persons to take positive action to promote equality where they reasonably think that (a) persons who share a protected characteristic suffer a disadvantage connected to the characteristic, (b) persons who share a protected characteristic have needs that are different from the needs of persons who do not share it, or (c) participation in an activity by persons who share a protected characteristic is disproportionately low (s 158(1)). This applies to all protected characteristics, including disability. The use of discretionary language in both sections, however, means that neither is mandatory to implement (see also Fredman, 2011). Critics have also attacked the failing of the law to impose a similar duty on the private sector (Hepple, 2011) which remains unregulated (Fredman, 2011). Fredman (2011) points out that the fact that discrimination is unlawful strongly suggests that the authority should have an express duty to eliminate it, rather than be given the discretion to do so.

The Chartered Institute of Personnel and Development ("CIPD") (2021) has suggested good employment practices based on the *Equality Act* (2010) to ensure everyone has fair access and opportunity to progress in work and that employers make reasonable adjustments to accommodate the needs of persons with disabilities. It also encourages employers to challenge stereotypical thinking and provides recommendations for positive progress. The practices suggest an inclusion and diversity in the workplace policy to help mitigate discrimination claims and illustrate a voluntary approach to equality by the employer. Legally, making reasonable adjustments is required but the CIPD (2021) recommends that they be made consultatively and be customised. While section 60 of the Act heavily circumscribes disability and health enquiries during the recruitment process, the CIPD (2021) describes the circumstances under which queries may be made. It advises employers to challenge stereotypical thinking about employing persons with disabilities and making accommodations for them. A final recommendation is for employers to be disability aware and understand how to make and implement reasonable adjustments. The CIPD (2021) further suggests voluntary reporting on how employers manage disability at work. The Department for Work and Pensions (2020) has also issued a guide for line managers on recruiting, managing and developing persons with disabilities or health conditions as persons with direct and regular interactions with members of this group. The Employment Statutory Code of Practice has been issued pursuant to the *Equality Act* (2006), as an authoritative, comprehensive and technical guide to the detail of law for those who need to understand and apply it (Equality and Human Rights Commission, 2011).

Discussion

Victimisation, harassment and direct and indirect discrimination provisions address non-discrimination and equality and are included in the legislation of the UK, Australia, Barbados, Guyana and St. Lucia; these, however, have not been included in this review but rather specific employment measures designed to assist persons with disabilities at work. The focus is on employment-specific measures adopted to promote and protect the rights of persons with disabilities in the workplace as noted in Table 8.1 as well as others that exist in Australian and UK law to provide a basis for recommending best practices.

The laws addressing disability and employment in the Anglophone Caribbean can be dissected into 15 main areas of employment, as illustrated in Table 8.1. These areas include alternative employment or redeployment; continuance of employment; compensation packages; disciplinary action; employment-related facilities; employment-related education and training; health and safety measures; medical testing as precondition for employment; promotion or transfer; reasonable accommodations or adjustments; recruitment and selection; special measures; terms and conditions of employment; undue or unjustifiable hardship or burden; and unfair termination or retrenchment. St. Lucia's law includes the most number of areas of employment out of all the countries; it addresses 11 of the 15 areas. Three countries cover 8 areas (Antigua and Barbuda, Guyana, The Bahamas); one includes 7 areas (Jamaica); two address 6 areas (Barbados, Trinidad and Tobago); Grenada's law covers two areas while Belize's law includes only one (see Table 8.2). The laws of three countries—Dominica, St. Kitts and Nevis, St. Vincent and the Grenadines—have no provisions in any of these areas. Notably, only

Antigua and Barbuda provides for continuance of employment. Remarkably, too, Barbados is the only country to prohibit health enquiries or medical testing as a precondition for employment, such as is done in the *Equality Act*, 2010 of the UK. This is important, as employers may either knowingly or inadvertently use this information to screen out people with disabilities resulting in otherwise qualified candidates being overlooked (Scott, 2016). Its rationale is the disproportionate disadvantage caused by pre-employment health checks to applicants with disabilities and the difficulty of legally challenging rejections made at this early stage of the recruitment process (Harpur et al., 2012; Lawson, 2011). While six countries promote the use of temporary, special measures designed to promote equality of opportunity for persons with disabilities in the workplace, The Bahamas is the sole one in the group that has legislated a quota of one per cent of persons with disabilities to be employed where there are more than one hundred employees; its implementation and effectiveness are not known. While an undoubtedly positive inclusion, as it provides a quantifiable measure, the effectiveness and need for disability quotas in employment (legislation) are questioned in the context of wider anti-discrimination policy and legal approaches (Sargeant et al., 2016). Interestingly, Trinidad and Tobago's law includes an unjustifiable hardship clause for the protection of employers in the absence of a provision specifically addressing reasonable accommodations to be made for employees with disabilities; all other countries with similar provisions have both.

Australian law addressing the employment of persons with disabilities is expansive and exhaustive relying on two principal pieces of

Table 8.2 Number of areas of employment addressed in equality and disability-specific legislation in relation to employment matters in Anglophone Caribbean Countries

Country	*No of areas covered*
Antigua and Barbuda	8
Barbados	6
Belize	1
Grenada	2
Guyana	8
Jamaica	7
St Lucia	11
The Bahamas	8
Trinidad and Tobago	6

legislation: the DDA and the *Fair Work Act*. The DDA covers standard employment matters in relation to persons with disabilities but also includes prohibitions not found in most Caribbean legislation, such as prohibiting discrimination against persons with disabilities who are commission agents, contract workers and partners. Additionally, qualifying bodies (professional bodies), organisations registered under the *Fair Work Act*, and employment agencies are prohibited from discriminating against a person with disabilities. Similar provisions exist in the UK law and St. Lucia's, which prohibits discrimination by qualifying and vocational bodies and employment agencies.

UK law addressing disability and employment is equally comprehensive in its approach with Scott (2016) commenting that the UK has adopted a stronger standards-based approach than Australia to disability discrimination regulation. Based on the review above, the *Equality Act* contains three main differences to Caribbean legislation. It covers prohibitions not found in most Caribbean legislation, such as prohibiting discrimination against persons with disabilities who are contract workers, partners and attorneys. Moreover, qualifying bodies (professional bodies), employment service providers, trade organisations and local authorities are prohibited from discriminating against persons generally, including those with disabilities (ss 53–59). Similar provisions exist in the DDA of Australia and St. Lucia's Labour Code. The second main difference is the restriction on the use of pre-work health questions which can lead to discriminatory recruitment outcomes and which, surprisingly, is included in the legislation of Barbados; and the third is the establishment of a public sector duty to promote equality, albeit discretionary. The Equal Opportunity Commission of Trinidad and Tobago, a creature of statute, has functions that reflect, in part, the UK's public sector equality duty. Among other functions, the Commission must work towards the elimination of discrimination; and promote equality of opportunity and good relations between persons of different status generally (s 27). Other Caribbean countries do not contain such legislative provisions.

The National Employment Standards of the *Fair Work Act* of Australia create minimum standards related to various areas of employment. Caribbean legislation contains the power to make regulations which, like standards, will provide specificity in addressing particular matters. Seven of the nine Caribbean countries' legislation include regulation-making powers, with the exception of Grenada and Trinidad and Tobago. Scott (2016) notes the difference in approach: regulations and rules are prescriptive, legal constructs with specific legal consequences. Regulations and rules can be negative or positive in nature depending on whether conduct is required or prohibited (Scott, 2016). Scott (2016) observes that standards, on the other hand, allow for some form of discretion in relation to conduct and context. They command the achievement of a value, goal, or outcome without specifying the required action undertaken to achieve it. In either case, both standards and regulations provide specificity to legal provisions and would be useful in Caribbean contexts. As it currently stands in the Caribbean, legal principles in relation to persons with disabilities in employment are stated at a very high level of generality which, while they are sufficiently flexible to cover a broad range of factual scenarios (Scott, 2016), are too vague to permit proper understanding and effective implementation of the measures.

Both Australia and the UK have issued national best practices, as well as some issued by professional organisations, that would benefit persons with disabilities in employment matters in the Caribbean. Notable are flexible working arrangements; consultation and cooperation in the workplace; use of individual flexibility arrangements; reasonable accommodations; disability awareness training for employers and employees alike; dispute resolution; and guidelines on implementing reasonable adjustments in the workplace which should include consultation and be individualised. While some of these matters might be addressed by individual employers in the Caribbean through workplace policies, such as flexible working arrangements, or sporadic practice, they are not mandatory. It should be noted that Antigua and Barbuda, Jamaica and Trinidad and Tobago promote alternative dispute resolution in discrimination complaints. These are generally less costly and adversarial than litigation and should be a preferred initial approach made available for disability discrimination complaints.

The *Fair Work Act* of Australia provides one more key best practice: reversing the burden of proof. In instances of complained adverse action in the exercise of a workplace right, it is the employer who bears the burden of proving that this did not occur (Harpur et al., 2012). This burden is both evidentiary and financial, making it difficult and costly for employees to take legal action. Adverse action becomes unlawful when it is taken *because of* a protected attribute the employee has, such as disability (Allen, 2018). Similar application would be useful in Caribbean jurisdictions making the complaints process much less onerous for employees with disabilities where the burden of proving discrimination rests with said employees. One notable exception is a very selective application of reversed burden of proof in the St. Lucia Labour Code (s 274); however, it applies very narrowly to employment membership bodies having to prove that it did not discriminate against applicants or members on the basis of their disability. In all other cases, the burden of proof lies with the employee alleging discrimination. Another shortfall of the complaints-led approach is that it is limited in its ability to address the structural causes of discrimination (Fredman, 2011), which is the whole point of non-discrimination legislation.

Conclusion

Work plays a major role in individual lives and has a positive influence on health, well-being, social inclusion and identity (Ruhindwa et al., 2016). This is true also for persons with disabilities who find themselves faced with limited employment opportunities due to a number of factors. Laws have been promulgated in many countries to address this disadvantage. Legal approaches often take the form of equality and non-discrimination legislation, designed to protect and promote the rights of persons with disabilities in employment. Such laws can be comprehensive, applying to different groups within the population, including persons with disabilities, or can be disability-specific addressing employment as one of several areas affecting persons with disabilities, or can be employment-specific with disability being one of the various protected characteristics. Laws that cater for persons with disabilities in employment, by whichever route, seek to mitigate the power disadvantages experienced by people with disabilities, while simultaneously empowering people with disabilities to claim their rights to equal access and participation (Fisher & Purcal, 2017). This is the approach generally adopted by Caribbean jurisdictions as well as Australia and the UK. Comprehensive laws are found in Australia, the UK, Guyana and Trinidad and Tobago. Four Caribbean countries each have disability-specific and employment-specific legislation.

Caribbean legislation addressing employment matters for persons with disabilities has a number of positive attributes, among which include alternative dispute resolution mechanisms, and the promotion of equality and equality of opportunity through, for example, provisions allowing for the implementation of special measures. For persons with disabilities in employment, equality of opportunity, to the extent that it is achievable, often requires different treatment (Haves, 2018); this is reflected in the special measures provisions. Nevertheless, there are a number of lessons that can be imported into Caribbean legislation and practice for matters addressing persons with disabilities from the experiences of Australia and the UK. These include expanding the categories of persons with disabilities against whom discrimination in employment is prohibited; restricting enquiries on disabilities during the recruitment process to avoid discriminatory recruitment outcomes; and the establishment of national standards, rules or regulations to provide specificity for understanding and implementing legislative measures designed to promote and protect the rights of persons with disability in employment. A final key lesson to implement would be the approach adopted in the *Fair Work Act* of Australia that reverses the burden of proof in discrimination claims so that it rests with the employer rather than the employee. This would improve the effectiveness of such legislation by encouraging workplace disability discrimination claims; it should simultaneously keep employers in compliance due to the ease of the complaints process which they should wish to avoid having initiated. Incorporating these lessons can lead to more meaningful and relevant employment outcomes for persons with disabilities in relation to employment in the English-speaking Caribbean.

References

Allen, D. (2018). Adverse effects: Can the *Fair Work Act* address workplace discrimination for employees with a disability? *UNSW Law Journal, 41*(3), 846–870.

Ambrosini, E. (2017). Reverse discrimination in EU law: An internal market perspective. In L. Rossi & F. Casolari (Eds.), *The principle of equality in EU law* (pp. 255–280). Springer International Publishing.

Ashtiany, S. (2011). The Equality Act 2010: Main concepts. *International Journal of Discrimination and the Law, 11*, 29–42.

Barnes, C., & Mercer, G. (2005). Disability, work, and welfare: Challenging the social exclusion of disabled people. *Work, Employment and Society, 19*(3), 527–545. https://doi.org/10.1177/0950017005055669

Bell, D., & Heitmueller, A. (2009). The Disability Discrimination Act in the UK: Helping or hindering employment among the disabled? *Journal of Health Economics, 28*, 465–480. https://doi.org/10.1016/j.jhealeco.2008.10.006

Besson, S. (2005). The principle of non-discrimination in the convention on the rights of the child. *The International Journal of Children's Rights, 13*, 433–461.

Bonaccio, S., Connelly, C., Gellatly, I., Jetha, A., & Ginis, K. (2020). The participation of people with disabilities in the workplace across the employment cycle: Employer concerns and research evidence. *Journal of Business and Psychology, 35*, 135–158.

Casolari, F. (2017). The acknowledgment of the direct effect of EU international agreements: Does legal equality still matter? In L. Rossi & F. Casolari (Eds.), *The principle of equality in EU law* (pp. 83–129). Springer International Publishing.

Central Statistical Office of Trinidad and Tobago. (2022). *Continuous sample survey of population*. Available from https://cso.gov.tt/subjects/continuous-sample-survey-of-population/

Chartered Institute of Personnel and Development. (2021). *Disability and employment*. Available from https://www.cipd.co.uk/knowledge/fundamentals/emp-law/disability-discrimination/factsheet#gref

Coleman, N., Sykes, W., & Groom, C. (2013). *Barriers to employment and unfair treatment at work: A quantitative analysis of disabled people's experiences* (Research Report no. 88). Equality and Human Rights Commission.

Corby, S., William, L., & Richard, S. (2019). Combatting disability discrimination: A comparison of France and Great Britain. *European Journal of Industrial Relations, 25*(1), 41–56. https://doi.org/10.1177/0959680118759169

Degener, T., & Quinn, G. (2021). A survey of international, comparative and regional disability law reform. *Disability Rights Education & Defense Fund*. Available from https://dredf.org/news/publications/disability-rights-law-and-policy/a-survey-of-international-comparative-and-regional-disability-law-reform/

Department for Work & Pensions. (2020). *Guide for line managers: Recruiting, managing and developing people with a disability or health condition*. Available from https://www.gov.uk/government/publications/disability-confident-and-cipd-guide-for-line-managers-on-employing-people-with-a-disability-or-health-condition/guide-for-line-managers-recruiting-managing-and-developing-people-with-a-disability-or-health-condition

Department of Social Services, Australia. (2012). *National standards for disability services*. Available from https://www.fairwork.gov.au/employment-conditions/national-employment-standards

Devine, A., Shields, M., Dimov, S., Dickinson, H., Vaughan, C., Bentley, R., LaMontagne, A. D., & Kavanagh, A. (2021). Australia's disability employment services program: Participant perspectives on factors influencing access to work. *International Journal of Environmental Research and Public Health 18*, 11485. https://doi.org/10.3390/ijerph182111485

Equality and Human Rights Commission. (2011). *Employment statutory code of practice*. Equality and Human Rights Commission. Available from https://www.equalityhumanrights.com/sites/default/files/employercode.pdf

Equality and Human Rights Commission, Equality Commission for Northern Ireland, Northern Ireland Human Rights Commission, Scottish Human Rights Commission. (2017). *Disability rights in the UK: UK independent mechanism. Submission to inform the CRPD. List of Issues on the UK*. Available from https://www.equalityhumanrights.com/sites/default/files/united_kingdom_main_submission_to_crpd_uk_loi_-_ukim13march.pdf

Equal Opportunity Commission of Trinidad and Tobago. (2018). *Guidelines for employers on disability in Trinidad and Tobago*. Equal Opportunity Commission of Trinidad and Tobago.

Fair Work Ombudsman. (2022). *Best practice guide*. Available from https://www.fairwork.gov.au/tools-and-resources/best-practice-guides

Fisher, K. R., & Purcal, C. (2017). Policies to change attitudes to people with disabilities. *Scandinavian Journal of Disability Research, 19*(2), 161–174. https://doi.org/10.1080/15017419.2016.1222303

Fredman, S. (2011). The Public Sector Equality Duty. *Industrial Law Journal, 40*(4), 405–427.

Goss, D., Goss, F., & Adam-Smith, D. (2000). Disability and employment: A comparative critique of UK legislation. *The International Journal of Human Resource Management, 11*(4), 807–821. https://doi.org/10.1080/09585190050075132

Gray, P. (2020). Disclosure of disability in the Australian Public Service: What the statistics tell us. *Australian Journal of Career Development, 29*(1), 3–11. https://doi.org/10.1177/1038416219843620

Griffiths, E. (2015). Would the 'reasonable accommodation' of religious belief in the work-place prevent a hierarchy of protected characteristics from developing? [PowerPoint Slides]. *University of Chester: 'The Equality Act 2010: Five-years on' - Presentation slides*. Retrieved February 24, 2020, from http://www.chester.ac.uk/node/31631

Handicap International. (2016). *Situation of wage employment of people with disabilities: Ten Developing Countries in Focus*. Handicap International.

Harpur, P., French, B., & Bales, R. (2012). Australia's Fair Work Act and the transformation of workplace disability discrimination law. *Wisconsin International Law Journal, 30*, 190.

Haves, E. (2018). Disability in the UK: Rights and policy. Debate on 28 June 2018. *House of Lords, library briefing*. Available from https://researchbriefings.files.parliament.uk/documents/LLN-2018-0071/LLN-2018-0071.pdf

Harwood, R. (2016). What has limited the impact of UK disability equality law on social justice? *Laws, 5*(42), 1–23. https://doi.org/10.3390/laws5040042

Hepple, B. (2010). The new single Equality Act in Britain. *The Equality Rights Review, 5*, 11–24.

Hepple, B. (2011). Enforcing equality law: Two steps forward and two steps backwards for reflexive regulation. *Industrial Law Journal, 40*(4), 315–335. https://doi.org/10.1093/indlaw/dwr020

International Labour Office. (2014). *Achieving equal employment opportunities for people with disabilities through legislation: Guidelines*. International Labour Office.

Jones, F., & Serieux-Lubin, L. (2018). *Disability, human rights and public policy in the Caribbean: A situation analysis*. ECLAC – Studies and Perspectives Series – The Caribbean – No. 64. UN ECLAC. Retrieved April 5, 2021, from https://www.cepal.org/sites/default/files/publication/files/43306/S1701279_en.pdf

Lawson, A. (2011). Disability and employment in the Equality Act 2010: Opportunities seized, lost and generated. *Industrial Law Journal, 40*(4), 359–383. https://doi.org/10.1093/indlaw/dwr021

MacNaughton, G. (2009). Untangling equality and non-discrimination to promote the right to health care for all. *Health and Human Rights, 11*(2). Retrieved November 8, from https://www.hhrjournal.org/2013/08/untangling-equality-and-non-discrimination-to-promote-the-right-to-health-carefor-all/

McDonnell, A. (2017). Equality for citizens in the EU: Where did all the flowers go? In L. Rossi & F. Casolari (Eds.), *The principle of equality in EU Law* (pp. 199–228). Springer International Publishing.

Mora, G., Elena, M., Orellana, S., & Freire, G. (2021). *Disability inclusion in Latin America and the Caribbean: A path to sustainable development*. World Bank.

Morris, J. (2011). Rethinking disability policy. *Joseph Rowntree Foundation*. Available from https://www.jrf.org.uk/sites/default/files/jrf/migrated/files/disability-policy-equality-summary.pdf

Office for National Statistics. (2021). *Outcomes for disabled people in the UK: 2020*. Available from https://www.ons.gov.uk/peoplepopulationandcommunity/healthandsocialcare/disability/articles/outcomesfordisabledpeopleintheuk/2020

Persadie, N. (2012). *A critical analysis of the efficacy of law as a tool to achieve gender equality*. University Press of America.

Powell, A. (2021). *Disabled people in employment*. House of Commons Library. Available from https://researchbriefings.files.parliament.uk/documents/CBP-7540/CBP-7540.pdf

Raymond, M., Olsen, J. E., Ainsworth, S., Lotia, N., Harbridge, R., & Holland, A. (2019). *Improving access and inclusion in employment for people with disabilities: Implementation of workplace adjustments in 'best-practice' organisations*. Centre for Workplace Leadership Research Report, University of Melbourne. Available from https://fbe.unimelb.edu.au/__data/assets/pdf_file/0004/3103771/Improving-Access-and-Inclusion-in-Employment-for-People-with-Disabilities-Report.pdf

Ruhindwa, A., Randall, C., & Cartmel, J. (2016). Exploring the challenges experienced by people with disabilities in the employment sector in Australia: Advocating for inclusive practice - a review of literature. *Journal of Social Inclusion, 7*(1), 4–19.

Sargeant, M., Radevich-Katsaroumpa, E., & Innesti, A. (2016). Disability quotas: Past or future policy? *Economic and Industrial Democracy, 1–18*,. https://doi.org/10.1177/0143831X16639655

Scott, P. (2016). Addressing Ableism in Workplace Policies and Practices: The Case for Disability Standards in Employment. *Flinders Law Journal, 18*, 121–159.

Secretary of State for Work and Pensions. (2021). *National Disability Strategy*. Available from https://assets.publishing.service.gov.uk/government/uploads/system/uploads/attachment_data/file/1006098/National-Disability-Strategy_web-accesible-pdf.pdf

Seetahal, K., & Charran, C. (2018). The unknown and unemployed masses with disabilities in Trinidad and Tobago. *Texas Education Review, 7*(1), 130–139. https://doi.org/10.26153/tsw/20

Stephenson, J. H., Persadie, N., Bissessar, A., & Esnard, T. (2020). *Diversity, equality, and inclusion in Caribbean organisations and society: An exploration of work, employment, education, and the law*. Palgrave Macmillan.

Stoevska, V. (2020). *International day of persons with disabilities: How disability affects labour market outcomes*. ILOSTAT, International Labour Organization. Available from https://ilostat.ilo.org/international-day-of-persons-with-disabilities-how-disability-affects-labour-market-outcomes/

United Nations. (1948). United Nations declaration of human rights. Adopted 10 December 1948. In I. Brownlie (Ed.), *Basic documents on human rights (1992)*. Oxford University Press.

United Nations. (2008). Convention on the rights of persons with disabilities, May 03, 2008. Available from https://www.un.org/disabilities/documents/convention/convoptprot-e.pdf

United Nations. (n.d. [a]). *Disability and employment*. Available from https://www.un.org/development/desa/disabilities/resources/factsheet-on-persons-with-disabilities/disability-and-employment.html.

United Nations. (n.d. [b]). *Disability laws and acts by country/area*. Available from https://www.un.org/development/desa/disabilities/disability-laws-and-acts-by-country-area.html

World Bank. (2021). *Inclusion of persons with disabilities is crucial for the sustainable development of Latin America and the Caribbean*. Press Release No: 2021/LAC. Available from https://www.worldbank.org/en/news/press-release/2021/12/02/la-inclusion-de-las-personas-con-discapacidad-clave-para-el-desarrollo-sostenible-de-america-latina-y-el-caribe

World Economic Forum. (2022). *Closing the disability inclusion gap with business leadership*. Available from https://www.weforum.org/impact/closing-the-disability-inclusion-gap-through-the-power-of-business-leadership/

Wouters, J., & Schmitt, P. (2017). Equality among member states and differentiated integration in the EU. In L. Rossi & F. Casolari (Eds.), *The principle of equality in EU law* (pp. 43–82). Springer International Publishing.

Zaccaroni, G. (2017). Differentiating equality? The different advancements in the protected grounds in the case law of the European Court of Justice. In L. Rossi & F. Casolari (Eds.), *The principle of equality in EU law* (pp. 167–195). Springer International Publishing.

Laws

Antigua and Barbuda

Disabilities and Equal Opportunities Act, 2017. Available from http://laws.gov.ag/wp-content/uploads/2019/04/No.-32-of-2017-Disabilities-and-Equal-Opportunities-Act-2017.pdf

Australia

Disability Discrimination Act, 1992. Available from https://www.legislation.gov.au/Details/C2016C00763

Fair Work Act, 2009. Available from https://www.legislation.gov.au/Details/C2017C00323

Barbados

Employment (Prevention) of Discrimination Act, 2020. Available from https://www.barbadosparliament.com/uploads/bill_resolution/06948a67143d62e36c426fbd077e1055.pdf

Employment Rights Act, 2012–9. Available from https://www.ilo.org/dyn/natlex/docs/ELECTRONIC/94144/110398/F-749620620/BRB94144.pdf

Belize

International Labour Organization Conventions Act, Cap. 304:01. (Revised Edition 2020). Available from https://www.agm.gov.bz/wp-content/uploads/2021/11/Cap.-304.01-International-Labour-Organization-Conventions-Act.pdf

Grenada

Employment Act, Cap. 89. Available from https://laws.gov.gd/

Guyana

Persons with Disabilities Act, Cap. 36:05. Available from https://mola.gov.gy/sites/default/files/Cap.%203605%20Person%20with%20Disabilities.pdf

Prevention of Discrimination Act, Cap. 99:08. Available from https://mola.gov.gy/sites/default/files/Cap.%209908.pdf

Jamaica

The Disabilities Act, 2014. Available from https://japarliament.gov.jm/attachments/341_The%20Disabilities%20bill%202014%20No.13.pdf

St. Lucia

Equality of Opportunity and Treatment in Employment and Occupation Act, Cap. 16.14. Available from https://www.ilo.org/wcmsp5/groups/public/---ed_protect/---protrav/---ilo_aids/documents/legaldocument/wcms_127741.pdf

Labour Code, 2006. Available from https://www.govt.lc/media.govt.lc/www/resources/legislation/SaintLuciaLabourCode2006.pdf

The Bahamas

Persons with Disabilities (Equal Opportunities) Act, 2014. Available from http://laws.bahamas.gov.bs/cms/images/legislation/principal/2014/2014-0031/PersonswithDisabilitiesEqualOpportunitiesAct2014_1.pdf

Trinidad and Tobago

Equal Opportunities Act, Ch. 22:03. (Revised Laws of Trinidad and Tobago, 2016). Available from https://agla.gov.tt/downloads/laws/22.03.pdf

United Kingdom

Disability Discrimination Act, 1995. Available from https://www.legislation.gov.uk/ukpga/1995/50/contents

Equality Act, 2010. Available from https://www.legislation.gov.uk/ukpga/2010/15/contents

CHAPTER 9

Experiences of Disabled Persons in Employment in the Caribbean Region

Introduction

This chapter consists of qualitative case reports based on the experiences of persons with differing disabilities across the Caribbean region. Each case study will outline the nature of the individual's disability and their experiences in seeking, obtaining and retaining full employment. Interviewees committed 30–40 min to the interviews which were conducted via Zoom, at their convenience. All protocols regarding vulnerable groups and ethics approvals were received from the University of the West Indies prior to the start of this project. All interviewees were asked to sign a consent form and were advised that they could withdraw consent at any time, even after the start of the interviews, and they were not compelled to reveal any sensitive information. Every effort was made by the interviewers to disguise the identity of the interviewees when providing the interview summaries. To this end the names used herein are pseudonyms and their professions were changed to preserve their anonymity. The accounts from three interviewees are described here along with an analysis of the relevant literature offering insights into employees with amputations, employees with non-work-related injuries and employees who have been diagnosed with a depressive disorder.

J. H. Stephenson and N. Persadie, *Disability in the Workplace*, Palgrave Explorations in Workplace Stigma,
https://doi.org/10.1007/978-3-031-19340-8_9

Depression

Depression is a common mental disorder and globally 5% of adults have been diagnosed with depressive disorders, which affect women more than men (Heinz et al., 2018; WHO, 2021). Depression and associated mental disorders can have a profound effect on all aspects of life, including employment, social, educational, personal and the ability to participate in the community. In the Caribbean, depression is one of the leading causes of disability (WHO, 2021) and within the organisational context, it is associated with a degradation in an employee's quality of life and levels of productivity and efficiency (Lagerveld et al., 2010; Madsen et al., 2017). Brosse et al. (2002) define depression as a "dysphoric mood state, comprised of a cluster of symptoms", which cause "*clinically significant distress or impairment in social, occupational, or other important areas of functioning*" (DSM-IV). The effects of depression can be long-lasting or recurrent. Depression varies in severity (from mild, moderate and severe), with the most severe form of depression referred to as clinical depression (major depression/major depressive disorder) (Brosse et al., 2002; Shani & Pizam, 2009). Clinical depression is referred to as "*a period of intense, often continuous feelings of sadness and hopelessness accompanied by cognitive and somatic symptoms requiring treatment* (i.e., psychotherapy and/or medication)" (Shani & Pizam, 2009: 448; *see also* Cassano & Fava, 2002; DSM-IV).

The causes of depression include complex interactions between social, psychological and biological factors (Cassano & Fava, 2002). Specifically, the probability of being diagnosed with a depressive disorder is contingent on one's: "*biochemistry (abnormalities of certain chemicals or networks in the brain), genetics (depression might be hereditary), personality (certain personal characteristics such as low self-esteem, being easily stressed, or pessimism), and environmental factors (e.g., exposure to violence, neglect, and poverty)*" (Shani & Pizam, 2009: 451). Depression is characterised by psychological, physical and social symptoms including but not limited to: - feelings of emptiness, worthlessness, guilt, hopelessness, sadness, irritability, frustration, sleep disturbances, loss of interest in routine activities, changes in appetite and weight, increased anxiety, difficulty concentrating, remembering or making decisions, recurrent thoughts of death and/or suicidal ideation, *inter alia* (Craft & Landers, 1998; APA, 2021; Shani & Pizam, 2008). Within the organisational context, this is manifested as difficulty in concentrating on assigned tasks, thinking clearly, processing information in a timely, efficient manner and the absence of effective time management (Shani & Pizam, 2009). As a consequence, depression can have an adverse relationship on the professional success of persons so diagnosed (Heinz et al., 2018).

According to the Diagnostic and Statistical Manual of Mental Disorders (DSM-IV), the criteria for major depressive episodes consist of five (5) or more of the following:

(A) Indicated symptoms must have been present during the same 2-week period, and represent a change from previous functioning; at least one of the symptoms is either:

  (1a) depressed mood or (2) loss of interest or pleasure.
  (1b) depressed mood most of the day, nearly every day, as indicated by either subjective report (e.g., feels sad or empty) or observation made by others (e.g., appears tearful);
  (2) markedly diminished interest or pleasure in all, or almost all, activities most of the day, nearly every day (as indicated by either subjective account or observation made by others);
  (3) significant bodyweight loss when not dieting or bodyweight gain (e.g., a change of more than 5% of bodyweight in a month), or decrease or increase in appetite nearly every day;
  (4) insomnia or hypersomnia nearly every day;
  (5) psychomotor agitation or retardation nearly every day (observable by others, not merely subjective feelings of restlessness or being slowed down);
  (6) fatigue or loss of energy nearly every day;
  (7) feelings of worthlessness or excessive or inappropriate guilt (which may be delusional) nearly every day (not merely self-reproach or guilt about being sick);
  (8) diminished ability to think or concentrate, or indecisiveness, nearly every day (either by subjective account or as observed by others);
  (9) recurrent thoughts of death (not just fear of dying), recurrent suicidal ideation without a specific plan, or a suicide attempt or a specific plan for committing suicide.

(B) The symptoms do not meet the criteria for a mixed episode.

(C) The symptoms cause clinically significant distress or impairment in social, occupational, or other important areas of functioning.

(D) The symptoms are not due to the direct physiological effects of a substance (e.g., a drug of abuse, a medication) or a general medical condition (e.g., hypothyroidism).
(E) The symptoms are not better accounted for by bereavement, i.e. after the loss of a loved one, the symptoms persist for longer than 2 months or are characterized by marked functional impairment, morbid preoccupation with worthlessness, suicidal ideation, psychotic symptoms, or psychomotor retardation.

Depression can occur for multiple reasons, both work and non-work related. Within the workplace, job challenges can result in stressors which affect an employee's physical and psychological well-being, these include but are not limited to an unreasonably high number of assigned tasks, with relatively short periods of time permitted, in which to complete them, toxic organisational culture, work-life imbalance, micromanagement by supervisors, lack of control, autonomy and decision-making authority, work effort-reward imbalance, an absence of organisational social support, job insecurity, bullying and harassment perpetrated by one or more organisational member, role conflict and ambiguity, post-traumatic stress (e.g. if there was a severe workplace accident resulting in death or injury) *inter alia* (Andrea et al., 2009; Brijnath et al., 2014; Heinz et al., 2018; Lerner et al., 2010; Madsen et al., 2017; Shani & Pizam, 2009).

Depression has been referred to as an invisible or hidden disability, due primarily to the ease with which symptoms may be easily disguised, unless the individual is having a severe episode, which may necessitate psychiatric, psychological or medical intervention to effectively address (Gignac et al., 2021). Importantly, a diagnosis of a depressive disorder is treatable, there are a number of treatments for depression and their efficacy depends on the severity and pattern of the diagnosed depressive disorder including medication (anti-depressants), psychotherapy (e.g. cognitive behavior therapy); brain stimulation therapies (e.g. electroconvulsive therapy), exercise (cardiorespiratory, strength training, flexibility etc.) however, where untreated, suicide may result (Bender & Farvolden, 2008; Brosse et al., 2002; Craft & Landers, 1998).

Some of the costs of mental health conditions such as depression, to organisations include *absenteeism* (days taken off due to their depressive symptoms), *presenteeism* (days where employees are less productive due to their depressive symptoms, partial disability days and reduced productivity) and *compensation claims* (made per year) (Australia, 2014; Bender & Farvolden, 2008; Lagerveld et al., 2010; Lerner et al., 2010). Depression severity influences employment outcomes and is positively correlated with workplace absences where employees have been diagnosed with other psychiatric disorders such as bipolar disorder (Lerner & Henke, 2008; Lerner et al., 2010). Where mental illnesses are compounded with physical illnesses, the adverse effects have a more significant impact on the affected employees (Lerner et al., 2004). In addition, there are other known *employment outcomes* for persons with depressive disorders, namely: stress, job dissatisfaction, burnout, job loss and depression (Bender & Farvolden, 2008; Lagerveld et al., 2010). Hence, untreated depressive disorders may result in lost productivity, accidents, conflict, aggression and potential suicide (Bender & Farvolden, 2008). In the Anglophone Caribbean, Guyana is the country with the leading incidence of suicide and is among the top five (5) countries globally, with the highest rate of suicide, according to the World Health Organisation (2021). In 2022, the reported rate of suicide per 100 k people in Guyana was 40.3, however, other islands have significantly lower suicide rates per 100 k people, hence, in Trinidad and Tobago, the rate of suicide was 8.7; in St. Lucia 7.9; in the Bahamas 3.5; in Jamaica 2.4; in St. Vincent and the Grenadines 1.0; in Antigua and Barbuda 0.4; in Barbados 0.6 and in Grenada 0.7 (WHO, 2021).

Persons with diagnosed depressive illnesses are hesitant to disclose their mental disorders as they fear the effects of discrimination and stigmatised attitudes and behaviour, on their job prospects and opportunities for growth and development at work (Alvarez-Galvez & Rojas-Garcia, 2019; Gould-Werth et al., 2018; Manning & White, 1995; Yoshimura et al., 2018). Consequently, failure to request and receive entitled accommodations may result in employees with depression performing sub-optimally. In the Caribbean, due to the recency of the passage of the anti-discrimination laws, this is further compounded by employees' lack of familiarity with their rights and entitlements provided by the Act, as well as the obligations and prohibitions of their employers, and are hesitant to request assistance as they may fear that it may be rejected by managers and/or misunderstood as the receipt of an unfair advantage by colleagues (Gould-Werth et al., 2018).

To create mentally healthy workplaces, employers are encouraged to create a positive working environment, building individual skills and resilience and supporting staff with mental health conditions which requires the successful implementation of an action to achieve a mentally healthy workplace is based on leadership commitment; develop and implement inclusive and flexible policies; making resources necessary for success (Australia, 2014; Heinz et al., 2018; Kline & Sussman, 2000; Shani & Pizam, 2009; Shani et al., 2014). Specifically, employee wellness programmes should include:—physical activity programmes, coaching and mentoring, mental health first aid and education, resilience training, Cognitive Behaviour Therapy (CBT) based return-to-work programmes, well-being checks or health screening and encouraging employee involvement (Australia, 2014). Such programmes are likely to result in the following organisational benefits: - reduced absenteeism, increased productivity or reduction in presenteeism, reduction in compensation claims, reduction in turnover, lower management costs, reduced incident costs and lower income insurance costs for the organisation (Reichel & Pizam, 1984; Shani & Pizam, 2009).

Interviewee—Aida Gutiérrez-Nurse

Aida is 35 years old and works in the public service. Aida has been diagnosed with clinical depression and anxiety. Aida was diagnosed by a psychiatrist and about 5 years prior to her diagnosis she found that she was always upset and sad about everything and nothing appeared to be giving her joy. She assumed that she was just a sad person and had to live with that reality. In her late 20s Aida was feeling particularly despondent and attempted suicide by overdosing on pills. After this occurred, her doctor recommended that she see a psychiatrist, which she did and continued to have regular appointments for a year. She stopped the sessions and only returned very occasionally.

Aida has always enjoyed going to work and her profession, but she has always had difficulty fitting in with her colleagues. This is largely because she does not enjoy socialising, engaging in pointless "small talk" and cannot understand the need for office gossip. She is honest about this with her colleagues and as a consequence has found herself the target of ridicule and disparaging comments. Aida has also had the experience of being micromanaged, which she detests immensely. These encounters have elicited several unkind responses from Aida, which have resulted in reprimands from supervisors.

Aida recalled a few incidents which occurred over her life at work. These include reporting her supervisor to senior management for what she perceived as unfair treatment, being obstinate and deliberately uncooperative to her supervisor and resigning with immediate effect from one of her roles.

Aida describes herself as conservative and guarded. For Aida, work is important, she values the opportunity to use the knowledge, skills and aptitudes which she has acquired in a productive way. While at work, as in life, she finds it difficult to observe injustices of any kind and feels compelled to intervene, much to the chagrin of her supervisors.

She often has periods of feeling isolated and abandoned and unable to cope, feelings of helplessness and hopelessness, guilt and intolerance, ill at ease with herself, trouble sleeping, low energy and low motivation. This has resulted in suicidal ideations during these times. Aida has asked her partner or parents to call into her job to report that she is unable to return to attend work that day.

Over time, her manager observed her difficulties and suggested the company's counselling service, which she did. The sessions helped for a while, but Aida eventually stopped attending, in part because she feared that the personal details which were being shared would not be kept confidential, despite assurances by the counsellor and the counselling service that they were not permitted to divulge any information.

Without support, stress from responsibilities at home and work collided and she was forced to take a leave of absence from work. Aida is contemplating whether she should explore opportunities elsewhere but is concerned that the pattern will continue.

Amputations

After amputation, jobseekers are concerned about finding suitable employment, and those with jobs to which they are returning are concerned with the recovery time required before returning to work, possibilities for promotion and development and these employees with disabilities are concerned with getting appropriate workplace accommodations (Schoppen et al., 2001). Amputations may be upper (arm, hand, finger, thumb) or lower extremities (leg, foot, toe) (Darter et al., 2018; Girdhar et al., 2001; Hawley et al., 2022; Sanders et al., 2018). Amputations within the Caribbean are typically associated with diabetes mellitus, which is one of the leading causes of disabilities in the Caribbean region, according to the World Health Organisation (WHO, 2021). With diabetes mellitus, complications related to nerve damage and poor blood circulation necessitate amputations to preserve the life of patients (Bennett et al., 2015; Boyne, 2017; Graz et al., 2018; Gregg et al., 2016; Holstein et al., 2000; Trautner et al., 1996, 2002). Within the Anglophone Caribbean, the incidence of "diabetic foot disease and the rates of lower extremity amputation are high" though the availability of prosthetics is limited (Sumpio et al., 2022).

According to the International Working Group on the Diabetic Foot[1] (IWGDF) have described diabetes complications as having significant societal costs, and a project that by 2035 the global prevalence of diabetes will rise to 600 million globally with 80% of affected patients residing in developing countries like the Caribbean (Bakker et al., 2015). Amputations have a significant impact on every aspect of a patient's life, and fundamentally change the way an individual functions socially and within employment (Brown, 2003; Darter et al., 2018; Girdhar et al., 2001). The increased individual economic burden is also significant as patients have to bear the direct and indirect medical costs associated with treating diabetes, required amputations and any attendant complications. In developing regions like the English-speaking Caribbean, patients rely on social services, government-funded health care services and charitable organisations to assist with the cost of prosthetics, appropriate footwear, disease management, after procedure care and recovery including the prevention of infections and wound healing.

The nature of the employment which persons with disabilities are able to effectively engage after amputations depends on the human resource policies and practices of the organisation (including the attitudes towards inclusion of management and staff), the sex and age of the affected employee, their psychological acceptance of the loss of limb, their level of education, degree of pain and discomfort, acceptance and use of prosthetics and amputation related complications (Arent et al., 2009; Balser, 2007; Darter et al., 2018; Girdhar et al., 2001; Hawley et al., 2022; Lee et al., 2022; McMahon, 2012; Murray, 2009; Sanders et al., 2018). The duration after the amputation and returning to work

[1] The International Working Group on the Diabetic Foot (IWGDF; www.iwgdf.org) was founded in 1996 and consists of experts from almost all disciplines involved in the care of patients with diabetes and foot problems. The IWGDF aims to prevent, or at least reduce, the adverse effects of foot problems in diabetes, in part by developing and continuously updating international guidance documents for use by all health care providers involved in diabetic foot care (*Source* https://iwgdfguidelines.org/wp-content/uploads/2017/10/website_development.pdf.).

may vary from 9 to 27 months, depending on the limp amputated, co-morbidities, the success of the amputation surgery and rehabilitation process, speed of access to and fitting of prosthesis and the recovery period required (Burger, 2009; Craig et al., 2017; Journeay et al., 2018; McMahon, 2012; Murray, 2009; Wang et al., 2013). Successful transitions back to gainful employment may therefore necessitate "retraining, further education and vocational rehabilitation and may require engagement in less physically demanding jobs" and accommodations made by the organisation (Darter et al., 2018, p. 660). These accommodations must be sensitively handled by organisations and include affected employees throughout the process and may vary contingent upon the type of amputation required, these include: alternative computer input devices, orthotic writing aids, tool grips, telecommunications aids and lifting and carrying items; adjustable desks, climbing assistance, standing supports, assistance lifting and carrying items, transport assistance (driving hand controls), walking assistance (such as rolling seats or wheelchairs), assistive equipment, providing personal assistants, transferring an employee to a different job/location, flexible schedules (Arent et al., 2009; Girdhar et al., 2001; Hashim & Wok, 2014; Hebert & Burger, 2016; Lee et al., 2022; McMahon, 2012; Padkapayeva et al., 2017; Shinall, 2019; Sundar, 2017). It is important to note that organisations are not required to offer accommodations which will result in undue financial hardship on organisations (Girdhar et al., 2001; see also Caribbean antidiscrimination laws[2]). In fact, unlike prevailing preconceived notions, the organisational costs of the average modification/accommodation required have been estimated between $100 and $500 USD (Burke et al., 2013; Chirikos, 1999; Girdhar et al., 2001; Kaye et al., 2011; MacDonald-Wilson et al., 2002; McFarlin et al., 1991; Schartz et al., 2006; Solovieva et al., 2011; Stein, 2003), this is in part because many of the aids required to make daily life and functioning, more comfortable after amputations, have already been acquired, by the employee before rejoining the workforce. While it might be necessary for some individuals to change jobs after amputations, this

[2] ***Antigua and Barbuda****—Disabilities and Equal Opportunities Act*, 2017 and Employment (Prevention) of Discrimination Bill, 2020. ***Barbados***—Employment (Prevention) of Discrimination Bill, 2020. ***Guyana***—Prevention of Discrimination Act, 1999 & *Persons with Disabilities Act*, 2010. ***Jamaica***—The Disabilities Act, 2014. ***St. Lucia***—Equality of Opportunity and Treatment in Employment and Occupation Act, 2000. ***Bahamas*** - Persons with Disabilities (Equal Opportunities) Act, 2014. ***Trinidad and Tobago*** - Equal Opportunities Act, 2001.

is not the outcome for all persons after amputations (Arent et al., 2009; Girdhar et al., 2001; Murray, 2009; Schartz et al., 2006).

Girdhar (2001, p. 107) suggests 8 key questions to be asked when organisations are considering accommodations for employees with amputations, and these are as follows:

1. What are the limitations of the amputee?
2. To what degree do these limitations affect the person and the person's job performance?
3. Is the person able to stand or walk without the aid of an assistive device, such as a wheelchair? If yes, how long can the person stand or walk unaided?
4. Does the person have full, partial, or no use of the upper extremities?
5. What specific tasks are problematic?
6. What accommodations are available to reduce or eliminate these problematic tasks? Are all possible resources being used to determine possible accommodations?
7. Once accommodations are in place, would it be useful to meet with the amputee to evaluate the effectiveness of the accommodations and determine whether additional accommodations might be needed?
8. Is education of supervisory personnel and coworkers regarding amputees who use these accommodations needed?

Interviewee—Rebecca Mondesir

Rebecca Mondesir is a 55-year-old Accountant, who has recently had to have one of her feet amputated due to diabetes. As a result of the amputation. Rebecca has had to request accommodation from her company and perhaps due to her fifteen (15) years of service and dedication, she was asked what would make her return to work easier and she was granted relocation to the first floor, and reconfiguration of her office to accommodate the use of her temporary wheelchair, until she was able to have the prosthesis fitted and transition to the use of a cane. Rebecca has always been an extrovert, the kind of person who "*never met a stranger*" and assumed that she had the total support of her company, including collegial support, but upon her return to work she began hearing rumours that some colleagues were wondering why she chose to return to work rather than taking early retirement, in order to create an opportunity for someone else in the company to be promoted.

As a result of these rumours Rebecca started to question her decision, and ultimately requested a meeting with senior management, where she shared her concerns and was reassured by management that she had successfully adapted to her new circumstances. With these assurances, Rebecca returned to her office and held a staff meeting where she asked staff to share any concerns they may have about her disability and her ability to do her job and any deficiencies which they observed since her return. The feedback was largely positive, and she was able to address those concerns shared at that time. Rebecca reports that she continues to enjoy a positive, transparent relationship with her staff and has not encountered any direct or indirect discrimination, and continues to be accommodated by the organisation, as her needs change over time.

Injuries

Persons with disabilities desire meaningful, full employment as do all other societal members (Hammel et al., 2008; Konrad et al., 2013; Lindsay et al., 2018). In contemporary societies, one's occupational status is an important determinant in social status and perceived prestige, therefore, employees in organisational posts where high skill levels and qualifications are required, are regarded as highly valued assets, and are positively correlated with well-being and self-esteem. Unfortunately, persons with disabilities face challenges in finding and retaining full employment (Weeden & Grusky, 2005). Persons with disabilities are typically underemployed, with temporary and/or part time work assignments, which are deficient in meeting their emotional, economic and social needs (Barnow, 2008; Burkhauser et al., 1998; Hammel et al., 2008; Konrad et al., 2013; 2018; Markel & Barclay, 2009).

By their nature, disabilities may be temporary, long-term or permanent (Čulík et al., 2020; Davis, 2005; Dias et al., 2018; González-Ramírez et al., 2017; Konrad et al., 2013). Temporary disabilities may occur as a result of sicknesses or injuries, which occur as a result of work-related causes, for example, accidents at work, which may occur as a result of failure to follow health and safety protocols (Martin-Fumado & Arimany-Manso, 2014; Vick & Lightman, 2010). As the name suggests, these disabilities are temporary in nature and while the average duration is one month, depending on the illness and/or injury, recovery may vary from two (2) days (gastroenteritis) to 365 days (depression), however, temporary disabilities may also result from non-work-related incidents, for example, sports injuries, domestic violence, vehicular accidents, falls at home, common ailments (Daigre et al., 2016; Davis, 2005; González-Ramírez et al., 2017; Macík et al., 2012). These temporary disabilities include but are not limited to migraines, skin disorders, back pain, anxiety, depression, broken bones (e.g. clavicle, arm, wrist, hip, ankle, foot, toe, hand), meniscus injuries, hernias, sciatica, gastroenteritis, carpal tunnel syndrome, tonsilitis, bronchitis, *inter alia* (González-Ramírez et al., 2017; Konrad et al., 2013; Macík et al., 2012).

Though these are not permanent impairments, persons who have been so diagnosed, may require temporary workplace accommodations to "minimize their impact on their ability to participate competitively in the workplace" (Davis, 2005: 309). As with permanent disabilities, the extent to which an organisation is successful at managing disabilities is contingent on its culture, its extant human resource policies and practices, health and safety policies and practices and the commitment by the organisation's management and staff to the pursuit of diversity, equality and inclusion, *inter alia* (Ahmed, 2012; Davis, 2005; Emens, 2008; Kirton & Greene, 2021; Popovich et al., 2003; Schur et al., 2005). Further, the costs associated with accommodations for persons with temporary disabilities are temporary and unlikely to result in undue financial hardships which will result in compromised organisational sustainability (Bruyere et al., 2002; Daigre et al., 2016; Davis, 2005; Kaye et al., 2011; Lengnick-Hall, 2008; Nevala et al., 2015; Sundar, 2017). During the recovery period it is also essential for organisations to acknowledge the incremental nature of the process, during which employees should feel valued by their employers and colleagues (Davis, 2005). Required accommodations should be provided by the organisation in consultation with the affected employee and are likely to be beneficial, where they address temporary changes in the employee's pace of work, ability to complete tasks on prescribed schedule, physical capacity (e.g. lower back pain, broken foot), which could affect access to their normal routine and the organisational conditions in which they are likely to be successful (Macík et al., 2012; Vick & Lightman, 2010).

Interviewee—Philip Mayers

Philip Mayers is a 40-year-old motorbike enthusiast and an automotive store employee. Philip works in the part department of the company. A few years ago, during a bike ride with friends, Philip got into an accident and seriously injured his foot. He was hospitalised as a result and had to have surgery to have the foot reconstructed. He has now recovered from the surgery but due to the multiple plates that were needed, he continues to experience some occasional discomfort when engaging in strenuous activities like running or standing for long periods, which is required for his job. When he was permitted to return to work by his doctors, Philip got in touch with his manager and requested a meeting. He told the manager that he was unwilling to aggravate his injury by standing all day or by walking back and forth in the stock room all day and asked to be reassigned to a less physically demanding job.

During the meeting the manager told Philip that he looks fine and it appeared as though he was ready to "pick up where he left off", but Philip protested and shared the advice from his doctor that he would need further surgery if he failed to follow his medical advice and he could not guarantee that those surgery outcomes would be just as favourable. Philip sought advice from his wife and decided that he would not return to that company. In his view, what occurred was effectively constructive dismissal as a result of his disability. He was able to find another job within 3 months of leaving, which was largely sedentary in nature and required less physical energy than his former post.

Conclusion

This chapter recounts three different outcomes for employees with disabilities in Caribbean organisations. The three jurisdictions represented by these cases, have all enacted laws prohibiting discrimination on the basis of disability, though with varying human resource policies and practices. In the case of Rebecca, the employer's primary concern was retaining an asset that was valuable to the company and they were successful in doing so. In her case all parties were satisfied with the outcome. With respect to Philip, he decided that it was not worth the effort to pursue a legal remedy, and he just wanted to get on with his life. Though from the perspective of self-preservation, his decision is understood, the effect is that his former employer's will continue to pursue organisational objectives, with their current employees until they are unable to function in the prescribed manner, at which time they will be forced to make a decision as to the sacrifices they are willing to make for the company. Aida's situation is one where long-term support is needed to ensure the restoration and maintenance of her mental health. There are resources that are available in her country, in addition to which she can access multiple online mental healthcare services. It was beyond the scope of this exercise to recommend any course of action to these interviewees, since the interviewer was not a trained attorney-at-law, psychologist or psychiatrist. Notwithstanding this, extant literature and available policy guidance offer some insight into their experience and possible recourse. Further, these accounts allow a practical perspective on the theoretical differences between disclosure and non-disclosure, and disabilities which are physical and psychological.

Regarding organisational changes, Laughlin (1991) proposed a change model,[3] suggesting that an environmental disturbance (for example, the enactment of legislation, merging of organisations, economic recessions *inter alia*) will not have the same effect across workplaces; thus, it should not be assumed that where change occurs it will do so at the same rate and manner across workplaces (Nelson, 2003). However, the Laughlin (1991) model is not without dissention, as for example Gray et al. (1995, *see also* Fennell & Arnot, 2008) contend that the model is too inflexible, and does not take into consideration, ambiguities and contradictions which may occur within an organisational environment. To this end, issues of organisational context and mediating factors are important considerations, including but not limited to: - the competitive nature of the market, the workplace culture structure, trade union influence, management style and strategies and current practice (Dickens, 1999; Wood et al., 2004). Thus,

[3] Prior to the incidence of environmental disturbance, Laughlin (1991) theorises that workplaces are in a state of inertia or equilibrium and proposes four types of change responses likely to occur after an environmental disturbance, which may be categorised as follows: (i) ***rebuttal***, where despite the environmental change there is an attempt by the workplace to maintain the status quo; (ii) ***reorientation***, where environmental change is accepted and incorporated into the way in which the workplace functions but is managed such that existing beliefs, values and norms remain unchanged; (iii) ***colonisation***, which occurs where change is imposed on the workplace and consequently beliefs and norms change along with the workplace ethos; and finally the (iv) ***evolution*** response to environmental change is where change occurs as a consequence of the relevant stakeholders within the workplace agreeing to adopt and pursue a new direction.

for example, where culturally accepted workplace practices are in contravention with equality legislation, ensuring compliance will be challenging, as adapting to legislative requirements may require comprehensive organisational adjustments (see Heery & Simms, 2005). Further, it has also been argued that the presence of a trade union can influence the extent of workplace change (Budd & Mumford, 2004). This is because according to Meager et al. (2002: 126) the organisational presence of a "trade union, affects the capacity to use and to comply with legislation and may provide a mechanism for monitoring and enforcement." Moreover, as it relates to workplace objectives, it has been argued that workplaces typically have a short-term outlook rather than a longer term vision in respect of equalities and anti-discrimination campaigns. This suggests that business imperatives may be quite influential in the immediate to short term, in relation to the fulfilment of legislative requirements, in part because of costs which could be incurred in order for workplaces to achieve full compliance (Dickens, 1999).

One area of commonality with respect to organisational change is that of commitment, *to wit*, commitment of organisations to making requisite change. This suggests that unless there is a significant degree of support from the workplace and its key managers, change beyond that of the superficial (e.g. change in policy statements) is unlikely to result. Another important consideration is that of implementation, indeed, it seems apparent that where policies to be implemented are not enforced and monitored, the likelihood for success would not be favourable. Justice may be seen to be done as a consequence of the bureaucratisation of policies but where non-discrimination is the desired outcome, commitment and thorough implementation is essential. Comprehensiveness is also important. In the Caribbean, the extant anti-discrimination laws do not permit positive discrimination and as a consequence where workers with disabilities are seen to receive more favourable treatment (except for training where positive action is permitted by the law), this may negatively impact the workplace. On the other hand, there are factors which are external to the workplace which may mediate the extent to which equality law is influential on workplace practice. Invariably the elements which comprise external influences are those over which the workplace typically has no control (e.g. government policies, technological changes, Convention on the Rights of Persons with Disabilities-CRPD) but may be obligated (as is the case with legislation) to make the required changes to employment practice, to mitigate their effect (Bennington & Wein, 2002; Gagnon & Cornelius, 2000; Laughlin, 1991; Smedley & Whitten, 2006; Taylor & Walker, 1998). It has been predicted that the labour pool of the future is likely to be comprised of a greater proportion of persons with disabilities, it would therefore be prudent and beneficial for Caribbean organisations to actively pursue an inclusive, diverse human resource agenda or fail to realise the benefits which are likely to be accrued by employing persons with disabilities, such as competitive advantage.

References

Ahmed, S. (2012). *On being included: Racism and diversity in institutional life.* Duke University Press.

Alvarez-Galvez, J., & Rojas-Garcia, A. (2019). Measuring the impact of multiple discrimination on depression in Europe. *BMC Public Health, 19*(1), 1–11.

American Psychiatric Association (APA). 2021. *Diagnostic and Statistical Manual of Mental Disorders IV (DSM-IVTR).* American Psychiatric Association Publishing.

Andrea, H., Bültmann, U., van Amelsvoort, L. G., & Kant, Y. (2009). The incidence of anxiety and depression among employees—the role of psychosocial work characteristics. *Depression and Anxiety, 26*(11), 1040–1048.

Arent, S., Dickson, M., & Dimick, B. (2009). *Employment considerations for people who have diabetes.*

Australia, P. (2014). Creating a mentally healthy workplace: Return on investment analysis.

Bakker, K., Apelqvist, J., Lipsky, B., Van Netten, J., & Schaper, N. C. (2015). *The 2015 IWGDF Guidance documents on prevention and management of foot problems in diabetes: development of an evidence-based global consensus.* International Working Group on the Diabetic Foot (IWGDF).

Balser, D. B. (2007). Predictors of workplace accommodations for employees with mobility-related disabilities. *Administration & Society, 39*(5), 656–683.

Barnow, B. S. (2008). The employment rate of people with disabilities. *Monthly Laboratory Review, 131*, 44.

Bender, A., & Farvolden, P. (2008). Depression and the workplace: A progress report. *Current Psychiatry Reports, 10*(1), 73–79.

Bennett, N. R., Francis, D. K., Ferguson, T. S., Hennis, A. J., Wilks, R. J., Harris, E. N., MacLeish, M. M., & Sullivan, L. W. (2015). Disparities in diabetes mellitus among Caribbean populations: A scoping review. *International Journal for Equity in Health, 14*(1), 1–17.

Bennington, L., & Wein, R. (2002). Aiding and abetting employer discrimination: The job applicant's role. *Employee Responsibilities and Rights Journal, 14*(1), 3–16.

Boyne, M. S. (2017). Diabetes in the Caribbean. In *Diabetes mellitus in developing countries and underserved communities* (pp. 127–149). Springer.

Brijnath, B., Mazza, D., Singh, N., Kosny, A., Ruseckaite, R., & Collie, A. (2014). Mental health claims management and return to work: Qualitative insights from Melbourne, Australia. *Journal of Occupational Rehabilitation, 24*(4), 766–776.

Brosse, A. L., Sheets, E. S., Lett, H. S., & Blumenthal, J. A. (2002). Exercise and the treatment of clinical depression in adults. *Sports Medicine, 32*(12), 741–760.

Brown, J. D. (2003). *Amputations: A continuing workplace hazard*. Bureau of Labor Statistics.

Bruyere, S., Erickson, W., & Ferrentino, J. (2002). Identity and disability in the workplace. *William & Mary Law Review, 44*(3), 1173–1196.

Budd, J. W., & Mumford, K. (2004). Trade unions and family-friendly policies in Britain. *Industrial and Labor Relations Review, 57*(2), 204–222.

Burger, H. (2009). Return to work after amputation. In *Amputation, prosthesis use, and phantom limb pain* (pp. 101–114). Springer.

Burke, J., Bezyak, J., Fraser, R. T., Pete, J., Ditchman, N., & Chan, F. (2013). Employers' attitudes towards hiring and retaining people with disabilities: A review of the literature. *The Australian Journal of Rehabilitation Counselling, 19*(1), 21–38.

Burkhauser, R. V. (1998). Policies to make work pay for people with disabilities. In *Growth in cash disability benefits: Explanations and policy implications* (pp. 365–371). Upjohn Press.

Cassano, P., & Fava, M. (2002). Depression and public health: An overview. *Journal of Psychosomatic Research, 53*(4), 849–857.

Chirikos, T. N. (1999). Will the costs of accommodating workers with disabilities remain low? *Behavioral Sciences and the Law, 17*(1), 93–106.

Craft, L. L., & Landers, D. M. (1998). The effect of exercise on clinical depression and depression resulting from mental illness: A meta-analysis. *Journal of Sport and Exercise Psychology, 20*(4), 339–357.

Craig, M., Hill, W., Englehart, K., & Adisesh, A. (2017). Return to work after occupational injury and upper limb amputation. *Occupational Medicine, 67*(3), 227–229.

Čulík, K., Hájnik, A., & Harantová, V. (2020, October). Improving the Mobility of People with Disabilities. In *2020 XII international science-technical conference automotive saFETY* (pp. 1–5). IEEE.

Daigre, C., Granell, A., Grau-López, L., Fadeuilhe, C., Calcedo-Barba, A., & Roncero, C. (2016). Risk factors for temporary work disability. *Actas Españolas De Psiquiatría, 44*(4), 119–124.

Darter, B. J., Hawley, C. E., Armstrong, A. J., Avellone, L., & Wehman, P. (2018). Factors influencing functional outcomes and return-to-work after amputation: A review of the literature. *Journal of Occupational Rehabilitation, 28*(4), 656–665.

Davis, L. (2005). Disabilities in the workplace: Recruitment, accommodation, and retention. *Aaohn Journal, 53*(7), 306–312.

Dias, A., Gómez-Salgado, J., Bernardes, J. M., & Ruiz-Frutos, C. (2018). Factors affecting sick leave duration for non-work-related temporary disabilities in Brazilian university public servants. *International Journal of Environmental Research and Public Health, 15*(10), 2127.

Dickens, L. (1999). Beyond the business case: A three-pronged approach to equality action. *Human Resource Management Journal, 9*(1), 9–19.

Emens, E. F. (2008). Integrating accommodation. *University of Pennsylvania Law Review, 156*(4), 839–922.

Fennell, S. and Arnot, M. (Eds) (2008). *Gender education and equality in a global context: conceptual frameworks and policy perspectives.* Routledge.

Fisher, K., Hanspal, R. S., & Marks, L. (2003). Return to work after lower limb amputation. *International Journal of Rehabilitation Research, 26*(1), 51–56.

Gagnon, S., & Cornelius, N. (2000). Re-examining workplace equality: Applying Sen and Nussbaum's capability approach. *Human Resource Management Journal, 10*(4), 68–87.

Gignac, M. A., Bowring, J., Jetha, A., Beaton, D. E., Breslin, F. C., Franche, R. L., Irvin, E., Macdermid, J. C., Shaw, W. S., Smith, P. M., Thompson, A., Tompa, E., Van Eerd, D., & Saunders, R. (2021). Disclosure, privacy and workplace accommodation of episodic disabilities: Organizational perspectives on disability communication-support processes to sustain employment. *Journal of Occupational Rehabilitation, 31*(1), 153–165.

Girdhar, A., Mital, A., Kephart, A., & Young, A. (2001). Design guidelines for accommodating amputees in the workplace. *Journal of Occupational Rehabilitation, 11*(2), 99–118.

González-Ramírez, C., Montanero-Fernández, J., & Peral-Pacheco, D. (2017). A multifactorial study on duration of temporary disabilities in Spain. *Archives of Environmental & Occupational Health, 72*(6), 328–335.

Gould-Werth, A., Morrison, K., & Ben-Shalom, Y. (2018). Employers' perspectives on accommodating and retaining employees with newly acquired disabilities: An exploratory study. *Journal of Occupational Rehabilitation, 28*(4), 611–633.

Gray, R., Walters, D., Bebbington, J., & Thompson, I. (1995). The greening of enterprise: An exploration of the (NON) role of environmental accounting and environmental accountants in organizational change. *Critical Perspectives on Accounting, 6*(3), 211–239.

Graz, H., D'Souza, V. K., Alderson, D. E., & Graz, M. (2018). Diabetes-related amputations create considerable public health burden in the UK. *Diabetes Research and Clinical Practice, 135*, 158–165.

Gregg, E. W., Sattar, N., & Ali, M. K. (2016). The changing face of diabetes complications. *The Lancet Diabetes & Endocrinology, 4*(6), 537–547.

Guimarães, B., Martins, L. B., & Barkokébas Junior, B. (2015). Workplace accommodation to people with disabilities: A case study in civil construction. *Fisioterapia Em Movimento, 28*, 779–791.

Hammel, J., Magasi, S., Heinemann, A., Whiteneck, G. B., & J & Rodriguez, E. (2008). What does participation mean? An insider perspective from people with disabilities. *Disability and Rehabilitation, 30*(19), 1445–1460.

Hashim, J., & Wok, S. (2014). Predictors to employees with disabilities' organisational behaviour and involvement in employment. *Equality, Diversity and Inclusion: An International Journal, 23*, 193–209.

Hawkins, A. T., Henry, A. J., Crandell, D. M., & Nguyen, L. L. (2014). A systematic review of functional and quality of life assessment after major lower extremity amputation. *Annals of Vascular Surgery, 28*(3), 763–780.

Hawley, C. E., Armstrong, A. J., Darter, B. J., Sima, A., & Fields, K. (2022). Veterans of operation enduring freedom and operation iraqi freedom: Employment status following traumatic amputation. *Journal of Applied Rehabilitation Counseling, 53*(1), 68–80.

Hebert, J. S., & Burger, H. (2016). Return to work following major limb loss. In *Handbook of return to work* (pp. 505–517). Springer.

Heery, E., & Simms, M. (2005). Union organising under certification law in the United Kingdom. In G. Gall (Ed.), *Union recognition: Organising and bargaining outcomes*. Routledge.

Heinz, A. J., Meffert, B. N., Halvorson, M. A., Blonigen, D., Timko, C., & Cronkite, R. (2018). Employment characteristics, work environment, and the course of depression over 23 years: Does employment help foster resilience? *Depression and Anxiety, 35*(9), 861–867.

Holstein, P., Ellitsgaard, N., Bornefeldt Olsen, B., & Ellitsgaard, V. (2000). Decreasing incidence of major amputations in people with diabetes. *Diabetologia, 43*(7), 844–847.

Journeay, W. S., Pauley, T., Kowgier, M., & Devlin, M. (2018). Return to work after occupational and non-occupational lower extremity amputation. *Occupational Medicine, 68*(7), 438–443.

Juurlink, T. T., Ten Have, M., Lamers, F., van Marle, H. J., Anema, J. R., de Graaf, R., & Beekman, A. T. (2018). Borderline personality symptoms and work performance: A population-based survey. *BMC Psychiatry, 18*(1), 1–9.

Kaye, H. S., Jans, L. H., & Jones, E. C. (2011). Why don't employers hire and retain workers with disabilities? *Journal of Occupational Rehabilitation, 21*(4), 526–536.

Kirton, G. & Greene, A. M. (2021). *The dynamics of managing diversity and inclusion: A critical approach*. Routledge.

Kleine-Budde, K., Müller, R., Kawohl, W., Bramesfeld, A., Moock, J., & Rössler, W. (2013). The cost of depression–a cost analysis from a large database. *Journal of Affective Disorders, 147*(1–3), 137–143.

Kline Jr., J., & Sussman, L. (2000). An executive guide to workplace depression. *Academy of Management Perspectives*, *14*(3), 103–114.

Konrad, A. M., Moore, M. E., Ng, E. S., Doherty, A. J., & Breward, K. (2013). Temporary work, underemployment and workplace accommodations: Relationship to well-being for workers with disabilities. *British Journal of Management, 24*(3), 367–382.

Lagerveld, S. E., Bültmann, U., Franche, R. L., Van Dijk, F. J. H., Vlasveld, M. C., van der Feltz-Cornelis, C. M., & Nieuwenhuijsen, K. (2010). Factors associated with work participation and work functioning in depressed workers: A systematic review. *Journal of Occupational Rehabilitation, 20*(3), 275–292.

Laughlin, R. (1991). Enviornmental disturbances and organisational transitions and transformations: Some alternative models. *Organisational Studies, 12*(2), 209–232.

Lee, C., Engdahl, S., Riegger, A., Davis, A., Kelly, B. M., & Gates, D. H. (2022). Employment status in individuals with upper-limb amputation: A survey of current trends. *JPO: Journal of Prosthetics and Orthotics*, *34*(2), 79–88.

Lerner, D., & Henke, R. M. (2008). What does research tell us about depression, job performance, and work productivity? *Journal of Occupational and Environmental Medicine*, *50*(4), 401–410.

Lengnick-Hall, M. L., Gaunt, P. M & Kulkarni, M. (2008). Overlooked and underutilized. People with disabilities are an untapped human resource. *Human Resource Management, 47*(2), 255–273.

Lerner, D., Adler, D. A., Chang, H., Berndt, E. R., Irish, J. T., Lapitsky, L., Hood, M. Y., Reed, J., & Rogers, W. H. (2004). The clinical and occupational correlates of work productivity loss among employed patients with depression. *Journal of Occupational and Environmental Medicine/american College of Occupational and Environmental Medicine, 46*(6), S46.

Lerner, D., Adler, D. A., Rogers, W. H., Lapitsky, L., McLaughlin, T., & Reed, J. (2010). Work performance of employees with depression: The impact of work stressors. *American Journal of Health Promotion, 24*(3), 205–213.

Lindsay, S., Cagliostro, E., Albarico, M., Mortaji, N., & Karon, L. (2018). A systematic review of the benefits of hiring people with disabilities. *Journal of Occupational Rehabilitation, 28*(4), 634–655.

MacDonald-Wilson, K. L., Rogers, E. S., Massaro, J. M., Lyass, A., & Crean, T. (2002). An investigation of reasonable workplace accommodations for people with psychiatric disabilities: Quantitative findings from a multi-site study. *Community Mental Health Journal, 38*(1), 35–50.

Macík, M., Sporka, A. J., & Slavík, P. (2012). An initial study of effects of temporary disabilities. *ACM SIGACCESS Accessibility and Computing, 103*, 3–13.

Madsen, I. E. H., Nyberg, S. T., Magnusson Hanson, L. L., Ferrie, J. E., Ahola, K., Alfredsson, L., Batty, G. D., Bjorner, J. B., Borritz, M., Burr, H., Chastang, J.-F., de Graaf, R., Dragano, N., Hamer, M., Jokela, M., Knutsson, A., Koskenvuo, M., Koskinen, A., Leineweber, C., ... Kivimäki, M. (2017). Job strain as a risk factor for clinical depression: Systematic review and meta-analysis with additional individual participant data. *Psychological Medicine, 47*(8), 1342–1356.

Manning, C., & White, P. D. (1995). Attitudes of employers to the mentally ill. *Psychiatric Bulletin, 19*(9), 541–543.

Markel, K., & Barclay, L. (2009). Addressing the underemployment of persons with disabilities: Recommendations for expanding organisational social responsibility. *Employee Responsibilities and Rights Journal, 21*(4), 305–318.

Martin-Fumadó, C., & Arimany-Manso, J. (2014). Temporary disability and its legal implications. *Medicina Clinica, 142*, 37–42.

McCaffrey, D. P. (1981). Work-related amputations by type and prevalence. *Monthly Laboratory Review, 104*, 35.

McFarlin, D. B., Song, J., & Sonntag, M. (1991). Integrating the disabled into the work force: A survey of Fortune 500 company attitudes and practices. *Employee Responsibilities and Rights Journal, 4*(2), 107–123.

McMahon, B. T. (2012). An overview of workplace discrimination and disability. *Journal of Vocational Rehabilitation, 36*(3), 135–139.

Meager, N., Tyers, C., Perryman, S., Rick, J. And Willison, R. (2002). *Awareness, knowledge and exercise of individual rights* (Employment Relations Research Series, No. 15). DTI and IES.

Murray, C. (Ed.). (2009). *Amputation, prosthesis use, and phantom limb pain: An interdisciplinary perspective* (Vol. 14). Springer.

Nelson, L. (2003). A case study in organisational change: Implications for theory. *The Learning Organisation, 10*, 1.

Nevala, N., Pehkonen, I., Koskela, I., Ruusuvuori, J., & Anttila, H. (2015). Workplace Accomodation among persons with disabilities: A systematic review of its effectiveness and barriers or facilitators. *Journal of Occupational Rehabilitation, 25*(2), 432–448.

Padkapayeva, K., Posen, A., Yazdani, A., Buettgen, A., Mahood, Q., & Tompa, E. (2017). Workplace accommodations for persons with physical disabilities:

Evidence synthesis of the peer-reviewed literature. *Disability and Rehabilitation, 39*(21), 2134–2147.
Pan American Health Organization—PAHO. (2021). *Methodological notes.* NMH Data Portal, Pan American Health Organization.
Pohjolainen, T., Alaranta, H., & Kärkäinen, M. (1990). Prosthetic use and functional and social outcome following major lower limb amputation. *Prosthetics and Orthotics International, 14*(2), 75–79.
Popovich, P., Scherbaum, C., Scherbaum, K., & Polinko, N. (2003). The assessment of attitudes toward individuals with disabilities in the workplace. *The Journal of Psychology, 137*(2), 163–177.
Reichel, A., & Pizam, A. (1984). Job satisfaction, lifestyle and demographics of US hospitality industry workers—versus others. *International Journal of Hospitality Management, 3*(3), 123–133.
Sanders, J. E., Redd, C. B., Larsen, B. G., Vamos, A. C., Brzostowski, J. T., Hafner, B. J., Allyn, K. J., Henrikson, K., McLean, J. B., & Hinrichs, P. (2018). A novel method for assessing prosthesis use and accommodation practices of people with transtibial amputation. *Journal of Prosthetics and Orthotics: JPO, 30*(4), 214.
Schartz, H. A., Hendricks, D. J., & Blanck, P. (2006). Workplace accommodations: Evidence based outcomes. *Work, 27*(4), 345–354.
Schoppen, T., Boonstra, A., Groothoff, J. W., de Vries, J., Göeken, L. N., & Eisma, W. H. (2001). Employment status, job characteristics, and work-related health experience of people with a lower limb amputation in The Netherlands. *Archives of Physical Medicine and Rehabilitation, 82*(2), 239–245.
Schur, L., Kruse, D., & Blanck, P. (2005). Corporate culture and the employment of persons with disabilities. *Behaviour Sciences and the Law, 23*(1), 3–20.
Shani, A., & Pizam, A. (2009). Work-related depression among hotel employees. *Cornell Hospitality Quarterly, 50*(4), 446–459.
Shani, A., Uriely, N., Reichel, A., & Ginsburg, L. (2014). Emotional labor in the hospitality industry: The influence of contextual factors. *International Journal of Hospitality Management, 37*, 150–158.
Shinall, J. B. (2019). Anticipating accommodation. *Iowa Law Review, 105*, 621.
Smedley, K. and Whitten, H. (2006). *Age matters—employing, motivating and managing older employees.* Gower Publishing.
Solovieva, T. I., Dowler, D. L., & Walls, R. T. (2011). Employer benefits from making workplace accommodations. *Disability and Health Journal, 4*(1), 39–45.
Stein, M. A. (2003). The law and economics of disability accommodations. *Duke LJ, 53*, 79.

Sumpio, B. E., McConnie, S., & Maharaj, D. (2022). Heterogeneity in the guidelines for the management of diabetic foot disease in the Caribbean. *PLOS Global Public Health, 2*(5), e0000446.

Sundar, V. (2017). Operationalizing workplace accommodations for individuals with disabilities: A scoping review. *Work, 56*(1), 135–155.

Taylor, P., & Walker, A. (1998). Policies and practices towards older workers: A framework for comparative research. *Human Resource Management Journal, 8*(3), 61–76.

Trautner, C., Haastert, B., Giani, G., & Berger, M. (1996). Incidence of lower limb amputations and diabetes. *Diabetes Care, 19*(9), 1006–1009.

Trautner, C., Haastert, B., Giani, G., & Berger, M. (2002). Amputations and diabetes: A case-control study. *Diabetic Medicine, 19*(1), 35–40.

Vick, A., & Lightman, E. (2010). Barriers to employment among women with complex episodic disabilities. *Journal of Disability Policy Studies, 21*(2), 70–80.

Wang, K., Sears, E. D., Shauver, M. J., & Chung, K. C. (2013). A systematic review of outcomes of revision amputation treatment for fingertip amputations. *The Hand, 8*(2), 139–145.

Wells, K. B., & Sturm, R. (1995). Care for depression in a changing environment. *Health Affairs, 14*(3), 78–89.

West, S. L., McMahon, B. T., Monasterio, E., Belongia, L., & Kramer, K. (2005). Workplace discrimination and missing limbs: The national EEOC ADA research project. *Work, 25*(1), 27–35.

Weeden, K. A., & Grusky, D. B. (2005). The case for a new class map. *American Journal of Sociology, 111*(1), 141–212.

Wood, G., Harcourt, M., & Harcourt, S. (2004). The effects of age discrimination legislation on workplace practice: A New Zealand case study. *Industrial Relations Journal, 35*(4), 359–371.

World Health Organization—WHO. (2020a). *WHO methods and data sources for country-level causes of death 2000–2019*. World Health Organization.

World Health Organization—WHO. (2020b). *WHO methods and data sources for global burden of disease estimates, 2000–2019*. World Health Organization.

World Health Organisation (WHO). (2021). *Depression*. WHO.

Yoshimura, Y., Bakolis, I., & Henderson, C. (2018). Psychiatric diagnosis and other predictors of experienced and anticipated workplace discrimination and concealment of mental illness among mental health service users in England. *Social Psychiatry and Psychiatric Epidemiology, 53*(10), 1099–1109.

CHAPTER 10

Conclusion

Introduction

Each of the foregoing chapters offers useful and insightful discussions on persons with disabilities who may be seeking employment, and employees with disabilities, through the exploration and analysis of the nature of disabilities, the provision and access to education for students with disabilities and the facilitation of assistive devices for employees with disabilities who might benefit from such accommodation. We have also comprehensively assessed the experiences of persons who have been diagnosed with mental disorders, employees who are neurodiverse, employees with amputations, as well as others with non-work-related injuries in Caribbean organisations. Given the challenges which we have discussed, as it relates to persons with disabilities seeking and desirous of retaining employment, multiple change catalysts have been examined, including, but not limited to, the effective enactment and implementation of anti-discrimination legislation in the Commonwealth Caribbean. Any acts or omissions which result in the exclusion of this group from the labour force, starting from early educational exclusion, will deny organisations the opportunity to access assets with the potential to contribute to their competitive advantage, and facilitate a different perspective from a segment of the population which is not typically represented.

J. H. Stephenson and N. Persadie, *Disability in the Workplace*, Palgrave Explorations in Workplace Stigma,
https://doi.org/10.1007/978-3-031-19340-8_10

Discriminatory Conduct and Employment Engagement

The hierarchy of impairments has emerged as a useful framework in aiding our understanding of the stereotypical perception of persons with disabilities. In fact, the hierarchy of impairments appears to permeate employment practice, such that some impairments are perceived to be less discriminated against relative to others. As a reminder, the hierarchy of impairments is structured such that "acquired injuries (e.g. spinal and visual impairments), are at the top of the hierarchy", and more accepted societally, than others "such as speech impairments, learning disabilities, mental disorders, facial disfigurements (*inter alia*)" (Smith, 2012). The hierarchy is so structured because, those impairments at the top of the hierarchy are not perceived to be barriers to social interaction and do not evoke fear and discomfort from others (Deal, 2003; Harpur 2017, 2019; Kelly, 2010; Smith, 2012). In short, this ranking system, which is dependent on the nature and severity of disabilities, results in some persons with disabilities facing more incidents of discrimination (I.e. those with the lowest ranked impairments), by both persons with disabilities and persons with no known disabilities.

As we have seen, although multiple models of disability exist, in the Caribbean, the medical model prevails, where the diagnosed medical condition is believed to be disabling and limiting for persons with disabilities (Retief & Letšosa, 2018; Smart & Smart, 2006). On the contrary, the social model of disability perceives socially erected barriers, as the primary challenge faced by persons with disabilities who are desirous of actively and productively engaging in employment and otherwise positively contributing to society (Llewelyn & Hogan, 2000). To this end, let us consider individuals with a hearing impairment, the above-mentioned hierarchal framework suggests that persons with hearing impairments face relatively higher incidents of discrimination, but why does this occur? The hierarchy's answer to this question, is because of fear and discomfort of others, and the erroneous belief that persons with hearing impairments are unable to socially engage.

Collectively, these illustrate presumptions about persons with disabilities,[1] which have been embedded in society over time, are pervasive,

[1] Cognitive distortions in relation to persons with disabilities are informed by culturally accepted information, which has become normalised as stereotypes about a societal group.

unchallenged and presumed to be true, by virtue of their frequent use and repetition, and despite an absence of empirical evidence to support them. These also demonstrate a complete disregard for the proven heterogeneity of societal groups of people.

Continuing with our example, there are different severity levels of hearing impairments, and hearing loss may be temporary or permanent. Further, hearing loss may be *mild* (loss of between 20 to 40 decibels); *moderate* (loss of between 41 and 60 decibels); *severe* (between 61 and 80 decibels); *profound* (more than 81 decibels) (Bance, 2007; Bussé et al., 2020; Killion et al., 2004; Michels et al., 2019). Notably only hearing loss of more than 40 decibels constitutes a hearing impairment (Humes, 2019; Mulrow et al., 1990; Olusanya et al., 2019) thus individuals with hearing impairments may range from those who hard are of hearing to profound deafness and may be unilateral (affecting one ear) or bilateral (affecting both ears), in nature. Loss of hearing may also affect speech depending on when it occurs, thus persons with prelingual[2] hearing impairments may have delays in language acquisition, while persons with post lingual hearing impairments, have already acquired language skills before their hearing was adversely affected, thus their speech is not as acutely affected (Campbell & Sharma, 2014; Cavender & Ladner, 2008; Firzst et al., 2012; Muigg et al., 2021; Nance et al., 2006; Raymond et al., 2021).

Notwithstanding the type of hearing loss, persons with hearing impairments are expected to accommodate their hearing colleagues by wearing hearing aids, learning to lip read and/or by subjecting themselves to surgical procedures where available, for example, to facilitate cochlear

Stereotypes are heuristics, and as such do not apply to all group members. Thus in the same way that it would be offensive and irrelevant to make a recruitment decision as to a candidate's suitability based on their height, all employment related decisions should be done on a meritorious basis, after evaluating the candidate, being considered, specifically their knowledge, skills, abilities, experience, qualifications and aptitudes for the job role, rather than what is believed to be known all persons with disabilities (Krieger, 1995; Reskin, 2000, 2018).

[2] The point of departure between pre- and post-lingual hearing impairments, with respect to the former, impairment occurs before spoken language acquisition in infancy, and with respect to the latter, impairment occurs after spoken language skills are acquired (Campbell & Sharma, 2014; Cavender & Ladner, 2008; Firzst et al., 2012; Nance et al., 2006). "With postlingual deafness, speech training is much easier and often successful while with pre-lingual deafness, speech training is much more difficult and often unsuccessful" (Cavender & Ladner, 2008: 28).

implants. This is assumed to be the most appropriate course of action, because from the perspective of the medical model of disability, if an individual has been diagnosed with a medical condition, the optimal solution is assumed to be a medical solution (Cavender & Ladner, 2008; *see also* Prietch & Filgueiras, 2015; Jain et al., 2019; Maboe et al., 2019). Notwithstanding this, through the lens of the social model of disabilities, persons with hearing impairments may be accommodated by: including closed captions on videos; facilitating the use of assistive technology including assistive listening devices; and facilitating the use of sign language to communicate, if organisational colleagues and leaders were willing to learn sign language, to facilitate ease of communication (Bowe et al., 2005; Cavender & Ladner, 2008; Fink, 2017; Kushalnagar, 2019). Indeed, the attainment of inclusive and diverse Caribbean societies, requires a united approach, by all organisational and societal stakeholders, as such, the responsibility should not fall solely on the shoulders of marginalised, disenfranchised societal group members.

In proposing the glass box theory, Purc-Stephenson et al. (2017) suggests that PWD face challenges which are similar to those facing women and persons from the lesbian, gay, bi-sexual, transgender, queer (LGBTQ) community in their employment experience, *to wit*, the glass ceiling and lavender ceiling (*respectively*) faced by employees, from these groups, which result in limitations on their participation and progression within organisations.

The seminal model regarding employment outcomes and treatment for PWD was proposed by Stone and Colella (1996) and continues to provide useful operational information for employers, PWD, policymakers and other stakeholders. By suggesting a comprehensive approach in order to effect the best outcomes for employees with disabilities, these researchers highlight the need for a collaborative approach, with each interested party working towards the achievement of the same goal, namely, to remove employment obstacles for PWD.

The productive engagement of persons with disabilities in the workforce increases their sense of well-being, self-confidence and dignity. To facilitate this, persons with disabilities must be afforded equal access to educational opportunities in their formative years, and through their life course, opportunities to engage in higher education and/or vocational training to facilitate their continued upskilling and career development.

Legislative Drivers Towards Inclusion

Anglophone Caribbean island states have followed their ascension to the CRPD[3] by enacting laws which protect and promote the rights of persons with disabilities in employment, whether through disability-specific legislation that prohibits discrimination against persons in different spheres of socio-economic activity, including employment, namely Antigua and Barbuda; Guyana; Jamaica; and the Bahamas; or employment-specific legislation that also prohibits discrimination against persons with disabilities and other specific characteristics and promotes access to equal opportunities in employment, namely Barbados; Grenada; and St Lucia. A more progressive approach has been adopted by Guyana and Trinidad & Tobago, through the enactment of laws that prohibit discrimination on multiple grounds (including but not limited to disability), with a view of ameliorating the position of disadvantaged societal groups.

Anomalously, the Bahamas has chosen to legislate a disability quota, such that the Persons with Disabilities (Equal Opportunities) Act, 2014 (Sec. 14(3)), requires employers with more than 100 employees to have on staff, no less than 1% qualified persons with disabilities. Conversely, Dominica, St Kitts and Nevis and St Vincent and the Grenadines, have retained some legal provisions, which may have a further divisive effect, relative to disparate treatment of employees with disabilities. Specifically, Dominica's Labour Standards Act, 1977 (Sec. 7) permits employees with disabilities to be paid at a rate which is below the prevailing minimum wage(unless fixed by statue).

Internationally, laws which prohibit discrimination on the grounds of disability provide a benchmark which Caribbean territories may wish to use, to improve the efficacy of the extant anti-discrimination laws in the region. Notably, the current equality laws in Australia and the United Kingdom, portend the following legislative amendments to the existing and developing comparable Caribbean laws: (i) expanding the categories of persons with disabilities against whom discrimination in employment

[3] Article 9, Convention on the rights of persons with disabilities, identifies the objective of the convention which is for signatories to "enable persons with disabilities to live independently and participate fully in all aspects of life, take appropriate measured to ensure to PWD, access on an equal basis with others to the physical environment, transportation and to information and communication inter alia, to include the identification and elimination of obstacles and barriers to accessibility".

is prohibited; (ii) restricting enquiries on disabilities during the recruitment process to avoid disparate treatment and outcomes; (iii) establishing national standards, rules or regulations to provide specificity for understanding and implementing legislative measures designed to promote and protect the rights of persons with disabilities in employment and (iv) reverting the burden of proof in discrimination claims to the employer rather than the employee.

Moreover, it would be reasonable to expect that the Caribbean governments in signing and ratifying the Convention on the rights of persons with disabilities, would take a leading role in enacting robust legislation, and monitoring the same, to ensure that breaches are met with swift punitive action, such that the message, that non-compliance will not be tolerated, is widely understood. In practice, this has been slow to be realised, in part because the Caribbean region is not as litigious as other international jurisdictions, and employees with disabilities are neither fully aware of their rights, nor of the employers' responsibilities, under the law.

Non-Legislative Drivers Towards Inclusion

Where discrimination has been institutionalised in a society or an organisation, prejudicial patterns of employment practice may be followed without question, as a result of established expectations and norms (Renskin, 2000). Indeed, the existence of widespread discrimination within society (Banaji, 1999) may make it more challenging for movement towards inclusion to occur. In addition to the attitudinal and prejudicial challenges, research (Dudzik et al., 2002; WHO, 2011) suggests that infrastructure, education, transportation and architectural barriers still exist across the Caribbean archipelago, including the limited availability of assistive technology across the region. This in turn, also has an adverse effect on the extent to which persons with disabilities may be integrated and are able to successfully live independently.

There is no reasonable expectation of an immediate and comprehensive transformation of employment practices towards those which are completely free from discrimination, on the basis of disability. Indeed, it is accepted that the effect of the passage of anti-discriminatory laws is the removal of the most egregious and obtrusive forms of discrimination (Crenshaw, 1988; Hornstein et al., 2001; Neumark, 2003), while circuitous and latent discriminatory practices which are deeply embedded, are more difficult to eliminate (Claes & Heymans, 2008; Duncan, 2003; Lahey, 2005). Thus requiring a change in culture which is more likely to occur over the medium to long-term rather than immediately after the enactment of anti-discrimination legislation.

Stone and Collela's (1996) models, (original—see Fig. 2.3 and updated—see Fig. 10.1) provide a framework for understanding the changes which may be effective, by illuminating "the way persons with disabilities are perceived and treated at work", and via the framework of the theory of social categorisation, where individuals categorise others into groups with the objective of identifying those who are similar to and/or different from themselves (Wenzel, 2001) and hence those with whom they anticipate successful work and other relationships (Kurzban et al., 2001).

Figure 10.1 is an updated version of Stone and Colella's (1996) model on the organisational treatment of persons with disabilities. The updated model proposed by Beatty et al. (2019—see Fig. 10.1), suggests that a collaborative, comprehensive approach is imperative in order to effect desired changes, such as the full employment, accommodation and inclusion of persons with disabilities within contemporary organisations in the Anglophone Caribbean.

The model suggests that organisational members and organisational stakeholders have a role to play in eliminating the *illusion of inclusion* (Barnes & Mercer, 2006). Thus, to improve organisational outcomes for persons with disabilities, it is important to note that they are heterogeneous, qualified and capable workers, who need: (i) to be protected by appropriately enacted and enforced laws; (ii) an organisational environment, where they are regarded as valuable employees by organisational members and leaders and are represented at every level within the organisation (from operational to executive); (iii) recruited and selected for jobs for which they are qualified, not underemployed and underpaid; (iv) inclusive human resource policies and practices, which may require re-education of employees (and leaders), in order to disabuse them of some of the previously accepted and unchallenged stereotypes and prejudicial attitudes; (v) organisations where organisational citizenship behaviour[4] is valued; and (vi) organisationally supported wellness

[4] Organisational citizenship behaviour (OCB) refers to a "set of helpful, discretionary and extra-role behaviours exhibited by employees that are not recognized formally, but have a positive effect on the operation of the organisation" (Organ, 1988).

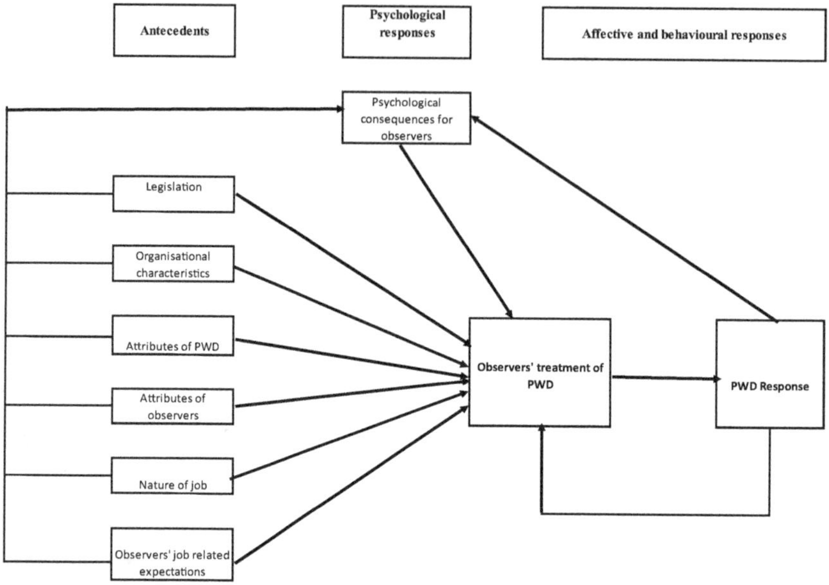

Fig. 10.1 Revised model of the factors affecting the treatment of people with disabilities in organizations (based on Stone & Colella, 1996). PWD: persons with disabilities (*Source* Beatty, J. E., Baldridge, D. C., Boehm, S. A., Kulkarni, M., & Colella, A. J. [2019]. On the treatment of persons with disabilities in organizations: A review and research agenda. *Human Resource Management*, *58*[2], 119–137)

programmes, designed to ensure the ongoing preservation of physical and psychiatric health and well-being (Beatty et al., 2019).

An organisation, which is committed to pursuing a human resource agenda of diversity, inclusion and equality, may preempt any reluctance by organisational members to embrace this by providing training to equip them with the skills and knowledge needed to reorient their thinking and correct previously held erroneous beliefs and misleading stereotypes regarding employees with disabilities (Warr, 1993; William & Klug, 1996). The role of training should not be underestimated, for where this is not provided or accessible, this could result in employees with disabilities who continue to: be underemployed, overrepresented in operational level organisational roles, feel marginalised and eventually withdraw from the labour force, to rely on state welfare agencies for support (Newton et al., 2005).

Concluding Comments

Drivers of change are wide and varied and may have a limited effect in isolation or a more significant effect when a combination is actioned. The failure of workplaces to realise changes in employment policies and practices, does not necessarily indicate a failure of equality legislation to attain its objective but could reflect a lack of awareness (by workplaces) of the applicable anti-discrimination legislation and consequently, the extent to which their current human resource practices diverge (Dickens, 2005; Loretto & White, 2006). Similarly, there are likely to be those workplaces which did not need to make any changes because they were continually reviewing and updating their policies to ensure equity and fairness prevailed.

In practice, non-discrimination is likely to be manifested within workplaces through the institutionalisation of fair procedures, bureaucratisation of the decision-making process and the implementation of non-discrimination employment practices. Likely changes by organisations include: (i) agenda setting by workplaces (this may include the realigning of the current workplace agenda to comply with legislative directives); (ii) the establishment and/or extension of coverage of equal opportunity policies within the workplace; and (iii) the collection of data and monitoring of the workplace with a view of detecting and addressing concerns regarding discrimination should they arise, and generally adjusting workplace policies and practices where required (Dickens & Hall, 2006). Moreover, Laughlin (1991) proposes a continuum of change, such that the organisation: (i) maintains the status quo; (ii) makes minimal required changes; (iii) makes changes to the workplace norms beliefs and ethos; and (iv) makes changes which facilitate the adoption and pursuit of a new direction, i.e. towards inclusion (see also Goss et al., 2000; Kirton & Greene, 2005).

Legislators and policymakers may wish to consider the analysis of this text in making legislative amendments or enacting new laws, with a view to broadening the range of persons protected as it relates particularly to disabilities. Moreover, organisational practitioners may find these discussions useful, where current policies/practices are shown to be unlikely to further their organisation's objectives vis-à-vis productivity and sustainability. Further, academics may also find this text useful in facilitating the delivery of contemporary data, literature and analysis as it relates to the current challenges faced by persons with disabilities in the region, how they are perceived within Caribbean society and community stakeholders and whether and the extent to which this has evolved over time. Additionally, academics and students may find this text useful in: (a) understanding the challenges faced by persons with disabilities as a marginalised group; (b) conducting comparative analyses in relation to the status of persons with disabilities and employment in the Caribbean; and (c) understanding the extent to which change is required in order to migrate towards greater equality and inclusion of employees with disabilities in the Anglophone Caribbean region.

Furthermore, this book establishes a benchmark for researchers, who may wish to explore further, the issues of discrimination in relation to persons with disabilities and the extent to which sustained employment of this group is affected. In the Caribbean region, specifically as it relates to persons with disabilities and much of what is accepted as representative of reality is based on anecdotal evidence and stereotypical assumptions about this marginalised group. The insights offered in this text, provide tools of clarification and direction for stakeholders across the Commonwealth Caribbean region to improve their knowledge and understanding of persons with disabilities and employees with disabilities. Finally, it is hoped that this text will also act as a catalyst for change, such that persons with disabilities are regarded as heterogenous, skilled, competent, productive and capable of making a significant contribution to the region's economies.

References

Banaji, M. R. (1999). *The roots of prejudice*. Kendon Smith Lectures, University of North Carolina, Greensboro.

Bance, M. (2007). Hearing and aging. *CMAJ: Canadian Medical Association Journal*, *176*(7), 925–928.

Barnes, C., & Mercer, G. (2006). *Independent futures: Policies, practices and the illusion of inclusion*. School of Sociology an Social Policy, University of Leeds, UK.

Beatty, J. E., Baldridge, D. C., Boehm, S. A., Kulkarni, M., & Colella, A. J. (2019). On the treatment of persons with disabilities in organizations: A review and research agenda. *Human Resource Management, 58*(2), 119–137.

Bowe, F. G., McMahon, B. T., Chang, T., & Louvi, I. (2005). Workplace discrimination, deafness and hearing impairment: The national EEOC ADA research project. *Work, 25*(1), 19–25.

Bussé, A. M., Hoeve, H. L., Nasserinejad, K., Mackey, A. R., Simonsz, H. J., & Goedegebure, A. (2020). Prevalence of permanent neonatal hearing impairment: Systematic review and Bayesian meta-analysis. *International Journal of Audiology, 59*(6), 475–485.

Campbell, J., & Sharma, A. (2014). Cross-modal re-organization in adults with early stage hearing loss. *PLoS ONE, 9*(2), e90594.

Cavender, A., & Ladner, R. E. (2008). Hearing Impairments. *Web Accessibility: A Foundation for Research*, 25–35.

Claes, R., & Heymans, M. (2008). HR Professionals' view on work motivation and retention of older workers: A focus group study. *Career Development International, 13*(2), 95–111.

Crenshaw, K. W. (1988). Race, reform and retrenchment: Transformation and legitimation in anti-discrimination law. *Harvard Law Review, 101*(7), 1331–1387.

Convention on the Rights of Persons with Disabilities (CRPD). (2006). Convention on the Rights of Persons with Disabilities and Optional Protocol. United Nations. https://www.un.org/development/desa/disabilities/convention-on-the-rights-of-persons-with-disabilites.html

Deal, M. (2003). Disabled people's attitudes toward other impairment groups: A hierarchy of impairments. *Disability & Society, 18*(7), 897–910.

Dickens, L. (2005). Walking the talk? Equality and diversity in employment. In S. Bach (Ed.), *Managing human resources: Personnel management in transition* (4th ed., pp. 179–208). Blackwell Publishing.

Dickens, L., & Hall, M. (2006). Fairness – Up to a point. Assessing the impact of New Labour's employment legislation. *Human Resource Management Journal, 16*(4), 338–356.

Dudzik, P., Elwan, A., & Metts, R. (2002). *Disability policies, statistics, and strategies in Latin America and the Caribbean: A review*. Inter-American Development Bank.

Duncan, C. (2003). Assessing Anti-ageism Routes to older worker re-engagement. *Work, Employment and Society, 17*(1), 101–120.

Fink, D. (2017, December). Disability rights aspects of ambient noise for people with auditory disorders under the Americans with Disabilities Act. In *Proceedings of Meetings on Acoustics 174ASA* (Vol. 31, No. 1, p. 015001). Acoustical Society of America.

Goss, D., Goss, F., & Adam-Smith, D. (2000). Disability and employment: A comparative critique of UK legislation. *International Journal of Human Resource Management, 11*(4), 807–821. https://doi.org/10.1080/09585190050075132

Harpur, P. (2017). Nothing about us without us: The UN convention on the rights of persons with disabilities. In A. Leithner & K. Libby (Eds.), *Oxford research encyclopedia of politics*. Oxford University Press. (pp. 1–20). https://doi.org/10.1093/acrefore/9780190228637.013.245

Harpur, P. D. (2019). *Ableism at work: Disablement and hierarchies of impairment*. Cambridge University Press.

Hornstein, Z., Encel, S., Gunderson, M., & Neumark, D. (2001). *Outlawing age discrimination foreign lessons UK Choices*. Policy Press.

Humes, L. E. (2019). The World Health Organization's hearing-impairment grading system: An evaluation for unaided communication in age-related hearing loss. *International Journal of Audiology, 58*(1), 12–20.

Jain, D., Lin, A., Guttman, R., Amalachandran, M., Zeng, A., Findlater, L., & Froehlich, J. (2019, May). Exploring sound awareness in the home for people who are deaf or hard of hearing. In *Proceedings of the 2019 CHI Conference on Human Factors in Computing Systems* (pp. 1–13).

Kelly, C. (2010). Wrestling with group identity: Disability activism and direct funding. *Disability Studies Quarterly, 30*(3), 1–19.

Killion, M. C., Niquette, P. A., Gudmundsen, G. I., Revit, L. J., & Banerjee, S. (2004). Development of a quick speech-in-noise test for measuring signal-to-noise ratio loss in normal-hearing and hearing-impaired listeners. *The Journal of the Acoustical Society of America, 116*(4), 2395–2405.

Kirton, G., & Greene, A. (2005). *The dynamics of managing diversity* (2nd ed.) Elsevier Butterworth Heinemann.

Krieger, L. H. (1995). The content of our categories: A cognitive bias approach to discrimination and equal employment opportunity. *Stanford Law Review, 47*(6), 1161–1248.

Kurzban, R., Tooby, J., & Cosmides, L. (2001). Can race be erased? Coalitional computation and social categorization. *Proceedings of the National Academy of Sciences, 98*(26), 15387–15392.

Kushalnagar, R. (2019). Deafness and hearing loss. In S. Harper & Y. Yesilada (Eds.), *Web accessibility* (pp. 35–47). Springer.

Lahey, J. (2005). Age, women, and hiring: An experimental study. *Journal of Human Resources, 43*(1), 30–56.

Laughlin, R. (1991). Enviornmental disturbances and organisational transitions and transformations – some alternative models. *Organisational Studies, 12*(2), 209–232.

Llewellyn, A., & Hogan, K. (2000). The use and abuse of models of disability. *Disability & Society, 15*(1), 157–165.

Loretto, W., & White, P. (2006). Employers' attitudes, practices and policies towards older workers. *Human Resource Management Journal, 16*(3), 313–330.

Maboe, M. J., Eloff, M., & Schoeman, M. (2019). Analysis of students with and without disabilities in an e-learning setting. In *Proceedings of the South African Institute of Computer Scientists and Information Technologists 2019* (pp. 1–7).

Michels, T. C., Duffy, M. T., & Rogers, D. J. (2019). Hearing loss in adults: Differential diagnosis and treatment. *American Family Physician, 100*(2), 98–108.

Muigg, F., Weichbold, V. W., Kuehn, H., Seebacher, J., & Galvan, O. (2021). Does cochlear implantation affect openness-to-experience in profound postlingual hearing loss? *The Journal of Deaf Studies and Deaf Education, 26*(1), 142–146.

Mulrow, C. D., Aguilar, C., Endicott, J. E., Tuley, M. R., Velez, R., Charlip, W. S., ... DeNino, L. A. (1990). Quality-of-life changes and hearing impairment: a randomized trial. *Annals of Internal Medicine, 113*(3), 188–194.

Nance, W. E., Lim, B. G., & Dodson, K. M. (2006). Importance of congenital cytomegalovirus infections as a cause for pre-lingual hearing loss. *Journal of Clinical Virology, 35*(2), 221–225.

Neumark, D. (2003). Age discrimination legislation in the United States. *Contemporary Economic Policy, 21*(3), 297–317.

Newton, B., Hurtsfield, J., Miller, L., Akroyd, K., & Gifford, J. (2005). *Training participation by age amongst unemployed and inactive people*. Department for Work and Pensions (DWP). Research Report No 291. DWP.

Olusanya, B. O., Davis, A. C., & Hoffman, H. J. (2019). Hearing loss grades and the International classification of functioning, disability and health. *Bulletin of the World Health Organization, 97*(10), 725.

Organ, D. W. (1988). *Organisational citizenship behaviour. The Good Soldier Syndrome*. USA.

Prietch, S. S., & Filgueiras, L. V. L. (2015, September). Technology acceptance evaluation by deaf students considering the inclusive education context. In *IFIP Conference on Human-Computer Interaction* (pp. 20–37). Springer.

Purc-Stephenson, R. J., Jones, S. K., & Ferguson, C. L. (2017). "Forget about the glass ceiling, I'm stuck in a glass box": A meta-ethnography of work participation for persons with physical disabilities. *Journal of Vocational Rehabilitation, 46*(1), 49–65.

Raymond, M., Barrett, D., Lee, D. J., Peterson, S., Raol, N., & Vivas, E. X. (2021). Cognitive screening of adults with postlingual hearing loss: A systematic review. *Otolaryngology-Head and Neck Surgery, 164*(1), 49–56.

Renskin, B. F. (2000). The proximate causes of employment discrimination. *Contemporary Sociology, 29*, 319–328.

Reskin, B. F. (2018). Rethinking employment discrimination and its remedies. In *Social Stratification* (pp. 849–858). Routledge.

Retief, M., & Letšosa, R. (2018). Models of disability: A brief overview. *HTS Teologiese Studies/Theological Studies*, *74*(1), 1–8.

Smart, J. F., & Smart, D. W. (2006). Models of disability: Implications for the counseling profession. *Journal of Counseling & Development*, *84*(1), 29–40.

Smith, A. (2012). Hierarchy of impairment: The impact. *Ethnicity and Inequalities in Health and Social Care.*, *5*(2), 70–71.

Stone, D. L., & Colella, A. (1996). A model of factors affecting the treatment of disabled individuals in organizations. *Academy of Management Review*, *21*(2), 352–401.

Sullivan, S. E., & Duplaga, E. A. (1997). Recruuiting and retaining older workers for the new millennium. *Business Horizons*, *40*(6), 65–69.

Warr, P. (1993). In what circumstances does job performance vary with age. *European Work and Organisational Psychologist*, *3*(3), 237–249.

Wenzel, M. (2001). A social categorization approach to distributive justice: Social identity as the link between relevance of inputs and need for justice. *British Journal of Social Psychology*, *40*(3), 315–335.

Williams, J. D., & Klug, M. G. (1996). Aging and cognition: Methodological differences in outcome. *Experimental Aging Research*, July–September, 219–244.

World Health Organisation (WHO) (2011). *World Report on Disability* – WHO.

List of Referenced Caribbean Laws

Antigua and Barbuda

Disabilities and Equal Opportunities Act, 2017. http://laws.gov.ag/wp-content/uploads/2019/04/No.-32-of-2017-Disabilities-and-Equal-Opportunities-Act-2017.pdf.

The Antigua and Barbuda Labour Code, Cap. 27. http://laws.gov.ag/wp-content/uploads/2018/08/cap-27.pdf.

The Social Security Act, Cap. 408. http://laws.gov.ag/wp-content/uploads/2018/08/cap-408.pdf.

The Workmen's Compensation Act, Cap. 475. http://laws.gov.ag/wp-content/uploads/2018/08/cap-475.pdf.

Barbados

Accidents and Occupational Diseases (Notification) Act, Cap. 338. http://www.barbadosparliament-laws.com/en/ShowPdf/338.pdf.

Casual Employees Pensions Act, Cap. 20. http://www.barbadosparliament-laws.com/en/ShowPdf/20.pdf.

Employment (Prevention) of Discrimination Bill, 2020. https://www.barbadosparliament.com/uploads/bill_resolution/06948a67143d62e36c426fbd077e1055.pdf.

Employment Rights Act, 2012–2019. https://www.ilo.org/dyn/natlex/docs/ELECTRONIC/94144/110398/F-749620620/BRB94144.pdf.

J. H. Stephenson and N. Persadie, *Disability in the Workplace*, Palgrave Explorations in Workplace Stigma,
https://doi.org/10.1007/978-3-031-19340-8

Factories Act, Cap. 347. http://www.barbadosparliament-laws.com/en/ShowPdf/347.pdf.
National Insurance and Social Security Act, Cap. 47. http://www.barbadosparliament-laws.com/en/ShowPdf/47.pdf.
Occupational Pension Benefits Act, Cap. 350B. http://www.barbadosparliament-laws.com/en/ShowPdf/350B.pdf.
Safety and Health at Work Act, Cap. 356. http://www.barbadosparliament-laws.com/en/ShowPdf/356.pdf.

Belize

International Labour Organization Conventions Act, Cap. 304:01. (Revised Edition 2020). https://www.agm.gov.bz/wp-content/uploads/2021/11/Cap.-304.01-International-Labour-Organization-Conventions-Act.pdf.
Labour Act, Cap. 297. (Revised Edition 2020). https://www.agm.gov.bz/wp-content/uploads/2022/05/Cap.-297-Labour-Act.pdf.
Social Security Act, Cap. 44. https://www.agm.gov.bz/wp-content/uploads/2021/11/Cap.-44-Social-Security-Act.pdf.
Workmen's Compensation Act, Cap. 303. (Revised Edition 2020). https://www.agm.gov.bz/wp-content/uploads/2021/11/Cap.-303-Workmens-Compensation-Act.pdf.

Dominica

Accidents and Occupational Diseases (Notification) Act, Cap. 89:51. https://www.dominica.gov.dm/laws/chapters/chap89-51.pdf.
Employment Safety Act, Cap. 90:08. https://www.dominica.gov.dm/laws/chapters/chap90-08.pdf.
Labour Standards Act, Cap. 89:05. https://www.dominica.gov.dm/laws/chapters/chap89-05.pdf.
Social Security Act, Cap. 31:01. https://www.dominica.gov.dm/laws/chapters/chap31-01.pdf.

Grenada

Employment Act, Cap. 89. https://laws.gov.gd/.
Labour Relations Act, Cap. 157A. https://laws.gov.gd/.
National Insurance Act, Cap. 205. https://laws.gov.gd/.
Social Security (CARICOM Agreement) Act, Cap. 307A. https://laws.gov.gd/.
Social Security (OECS Convention) Act, Cap. 307A. https://laws.gov.gd/.

Guyana

Equal Rights Act, Cap. 38:01. https://mola.gov.gy/sites/default/files/Cap.%203801.pdf.

Labour Act, Cap. 98:01. https://mola.gov.gy/sites/default/files/Cap.%209801.pdf.

National Insurance and Social Security Act, Cap. 36:01. https://mola.gov.gy/sites/default/files/Cap.%2036.01%20National%20Insurance%20%26%20Social%20Security.pdf.

Occupational Safety and Health Act, Cap. 99:06. https://mola.gov.gy/sites/default/files/Cap.%209906.pdf.

Persons with Disabilities Act, Cap. 36:05. https://mola.gov.gy/sites/default/files/Cap.%203605%20Person%20with%20Disabilities.pdf.

Prevention of Discrimination Act, Cap. 99:08. https://mola.gov.gy/sites/default/files/Cap.%209908.pdf.

Jamaica

The Disabilities Act, 2014. https://japarliament.gov.jm/attachments/341_The%20Disabilities%20bill%202014%20No.13.pdf.

The Factories Act. https://laws.moj.gov.jm/library/statute/the-factories-act.

The National Insurance Act. https://laws.moj.gov.jm/library/statute/the-national-insurance-act.

The Workmen's Compensation Act. https://laws.moj.gov.jm/library/statute/the-workmens-compensation-act.

St. Kitts and Nevis

Accidents and Occupational Diseases (Notification) Act, Cap. 9.01. https://aglcskn.info/wp-content/documents/Act02and09TOC/Ch-09_01-Accidents-Occupational-Diseases-Notification-Act.pdf.

Factories Act, Cap. 18.12. https://aglcskn.info/documents/Act02and09TOC/Ch%2018.12%20Factories%20Act.pdf.

Labour Act, Cap. 18.18. https://aglcskn.info/wp-content/documents/Act02and09TOC/Ch-18_18-Labour-Act.pdf.

Social Security Act, Cap. 22.10. https://aglcskn.info/wp-content/documents/Act17TOC/Ch-22_10-Social-Security-Act.pdf.

St. Lucia

Employees (Occupational Health and Safety) Act, Cap. 16.02. https://www.govt.lc/media.govt.lc/www/resources/legislation/EmployeesOccupationalHealthandSafetyAct.pdf.

Equality of Opportunity and Treatment in Employment and Occupation Act, Cap. 16.14. https://www.ilo.org/wcmsp5/groups/public/---ed_protect/---protrav/---ilo_aids/documents/legaldocument/wcms_127741.pdf.

Labour Code, 2006. https://www.govt.lc/media.govt.lc/www/resources/legislation/SaintLuciaLabourCode2006.pdf.

National Insurance Corporation Act, Cap. 16.01. https://www.ilo.org/dyn/natlex/docs/ELECTRONIC/60635/128159/F781131238/LCA60635%202005.pdf.

St. Vincent and the Grenadines

Factories Act, Cap. 335 (Revised Edition 1990). https://www.ilo.org/dyn/legosh/en/f?p=14100:1100:0::NO::P1100_ISO_CODE3,P1100_SUBCODE_CODE,P1100_YEAR:VCT,,2015.

National Insurance Act, Cap. 296. https://www.ilo.org/dyn/natlex/docs/ELECTRONIC/54275/88412/F1313009582/VCT54275%202007.pdf.

National Insurance (Employment Injury Benefits) Regulations, 1997. https://www.ilo.org/dyn/natlex/natlex4.detail?p_lang=en&p_isn=54275.

Protection of Employment Act, 2003. https://www.ilo.org/dyn/natlex/docs/ELECTRONIC/80807/87478/F414224706/VCT80807.pdf.

The Bahamas

Employment Act, Cap. 321A. http://laws.bahamas.gov.bs/cms/images/legislation/principal/2001/2001-0027/EmploymentAct_1.pdf.

National Insurance Act, Cap. 350. http://laws.bahamas.gov.bs/cms/images/LEGISLATION/PRINCIPAL/1972/1972-0021/NationalInsuranceAct_1.pdf.

Persons with Disabilities (Equal Opportunities) Act, 2014. http://laws.bahamas.gov.bs/cms/images/LEGISLATION/PRINCIPAL/2014/2014-0031/PersonswithDisabilitiesEqualOpportunitiesAct2014_1.pdf.

Trinidad and Tobago

Equal Opportunities Act, Cap. 22:03. (Revised Laws of Trinidad and Tobago, 2016). https://agla.gov.tt/downloads/laws/22.03.pdf.

National Insurance Act, Cap. 32:01. (Revised Laws of Trinidad and Tobago, 2016). https://agla.gov.tt/downloads/laws/32.01.pdf.
Occupational Safety and Health Act, Cap. 88:08. (Revised Laws of Trinidad and Tobago, 2016). https://agla.gov.tt/downloads/laws/88.08.pdf.
Workmen's Compensation Act, Cap. 88:05. (Revised Laws of Trinidad and Tobago, 2016). https://agla.gov.tt/downloads/laws/88.05.pdf.

Index

J. H. Stephenson and N. Persadie, *Disability in the Workplace*, Palgrave Explorations in Workplace Stigma,
https://doi.org/10.1007/978-3-031-19340-8

Kolibri 360 GmbH
Ferdinand-Jühlke-Straße 7
99095 Erfurt, Deutschland
produktsicherheit@kolibri360.de